Sex
and
Rockets

ISBN 978-0-922915-97-2

Design by Linda Hayashi
Cover design by Sean Tejaratchi

10 9 8 7 6 5

Feral House
1240 W. Sims Way Suite 124
Port Townsend, WA 98368

www.feralhouse.com

Sex
and
Rockets

The Occult World of Jack Parsons

John Carter
Introduction by Robert Anton Wilson

**feral
house**

Contents

v

contents

A Marvel Walked Among Us
by *Robert Anton Wilson*

"I seem to be living in a nation that simply does not know what freedom is."
—*John Whiteside Parsons*[1]

This book tells the life story of a very strange, very brilliant, very funny, very tormented man who had at least three major occupations (or vocations); he also had no less than four names. He acted as scientist, as occultist, as political dissident and often as a simple damned eejit (just like you and me).

Scientists, aware of his tremendous contributions to space science, generally call him John Parsons, and they've even named a crater on the moon after him. Those occultists who know of his work in their very specialized arts call him Jack Parsons, the name he himself preferred; in some magick lodges they consider him second only to Aleister Crowley as a progenitor of the New Aeon. His best-known book, *Freedom Is A Two-Edged Sword*, which increasingly influences the libertarian and anarchist movements, gives his name as John Whiteside Parsons on the cover and title page. And, as the present biography documents, this odd bird actually had the legal name Marvel Whiteside Parsons imposed on him at birth.

Oh, well, if my parents had named me "Marvel," I would have changed my name, too, perhaps as often as Parsons did.

For utmost scientific clarity about matters usually left in mystic murk or psychobabble, I shall use all four of Our Hero's names: John Parsons for the scientist, John Whiteside Parsons for the libertarian philosopher, Jack Parsons for the occultist, and Marvel Parsons for the original template: an alienated and sometimes naive boy, a child of divorce, who tried to find and liberate what occultists call his True Self by creating the other three Parsonspersons and permitting them

vii

introduction

---

1. *Freedom Is A Two-Edged Sword*, by John Whiteside Parsons, Falcon Press, Las Vegas, 1989, p 10.

to fight brutal wars in the loneliness of his passionate brain until all three became One. When endured helplessly by a truly fractured personality, we generally call this civil war in the psyche Multiple Personality Disorder: when deliberately pursued as a path of Illumination leading through Hell and Purgatory toward a vision (at least) of Paradise, we have no name for it in our current culture but those few who, like Parsons, have taken the hermetic oath to Will and Dare and Know and Keep Silence simply call it magick (pronounced mage-ick, as in the Three Magi).

Marvel Parsons, born in 1914 in Los Angeles but raised mostly in the nearby town of Pasadena, began life like all of us in what Tibetans call the Void and the Chinese call *wu-hsin* (no mind). Gradually, out of the Void, form emerged. He made the distinction between Marvel and Everything Else; a glass wall then separated Marvel from Everything Else. He gradually identified various parts of Everything Else, as soon as he learned their names.

Fatherless, Marvel had a conservative middle class mother who loved him a bit too ardently (she committed suicide within a few hours after his death, 17 June 1952). She also taught him to hate his absent father, a proven "adulterer." (Horrors!) Developing an early interest in psychology, Marvel diagnosed himself as having a classic Oedipus complex, a compulsive antipathy to "Patriarchy" (he used the word before the Feminists made it trendy) and an equally intense loathing for any and all Authority symbols, especially "God the Father."

But let us look at 1914, the year of Parsons' birth, more closely. Whatever you think of astrology, with its extraterrestrial bias, a "secular horoscope" limited to Earthly portents always provides amusing insights. The terrestrial world that shaped Marvel Parsons looked like this:

The First World War had started on July 28 that year; before 1914 ended the first aerial bombing of civilian populations occurred (Germany did it to France), and the bloody battles of the Marne, Tannerberg, Ghent and especially Ypres demonstrated that "civilized" modern humans could act even more inhumanely and insanely than any barbarians of the past.

Police arrested the legendary labor hero Joe Hill in Utah on January 13 for a murder he almost certainly did not commit, and the State executed him the following year. His last words, "Don't weep for me, boys—organize!" became a mantra to union members for decades after.

In Colorado, John D. Rockefeller's hired goons killed 21 people (including 11 children) in a clash with other labor "radicals." Leftists protested outside Rockefeller's New York office and got arrested for it: a court order banned any other people with signs or banners from parading in front of that sacrosanct shrine of the Almighty Dollar. Novelist Upton Sinclair appeared the next day with a blank sign, telling reporters that free speech had died. Suffragettes marched on Washington June 28, demanding equal rights for women.

In England, *Dubliners*, the first book by an Irish author named James Joyce, appeared; and in America Edgar Rice Burroughs brought forth *Tarzan of The Apes*. Musically, we all acquired three major treasures, "The Colonel Bogey March," "Saint Louis Blues" and "12th Street Rag." In film, D.W. Griffith's *The Mother and the Law* rawly showed the abuse of women by "the Patriarchy."

Margaret Sanger introduced the term "birth control" in *The Woman Rebel* and then fled to England to avoid imprisonment for the "crime" of publishing explicit details on contraception.

Charles Taze Russell, founder of the Jehovah's Witnesses, announced that the apocalypse would begin on October 2—coincidentally or synchronistically, the very day Marvel Whiteside Parsons [who would later, as Jack Parsons, call himself the AntiChrist] emerged from his mother's womb, or from even darker places, and began to investigate and meddle with this planet.

Going back to England again: also in 1914, Aleister Crowley (rhymes with "holy") and his current mistress, violinist Leila Waddell, staged something called "The Rites of Eleusis" in London—several nights of quasi-masonic ritual, music, poetry, ballet and drama. On the first night, the actors informed the audience, Nietzsche-fashion, that "God is dead" and mourned and grieved over the departed deity: things became even stranger after that, like the bardos in the *Tibetan Book of the Dead*, and on the last night the audience received "The Elixir of the Gods," a wine containing a high dosage of the psychedelic drug mescaline. While they willynilly entered Chaos and the Void a chorus announced the dawning of a New Aeon based on Rabelais' Law of Thelema—"Do What Thou Wilt" . . .

And Doublemint chewing gum appeared on the market, produced by William Wrigley . . .

All of this undeniably influenced Marvel as much as, or more than, any distant stars or planets. The horrors of World War imprinted him with a wounded perception of the dark side of "human nature": some parts of *Freedom Is A Two-Edged Sword* sound as bitter as Swift or Twain at their most misanthropic. Marvel also acquired a genuine sympathy for working people, and an awareness of the brute force behind Capitalism and Capitalist Governments never left him: although an ultra-individualist himself. he had more than one Marxist friend (which got him virtually tarred and feathered during the McCarthy era).

> Standing there as big as life
> And smiling with those eyes:
> "What they forgot to kill," said Joe
> "Went on to organize."

Margaret Sanger and the suffragettes also left a mark: no male writer since John Stuart Mill in the 19th Century has shown more empathy for Feminism than John Whiteside Parsons.

"Saint Louis Blues" helped create the Jazz Age in which Marvel began to evolve from boy to man. And, like Russell and the Jehovah's Witnesses, he grew up convinced that the world had entered a life-and-death battle between Cosmic (or at least Archetypal) Forces—but he enlisted on the side of the rebels, since he hated what we now call the logophallocentrism of "God the Father" even more than our current crop of Feminist theologians do. Although (as noted) he could see the Oedipal roots of this bias, he also perceived/conceived it as a decision for Light and Liberty against Tyranny and Superstition.

Aleister Crowley and his New Aeon would later transform Marvel into Jack Parsons.

I don't know how Wrigley's Doublemint gum fits into this list of terrestrial Signs and Omens surrounding the genesis of Marvel Parsons. But I feel sure some student of Crowleyana will write to me and explain it after this book appears.

Then another major influence mutated Marvel Parsons into John Parsons and John Whiteside Parsons and Jack Parsons: in his teens he discovered a despised and disreputable genre of pulp literature confusingly known (at the time) as either science-fiction or science-fantasy. Seen from the present, the sci-fi crowd of that age look like closet surrealists who had re-invented the Novel Of Ideas and tailored it for magazines with names like *Thrilling Wonder Tales*. The uncertainty about what to call their product typified the age of accelerated change in which Parsons and this literature both matured: after Jules Verne's "fantasy" submarine appeared in the world's real seas, nobody with more brain cells than a chimpanzee or a Fundamentalist felt totally secure about the differences between the probable, the improbable and the totally impossible.

If Verne's submarine could become materialized, why not his rocket to the moon? The question excited a lot of other boys besides Marvel Parsons: but, unlike most of them, he did something about it. He became John Parsons, almost certainly (as this book documents) the one single individual who contributed the most to rocket science. Two of the institutions he helped organize, the Jet Propulsion Laboratory at Pasadena and the Aerojet Corporation, still play large roles in space exploration.

You will learn more about John Parsons' acknowledged scientific achievements in the text to follow: I will concentrate on his other, still controversial labors. Just remember that when he started building rockets they seemed as "wacko" to most people as anything else he did. Yet his careful scientific experiments and theories liberated humanity from Terracentrism and showed us the path to a starry destiny.

Rocket engineer John Parsons also became friendly with the leading "fantasy" and "sci-fi" writers in the Los Angeles/Pasadena area and entered a subculture in which no idea seemed too crazy to discuss: a world where established science, fringe science, pseudo-science, philosophic speculation and visionary imagination all ran wild—in short, a world which anticipated and helped generate most of the "weird and kooky" ideas which have now infiltrated every aspect of our culture, except for the most reactionary Stone Age enclaves of Mississippi and the U.S. Congress.

It did not require much of a jump, then or now, to move from the Futurist-Fantasist world into Sex, Drugs and Magick. If you really enjoyed the *Star Trek* and *Star Wars* movies; or if you ever, even in fun, told a friend "Live long and prosper" or "May the Force be with you"; or played Dungeons and Dragons, smoked a joint now and again, participated to any degree in the New Age and/or the Neo-Pagan revival—two popularized (diluted) aspects of Crowley's New Aeon—or even if you ever wanted to get the government off our fronts (sexual freedom) as well as off our backs (market freedom)— you have received part of the huge legacy of Jack Parsons and his merry crew of science buffs, sorcerers and subversives.

Look at it this way: in John Parsons' 1930s–1940s sci-fantasy world, everybody he knew had already started discussing the possible "humanity" and "human rights" of extraterrestrials and robots;

they created alternate societies much more rational and adventurous than most "normal" people of that time could possibly imagine; they assumed (partly due to the influence of Alfred Korzybski and General Semantics) that information and technology would further accelerate their synergetic accelerations even faster than they had in the previous century (Parsons' friend, sci-fi-psi author A.E. van Vogt had studied with Korzybski personally); they created Alternative Worlds where anything currently considered goofy—from new economic systems to long-suppressed Gnostic doctrines—might function as efficiently as the pencil sharpener.

Robert Anson Heinlein, another friend of Parsons, wrote a novel, *Waldo*, in which all the arts of magick have not only won scientific acceptance but have become technologies used daily by everybody. Heinlein also wrote, a bit later, *Stranger In A Strange Land*, the first sci-fi novel to reach the *New York Times* bestseller list, and some still say Jack Parsons' magick/libertarian ideas permeate every page of it—*pax*, Mr. Carter!

To leave the heady and trippy environment of chaps like van Vogt and Heinlein, and to encounter and endure the Official Reality of the U.S. of those days probably seemed to Parsons like time travel back to the Dark Ages.

In that Official Reality, Christian piety and Capitalist predation co-existed as equally sacred Idols, even though they totally contradict each other. Stupidity, superstition and intolerance imprisoned most Americans in medieval squalor, both mental and economic: many humans did not have the "humanity" or "human rights" that Parsons' friends would grant to technically sophisticated robots (e.g. all those humans who had darker complexions than Snow White ranked as *non or-sub-human* in popular opinion and in law. We actually fought a war against fascism with a racially segregated army.) Almost all rational or adventurous ideas encountered blind bigotry and often violent persecution; contraception, divorce and abortion still remained illegal either locally or federally; homosexuality and bisexuality did not exist, or at least nobody in the major media could admit that they did exist; sex in general seemed so "dirty" that in the films of that time even married couples slept in separate beds, lest anyone suspect that they might occasionally fuck each other; all of the other delights of love enjoyed by most spouses remained illegal with penalties ranging as high as 20 years imprisonment; religious nutcases similar to Falwell and Robertson not only peddled hatred and intolerance to a gullible public, but nobody dared to fight back or even make cynical jokes about them; when the first scientific report on human sexuality appeared, its author, Dr. Alfred Kinsey, got hit with everything but flying monkey-shit—according to his research associate, Dr. Pomeroy, Kinsey literally died prematurely from the abuse he suffered.

Of course, irrational fear and superstition still stalk this nation; but in those days, they totally *dominated* it.

Parsons could only conclude that Americans, who claimed to love freedom, actually feared it, hated it and wanted to smother it with more and more tyrannical laws. They had willingly surrendered their liberty to "lying priests, conniving judges, blackmailing police" and other servitors of tyranny, as he wrote in 1946.

But John Parsons, jet propulsion pioneer, had by then become Jack Parsons, sex-magician—after he discovered and joined the Ordo Templi Orientis.

The Ordo Templi Orientis alleges that it descends directly from the 18th Century Illuminati of Bavaria. Let us look into that for a moment.

WHO PUT THE LIGHT IN EN-LIGHT-ENMENT?

"I need not add that freedom is a dangerous thing. But it is hardly possible that we are all cowards."

—*John Whiteside Parsons*[2]

Amid endless controversy about them, all agree that the Bavarian Illuminati began on May 1, 1776, in Ingolstadt, Bavaria, created by a Freemason (and former Jesuit) named Adam Weishaupt. According to the *Encyclopedia Britannica*, the Illuminati managed to influence many masonic lodges and gained "a commanding position" in the movement of anti-royalist, anti-Papist and pro-democratic "secular humanism." They attracted such literary men as Goethe and Herder but the whole movement came to an end when the Bavarian government banned the Illuminati in 1785. So says the standard reference.

Many conspiracy hunters have more faith in the decidedly paranoid *Memoirs Of Jacobinism* of Abbe Augustin Barruel, who believed that the Illuminati merely regrouped under other front names after

---

2.   *Freedom*, op. cit., p. 10.

1785, masterminded the French Revolution and still continued until the time he wrote (1806). Modern anti-Illuminists think it still continues today, although they often disagree as to whether the Illuminati really promotes secular humanism. Most Fundamtalists think they do, but others with livelier fantasies suspect them of unleashing Jazz, Rock 'n' Roll, communism, fascism, anarchism, Satanism, international banking, ritual child abuse, or some combination thereof.

According to masonic historian Albert G. Mackey, the Illuminati at its peak had only 2000 members in masonic lodges in France, Belgium, Holland, Denmark, Sweden, Poland, Hungary, and Italy. Mackey emphasizes that Baron Knigge, one of the most powerful and active members of the Illuminati, remained a devout Christian all his life and would not have worked so hard for the order if it really intended, as Abbe Barruel and others claim, the abolition of Christianity.

A new Order of the Illuminati appeared in 1880, founded by Freemasonic druggist Theodor Reuss in Munich. In 1896 Reuss, and fellow occultists Leopold Engel and Franz Hartmann co-founded the Theosophical Society of Germany, and in 1901 Engel and Reuss produced or forged a charter giving them authority over the re-established Illuminati of Weishaupt. In 1901, Reuss, Hartmann and metallurgist Karl Kellner founded the Ordo Templi Orientis and about 1912 Reuss conferred the 9th degree of the Ordo Templi Orientis upon Aleister Crowley, claiming that Crowley already knew the occult secret of that degree. (Crowley—rhymes with holy, remember?—already possessed the 33rd degree of the Scottish Rite and the 97th degree of the Order of Memphis and Mizraim.) Reuss later appointed Crowley his successor as Outer Head of the Ordo Templi Orientis. The Inner Head presumably remains invisible and unavailable to the un-Illuminated. (Hint: meditate on the Zen koan, "What wonderful magician makes the grass green?")

Crowley includes Adam Weishaupt, the founder of the 18th Century Illuminati, among the Holy Saints in his Gnostic Catholic Mass, performed regularly in all Ordo Templi Orientis lodges. But that list of Holy Saints also includes also such odd blokes as King Arthur, Mohammed, Parsifal, Buddha, Rabelais, Pope Alexander Borgia, Swinburne, Paracelsus, Sir Francis Bacon, John Dee, Goethe, Wagner, Nietzche, Simon Magus, King Ludwig II ("the mad king of Bavaria") and painter Paul Gauguin . . .

Before dying, Crowley appointed one Karl Germer (a survivor of a Nazi concentration camp) his successor as Outer Head, but Germer himself neglected to attend to that little detail, and when he died suddenly several claimants arose. I counted 1005 competing Outer Heads at one time in the mid-1980s, myself among them. (I had received that honor from a group of rebels against Kenneth Grant, an embattled Outer Head in London, who still calls himself the only real Outer Head. I always carry the card Grant's disloyal opposition sent me; it says "The Bearer of This Card is a Genuine and Authorized Outer Head of the Ordo Templi Orientis, so PLEASE treat him right" and magically/anachronistically has the signature of Aleister Crowley—or of a skillful forger.)

Over on this side of the pond, the federal courts have ruled that the title of Ordo Templi Orientis belongs only and always to the guys and gals represented on the World Wide Web and have further granted it tax-exempt status as a charitable corporation and religious entity. This group descends directly from the 1930s–1940s Agape Lodge of the OTO, the one that Jack Parsons once led.

As we mentioned, Aleister Crowley became an initiate of the OTO in 1912. This happened because he had published a mystic treatise and/or book of dirty jokes perversely or paradoxically entitled *The Book Of Lies (Falsely So Called)*. The Outer Head at that time, Theodore Reuss came to Crowley and said that, since he, Crowley, knew the secret of the 9th degree, he had to accept that rank in the OTO and its attendant obligations. Crowley protested that he knew no such secret but Reuss showed him a copy of *The Book Of Lies* and pointed to a chapter which revealed the great secret quite openly. Crowley looked at his own words and "It instantly flashed upon me. The entire symbolism not only of Free Masonry but of many other traditions blazed upon my spiritual vision . . . I understood that I held in my hands the key to the future progress of humanity."[3] Crowley, of course, does not tell us which chapter contains the secret. You can spend many happy hours, days, maybe even months or years, pouring over that cryptic volume seeking the right chapter and the final secret.

We should remember at this point that even before his involvement with the OTO Aleister Crowley also received training, sometimes briefly and sometimes lasting much longer, in such traditions as Taoism, Buddhism, Hinduism and Sufism; and we should note that he majored in organic chemistry at Cambridge University. He often reiterated his commitment to "the method of science, the aim of reli-

---

3. *The Book Of Lies*, by Aleister Crowley, Samuel Weiser Inc., York Beach, 1988. Introduction, p. 7.

gion." His work as Outer Head turned the OTO in radical new directions, both scientific and sexual.

Now it gets really scary for the Fundamentalists.

SEX AND DRUGS AND ROCK AND ROLL

"In these experiences the ego will be totally altered or completely destroyed in the death that must precede a rebirth into life. The terror, agony and despair that accompany this process cannot be minimized."
—John Whiteside Parsons[4]

Two recent books that shed some light on all these murky matters deserve some attention at this point—*The Hiram Key and The Second Messiah*.[5] The authors of both books, Knight and Lomas, both Freemasons themselves, claim that they have received "support and congratulations" from "hundreds" of other masons—athough they admit that their research has been greeted with hostile silence by the United Grand Lodge of England, one of the more conservative masonic bodies.

Basically, Knight and Lomas try to prove that masonry not only dates back to ancient Egypt—as only the most Romantic masons have hitherto claimed—but that it also served as a major influence on "Jerusalem Christianity," the earliest form of the Christian faith, which St. Paul and other sex-maniacs persecuted and drove underground. When the official Romish Christianity became dominant, primordial or "Jerusalem" Christianity survived by hiding within various Gnostic "heresies," Knight and Lomas say, and became a major force again only when rediscovered and accepted as their own secret inner doctrine by the Knights Templar. When the Templars were condemned by the Inquisition (1308) the surivivors used various other names until emerging again as "Freemasons" in the 17th or 18th Centuries.

Parts of this thesis have appeared in other books—the underground survival of primordial Christianity, for instance, underlies the entire argument of the famous *Holy Blood, Holy Grail* by Baigent,

---

4. *Freedom*, op. cit., p. 56.
5. *The Hiram Key* by Christopher Knight and Robert Lomas, Century, 1996; *The Second Messiah*, by Christopher Knight and Robert Lomas, Element Books, 1997.

Lincoln and Leigh—but Knight and Lomas have put the puzzle together in a more convincing way an any of their precursors.

But what about the original Egyptian "mystery" out of which this underground tradition emerged? Do Knight and Lomas attempt to delve that far back and claim to find a convincing answer?

Indeed they do.

The central masonic "myth" of the widow's son, Hiram—the builder of Solomon's temple, murdered for refusing to reveal "the mason word" to three ruffians—derives from actual events in Egypt, they aver. The "mason word" does not mean a "word" in the usual sense but acts as coded euphemism indicating a secret. ("Another damned secret?" I can hear you howl. Patience!)

Every new pharaoh, before ascending the throne, had to visit heaven and become accepted among the gods. Only after this otherworldly journey could the pharoah be accepted by the priests, *and by himself*, as one fit to fulfill the divine, as well as political, functions of kingship, as conceived in those days. This voyage to the highest stars, where the gods live, involved a magick ritual employing what Knight and Lomas call a "narcotic." When the last pharaoh of the native dynasty refused to reveal the secrets of this ritual to the new Hyskos dynasty, they killed him in the manner of the widow's son. The lost "word" = the details of the Ritual of Illumination and the name of the "narcotic" used.

It seems to me that Knight and Lomas have this last detail wrong, due to their ignorance of psycho-pharmacology. Narcotics do not allow you to walk among the stars and communicate with superhuman intelligences. They kill pain, they numb anxiety, they knock you unconscious; and they usually get you addicted: that's all they do. Almost certainly, the magick potion used in the ritual did not belong to the narcotic family but to the entheogens—the type of drugs also called psychedelics. Entheogens produce "mystic" and godly experiences, and at least one of them, and perhaps two, had widespread religious usage among the Indo-European peoples from ancient times, *Amanita muscaria* definitely and *psilocybin* possibly, both of them members of the "magic mushroom" group.

You can easily find learned works supporting this interpretation of how humanity first became aware of Higher Intelligences. See especially Pujarich's *The Sacred Mushroom,* Allegro's *The Sacred Mushroom and the Cross,* Wasson's *Soma: Divine Mushroom of Immortality,* Wasson et al., *Persephone's Quest: Entheogens and the Origins of Religion,* LeBarre's *Ghost Dance: Origins of Religion,* Peter

Lamborn Wilson's *Ploughing the Clouds: The Search for Irish Soma,* my own *Sex, Drugs and Magick*—and especially see Terence McKenna's *Food of the Gods,* which argues that all existing religions evolved from paleolithic rituals using entheogens and group sex to achieve ego-transcendence and cosmic consciousness. You can still see the ancient sexual symbolism even in such romish ikons as the Sacred Heart and the Cross: the former does not look like a heart at all but like a tumescent vagina and the latter has the shape of a penis and testicles.

Jack Parsons' magick and John Parsons' science have a closer unity than most people can imagine. They both aimed at the stars.

By the way, all over northern Europe traditional art shows the fairy-people and sorcerers surrounded by mushrooms, usually the "liberty cap" mushroom, now identified as psilocybin, the same used by Native American shamans for around 4000 years. The Irish Gaelic name for this fabulous fungus, *Pokeen,* means little god. ("Little fairy" in modern Gaelic, but *pook* derives ultimately from *bog,* the Indo-European root for "god.")

Crowley spoke for this tradition when he said true religion always invokes Dionysus, Aphrodite and the Muses, which he also called "wine, women and song."

Nowadays we call this magick trinity Sex and Drugs and Rock 'n' Roll, and celebrate them at Raves that hauntingly resemble the earliest stirrings of cosmic questing by ancestors who dressed in animal skins and looked even more like gorillas than we do.

I have saved the worst shock to "good, decent Americans" for the end of this section. In 1986, researchers found another (approximately) 2000-year-old manuscript near the same Nag Hammadi caves where the "Dead Sea Scrolls" had come to light. Translated into English by Mohammed al-Murtada and Francis Bendik under the title *The Secret Book Of Judas Of Kerioth,* this text depicts Jesus as the bisexual lover of both Mary Magdelene and St. John, and also describes the Last Supper as an entheogenic sacrament involving magic mushrooms. It has an introduction and running commentary by Dr. Maxwell Selander of Briggs-Melton Theological Seminary and you can get a copy from Abrasax Books in Corpus Christi, Texas. It will blow the circuits of any Fundamentalists you know . . .

Sort of sounds like the historical Jesus (as distinguished from the mythical Christ) had a lot in common with Jack Parsons, doesn't it?

"The time to fight for freedom is the time when freedom is threatened, not the time when freedom is destroyed, for that later time is too late. Freedom is threatened now, the destruction of freedom is not far off. Now is the time to fight."

—John Whiteside Parsons[6]

In every state of the Union, Fundamentalists still fight to ban all the science they dislike and prosecute all who teach it. To them, "traditional family values" denotes their right to keep their children as ignorant as their grandparents (and to hate the same folks grand-dad hated.)

Our government's war against "sin," i.e. against all forms of individual taste and whimsy, currently costs the taxpayers (federal and local) 450 billion dollars ($450,000,000,000) *every year*, according to Peter McWilliams.[7] This makes up the bill for all forms of government interference in people's private lives—i.e. the footless and hopeless attempt to stomp out "consensual" or "victimless" crimes—porno, prostitution, gambling, recreational or religious use of entheogens, etc. Who decides what consensual or victimless acts should become "crimes"? The so-called Christians who drove original "Jerusalem Christianity" underground, established the Holy Inquistion and still seem to suffer from what H.L. Mencken called "the haunting fear that somebody, somewhere, might be having a good time": the "lying priests, conniving judges, blackmailing police" denounced by John Whiteside Parsons in 1946. (Crowley, with his usual flair for humorous melodrama, called them the Black Brotherhood in his books, and it took me years to figure out whom he meant . . .)

In Newark, California, recently, police broke into the home of a Korean family, beat them all up and smashed all their furniture and dishes while allegedly looking for *verboten* drugs. They found no drugs, but the narcs explained to the press, "This is war."[8]

In Minneapolis, more tragically, the police also broke into the home of an elderly black couple, using flash-bang grenades which set the building on fire and killed both husband and wife. They offered the same "explanation" as in Newark: "This is war."[9]

6. *Freedom* op. cit. p. 39.
7. http://www.mcwilliams.com.
8. *Pissing Away The American Dream*, ed. by David Ross, Digit Press, Norcross, Georgia, 1991.

As Oliver Steinberg wrote, "It is inaccurate to speak of a War on Drugs . . . You don't lock drugs up in jail, you lock up people . . . You can't kill drugs—you kill people. Our government is not waging a war on drugs—it is waging a war on the people."[10]

Due to a strange and nefarious union of the Fundamentalists and the fanatic wing of Feminism, we have had more than 60 witch-hunts or Satanic Panics since 1980. Thousands of lives ruined, mass hysterias, millions of dollars wasted on prosecutions that usually collapsed in court for lack of real evidence: a large price to pay for the destruction of the Bill of Rights. After digging in countless "mass graves" of alleged victims of human sacrifice, the FBI's Behavioral Science Unit, which deals with serial killers, found no victims at all, at all, and concluded that the whole mania had no basis in fact—which led, of course, to charges that the FBI itself functioned as part of the Satanic conspiracy.[11]

And none of this has anything to do with the original Jerusalem Christianity. It emerged only from the Papist pretenders in Rome and their Protestant imitators, who make up the whole of what most people think of as "Christianity."

Nietzsche, who lived too soon to learn of that original Christianity, regarded what passes under that label as the worst disaster to ever befall humanity. As he wrote in *The Antichrist*:

> The hatred of intellect, of pride, courage, freedom of intellect, is Christian; the hatred of the senses, of the delights of the senses, of all delight, is Christian . . . the concepts of "the other world," "the last judgement," "the immortality of the soul," "soul" itself: they are torture instruments, they are systems of cruelty by which the priests became masters.[12]

Against this system of cruelty Nietzsche rebelled; and Crowley rebelled; and Jack Parsons rebelled: and because of them we now stand on the brink of an explosion of consciousness that literally can extend our minds and carry our bodies to the farthest stars.

9. Ibid.
10. Ibid.
11. *Satanic Panic*, by Jeffrey S. Victor, Open Court, Chicago, 1993.
12. As cited in *The Heretic's Handbook Of Quotations*, ed. by Charles Bufe, Sea Sharp Press, San Francisco, 1988, p. 177.

"No God. No Master."

—Margaret Sanger[13]

As you have gathered by now, I do not regard Parsons and Crowley as Black Magicians or Satanists or anything of that sort. Magick has many aspects, but primarily it acts as a dramatized system of "psychology" (or neuro-linguistic meta-programming) to train us to break out of the cage of the socially conditioned ego and, by plunging directly into the Chaos and Void from which we emerged, experience a rebirth into a new sense of self, of world, and of chaos and void, knowing directly, by experience, that all these names hide the same hidden unity—the wonderful magician who makes the grass green, makes the sad man sad, makes the angry woman angry, and makes the loving heart overflow with further love endlessly.

Dr. John Lilly called this process "metaprogramming the human bio-computer"; Dr. Timothy Leary, conscious of his debts to both Crowley and Parsons, called it "serial re-imprinting" of our "reality-tunnel."

As Terence McKenna often says in his lectures, you can do all this by yoga—but only if you can spare seven years of your life, or longer, sitting around an ashram meditating. Magick works faster, especially when united with the ancient shamanic ecstasies of full sexual release and the proper en-theo-gens.

Crowley said, and Parsons liked to quote him on this, "THERE IS NO GOD BUT MAN." (That sounds "sexist" these days, but you all know what he meant. He also said "EVERY MAN AND EVERY WOMAN IS A STAR.") To confuse this with atheism seems to me as wildly off the mark as confusing it with "Satanism." It quite simply means that all ideas/perceptions/experiences of the divine or the immortal refer directly back to the latent powers of the mind that contains them. (In this context, see John 10:34.)

As Jack Parsons knew, and as Freudians will readily see for themselves, the whole magickal struggle in Parsons' Babalon Working recounted in Chapters Seven and Eight unleashed, on one level, a violent confrontation with Marvel's Oedipus Complex. Babalon repre-

---

13. Cited in *Heretic's Handbook*, op. cit. p. 105.

sents the Mother and the Whore, the opposite archetypes of the male mind. To say it aloud, when making love to Babalon as Cameron, Jack Parsons did consciously what all men do unconsciously: he fucked his mother. After 2000 years of Christian sex-hate and sex-guilt, only in that total life-and-death battle with all inner inhibitions could he achieve that liberation which all of us seek, all of us fear, and all of us confront eventually, in the hour of our death, when we finally don't give a damn anymore about what other people think.

"Only in the irrational

and unknown direction

can we come to

wisdom again."

—John Parsons, letter to Cameron, 1946

Preface

"How shall I write of the mystery and the terror, of the wonder and pity and splendor of the sevenfold star that is Babalon?" I shall tell of the tragic life of her most devoted disciple and beloved son—known to her as Frater Belarion, and to the world of men as Jack Parsons.

In *The Rebirth of Pan*, Jim Brandon says that "Parsons" is one of the few names that turns up repeatedly in reports of anomalous phenomena. He does not mention Jack Parsons by name, but I think we shall see that the attribution is fitting. "Parson Jack," for instance, was a devil along the lines of the better known "Springheel Jack" who accosted astonished villagers. Our Jack was likewise hounded by his own devils.

In the aerospace world, there is a joke that "JPL"—the initials for Jet Propulsion Laboratory—actually stand for "Jack Parsons' Laboratory" or even "Jack Parsons Lives." How would you react to the statement that one of the Jet Propulsion Laboratory's founding fathers was a practicing ceremonial magician who attempted to summon a dangerous spirit and incarnate it into human form by impregnating a woman during one of his rites? The rite failed, and just a few years later this same Parsons would sign an oath stating he was the Antichrist. This man was at the same time the author of several once-classified government documents on explosives and patented means of rocket propulsion, and the Aerojet Corporation—which he personally founded—now produces solid-fuel rocket boosters for the Space Shuttle based on his innovations. The remarkable Parsons died at the early age of 37 in a mysterious explosion that even today is not definitively explained. Was it murder, suicide, or simply an accident?

I'd like to thank the following people for their contributions during the preparation of this manuscript: Carl Abrahamsson, Acharya (my copy editor), Judith Bauer, Greg Bishop, John Bluth, Peter Breton, Stephen Emmons, Allen Greenfield, Amy Lawrence, Marjorie Malina, Roger Malina, Adam Parfrey, Dave Reimer, Peter Stenshoel, Mick Taylor, Jourrie Van Der Woude, and all the unnamed others who helped make this book the best it could be. I'd also like to thank the staff of the following organizations: GenCorp Aerojet, Jet Propulsion Laboratory, Los Angeles Public Library, Pasadena Central Library, Pasadena Historical Museum, and Sherikon Space Systems.

A special thanks goes to my wonderful wife, Judy, for all her love and support throughout this entire endeavor. I couldn't have done it without her.

STATE OF CALIFORNIA
DEPARTMENT OF HEALTH SERVICES

P-625

W-323

Form 2. 12-13-10M

California State Board of Health
Bureau of Vital Statistics

State Index No. **608** 6549

PLACE OF BIRTH

COUNTY OF LOS ANGELES

CITY OF LOS ANGELES

Local Registered No.

[If birth occurred in a Hospital or Institution, give its NAME instead of street and number.]

ORIGINAL CERTIFICATE OF BIRTH

14-018214

(No. _Good Samaritan Hospital_ St.; _____ Ward)

Full Name of Child _Marvel Whiteside Parsons_

[If child is not yet named, make supplemental report, as directed.]

PERSONAL AND STATISTICAL PARTICULARS

SEX OF CHILD _Male_	**Twin, Triplet, or Other?** (To be answered only in event of plural births)	**Number in Order of Birth** _1_	**Legitimate?** _Yes_	**DATE OF BIRTH** _Oct_ _2_ _1914_ (Month) (Day) (Year)	

FATHER	MOTHER
FULL NAME _Marvel H. Parsons_	**FULL MAIDEN NAME** _Ruth Whiteside_
RESIDENCE _2401 Romeo St Los Angeles California_	**RESIDENCE** _(Same)_
COLOR OR RACE _White_ **AGE AT LAST BIRTHDAY** _23_ (Years)	**COLOR OR RACE** _White_ **AGE AT LAST BIRTHDAY** _23_ (Years)
BIRTHPLACE (State or Country) _Mass_	**BIRTHPLACE** (State or Country) _Illinois_
OCCUPATION _Auto Accessories_	**OCCUPATION** _Housewife_

Number of children born to this mother, including present birth _1s_   Number of children of this mother now living _1_

CERTIFICATE OF ATTENDING PHYSICIAN OR MIDWIFE

I hereby certify that I attended the birth of this child, who was _Born alive_ *at* _8 45_ P. M.
on the date above stated. (Born alive or Stillborn)

When there was no attending physician or midwife, then the father, householder, etc., should make this return. A stillborn child is one that neither breathes nor shows other evidence of life after birth.

(Signature) _Julian Coffey_
(Physician or midwife)

Given name added from a supplemental report _____, 191_

Address _926 Marsh George Bld_

FILED

Registrar. **OCT 7 1914** 191_

588770

one

The Early Years: 1914–1936

Marvel H. Parsons was from the Boston area, born circa 1894, the son of an egg merchant. Marvel does not appear in the Boston city directories for the years 1910 through 1913, so he was either living at home with his parents or he was from a small town just outside of Boston. When Marvel reached the age when men have to make a living for themselves, he realized there was no way he could do it selling eggs with his father. So Marvel decided to head west—to California, the land of sunshine and opportunity.

Marvel arrived in Los Angeles in 1913, a fact known because his name shows up in the 1914 city directory as residing at 2375 Scarrf, where he was a tenant. He was employed by the English Motor Car Company of 1132 S. Grand Ave., which was not an imported car dealer but named for its president, P.A. English. On a 1914 document, Marvel listed his occupation as "auto accessories," so he was probably employed in sales.

Parsons met Ruth Virginia Whiteside when he arrived in California and married her soon after. Ruth was from Ohio, but was born in Chicago, Illinois, in late 1893 or early 1894. Ruth had lived in several cities around the country and had also traveled to Europe with her parents on different occasions. I was unable to find her in any of the Los Angeles or Pasadena city directories prior to her marriage. Marvel and Ruth Parsons gave birth to a son on October 2, 1914 and named him Marvel Whiteside Parsons. He was their second child, the first having died at birth or in infancy. The younger Marvel was born at Good Samaritan Hospital, 1225 Wilshire Blvd., Los Angeles, California, at 8:45 p.m. The attending physician was Julian Coffey.

About this time the senior Marvel did something that was less common in 1914 than it is today. It was certainly less talked about then, and not condoned at all. Marvel had an affair with another woman. Ruth responded to his affair by doing something equally shocking: she divorced her new husband. Marvel can be found in the 1915 Los Angeles city directory, living alone at 2401 Romeo St., listed as owner of this home, where Ruth, listed as a housewife, and their son also lived for a while.

Embittered by her ex-husband's adulterous affair, Ruth began calling the boy "John" rather than "Marvel," but she never legally changed his name. As the boy grew, close friends and family would come to call him "Jack," which is how he is often remembered today. Because of these name changes, it is possible to tell at a glance whether a biographical account of Parsons originates from the scientific community or the occult community, as the latter uniformly calls him "Jack." Members of the scientific community call him "John," which is how he will be referred to throughout this book.

Curiously, Ruth Parsons kept her ex-husband's surname for herself and the boy, for she is consistently referred to as Mrs. Ruth Parsons for the rest of her life. It may be that there was no legal divorce at all, as one of her son's later documents makes reference to a "separation," which may mean that his mother may have merely kicked Marvel out.

In an ominous coincidence, Charles Taze Russell, whose "Russellites" now call themselves the Jehovah's Witnesses, predicted the end of the world would happen on October 2, 1914, the day of John Parsons' birth, and just a couple months after the start of World War I. When Russell announced to his congregation in Brooklyn, New York, that the end had begun, he meant the finale was not an instantaneous end to all things, but rather the beginning of the end as outlined in the Book of Revelation—the appearance of the Antichrist and the harlot, Babylon the Great, being two of the key events. It is ironic that John Parsons, who would later attempt to incarnate Babylon and who would also sign an oath stating that he was the Antichrist, was born the very day of Russell's eschatological event.

Of his own birth, the mystical Parsons wrote in *Analysis By A Master of the Temple* 34 years later, "I chose this constellation [Libra] in order that you might have an innate sense of balance and ultimate justice, responsive and attractive nature, a bountiful environment & sense of royalty and largesse, strength, courage & power combined with cunning and intelligence. Saturn [time] was bound [i.e., the planet was at aphelion] in order that you might not easily formulate a lower will which would have satisfied and overwhelmed you with its spectacular success."

Parsons' mother, Ruth, first appears in the Pasadena city directory in 1916, shown as living with her parents, Walter H. and Carrie Whiteside at 537 S. Orange Grove Ave., where Walter is listed as homeowner. After Marvel and Ruth separated, Ruth's parents apparently made the big sacrifice and moved west to help care for their daughter and grandson. Whatever occurrence or sentiment that had brought Ruth to California to begin with was evidently strong enough to make her want to stay. Rather than packing up and moving home after separating from Marvel, her home moved to her.

South Orange Grove Avenue was known locally as "Millionaire's Mile," and the family's presence here indicates Walter Whiteside was a successful man. Ruth's obituary lists Walter's occupation as president of both Stevens Duryea and the Allis Chalmers Manufacturing Company. Ruth and her parents, along with young John, stayed at 537 S. Orange Grove for a number of years. Ironically, John Parsons' life would end 37 years later just blocks from the very place where he grew up, at 1071 S. Orange Grove. The path he took to get there was a very interesting one, as we shall see.

John's father, Marvel H. Parsons, drops out of sight after 1915 and does not appear in any of the Los Angeles or Pasadena city directories again. We do know that he joined the army, and though it is thought that he did so after World War I ended in November 1918, the Department of Veterans Affairs has a record of a Marvel H. Parsons who enlisted in August 1917, one year before the war ended. This is the only Marvel Parsons in the VA's files. The army seems a natural refuge for a former salesman who had lost his wife, his son, and possibly his home.

John Parsons' FBI files refer to his father as a captain (i.e., "Captain Marvel"), and one of the newspaper articles written at the time of John's death refer to his father as a major. It has been said that Marvel worked for Woodrow Wilson (President, 1913–1921) or Warren G. Harding (President, 1921–1923), but this information is unconfirmed.

Marvel may have passed away in 1922, because the 1923 Pasadena city directory lists Ruth Parsons as a widow for the first time. However, the Marvel H. Parsons in the VA records was retired from active duty in October 1939 and didn't die until May 12, 1947, although he is evidently not buried in any of the VA's national cemeteries. Rather than his having passed away in 1923, it seems more likely that a man who rose from enlistee to captain or even major would require an entire career to do so, and four or five years just isn't enough. It may be that Ruth Parsons fibbed a little to cover up the stigma attached to her divorce.

According to John, Ruth (and perhaps her parents) cultivated a hatred in her son for the father he never knew. In his essay *Analysis By A Master of the Temple* he wrote (in the third person), "Your father separated from your mother in order that you might grow up with a hatred of authority and a spirit of revolution necessary to my work. The Oedipus complex was needed to formulate the love of witchcraft which would lead you into magick, with the influence of your grandfather active to prevent too complete an identification with your mother."

Of his childhood he wrote, "Your isolation as a child developed the necessary background of literature and scholarship; and the unfortunate experiences with other children [developed] the requisite contempt for the crowd and for the group mores. You will note that these factors developed the needful hatred for christianity [sic] (without implanting a christian [sic] guilt sense) at an extremely early age."

In *The Book of AntiChrist* (written by him just prior to *Analysis By A Master of the Temple*) John Parsons alleges to have invoked Satan at age 13, cowering in fear when he appeared. This event would have occurred in late 1927 or sometime in 1928. The reason for the invocation is not given, but it may have had to do with his problems with other children. It seems that in moments of distress not a few children have turned to magic, witchcraft or called upon "the devil."

In the directory listing of 1928 the Parsons and the Whitesides show up at 1105 Glen Oaks Blvd., Pasadena, where Walter Whiteside was listed as homeowner. Glen Oaks was a brand new street that year, not listed in any of the previous city directories. There was only one other house on the street, which must have been the start of a new housing development. Evidently Walter was doing very well at work, selling the old place and having a brand new home built for himself.

Around this time, when he was in the eighth grade, John made a lifelong friend when he found himself at the wrong end of a bully's attention. One young fellow, Edward S. Forman, intervened on Parsons' behalf, and the two were inseparable after that. Parsons and Forman soon learned they shared other interests: For example, both read the works of Jules Verne, especially *From the Earth to the Moon*, and Hugo Gernsback's new magazine of "scientifiction" called *Amazing Stories*.

The boys shared an interest in rockets that was more than theoretical. They loved to blow off fireworks in Parsons' backyard, and in 1928 they began to experiment with small, solid-fuel rockets. People who knew Parsons at the time said his yard was full of holes and burn spots from the constant activity. Interestingly, Forman later stated that he and Parsons often used glue as a binder to hold together the various gunpowder mixtures they prepared for their little rockets, a fact that will be important later on.

The adult male role model in Parsons' life was his grandfather Walter, though Parsons' own writings show that Ruth was clearly the major influence in his life. It seems Parsons never knew his birth father, growing up from infancy with Walter and Carrie Whiteside in their house. John Bluth, archivist of NASA's Jet Propulsion Laboratory, has speculated that some adult must have encouraged Parsons' early interest in rockets and fireworks. Perhaps it was merely a neighbor or a teacher, but it may have been his grandfather Walter.

For some reason the family moved very quickly, appearing in the Pasadena city directory of 1929 at 285 N. San Rafael Ave. This address was a new number on this street in this year, which leads one to assume that Walter Whiteside was taking advantage of the expansion taking place in Pasadena. For the first time the city directory lists Walter's occupation. Here he's shown to be the manager of Annandale Corporation, indicating a probable promotion.

Years later, John Parsons would tell the FBI that he toured Europe in 1929 with his "parents," a reference that must have been to his mother and grandparents, who were the only parents he had. Such a trip would be affordable for a well-to-do man like Walter. Ruth's obituary said she traveled to Europe on several occasions with her parents. At least one of these trips must have included her son.

Of his teenage years, Parsons wrote in *Analysis By A Master of the Temple*, "Early adolescence continued the development of the necessary combinations. The awakening interest in chemistry and science prepared the counterbalance for the coming magical awakening, the means of obtaining prestige and livelihood in the formative period, and the scientific method necessary for my manifestation. The magical fiasco at the age of 16 [1930 or '31, reference uncertain] was needful to keep you away from magick until you were sufficiently matured."

Around the time of this mysterious "magical fiasco" in 1931, John's grandfather, Walter, passed away. Carrie Whiteside subsequently listed herself as a widower in the 1932 directory. John Parsons, just turning 17, had now lost his father figure and role model. Most of his adult life John sought out others to fulfill this role.

In the year after his grandfather's death, Parsons and his boyhood friend Ed Forman devised a successful experiment that shows their interest in rockets was more than an amateur concern: they heated black powder—which involved no little danger—and cast it into a wax matrix. Aluminum (presumably aluminum oxide powder) was also added as an oxidizer. During the heat of combustion, the mixture would release oxygen, which further fueled the burn. Parsons and Forman remembered these early experiments later, when they began to work on rockets as a profession.

That same year, 1932, Parsons took a job with the Hercules Powder Company of Pasadena, where Ed Forman may have worked as well, as certainly he did later on. In 1933 Parsons graduated from the University School, which some have confused with University High School in West Los Angeles. The University School John Parsons attended was a small, private establishment located at 985 E. California St. in Pasadena. Attendance at such a private school is another indication of the Whiteside-Parsons family's wealth.

Parsons and Forman attended Pasadena Junior College together, and though it remains is unclear what subjects they studied, both spent two years at the expensive private college, USC (University of Southern California) but neither man graduated.

As they continued to indulge their passion for rockets, Parsons and Forman corresponded with Robert Goddard and some of the Germans and Russians working in the field. One of the Germans was science writer Willy Ley, who later fled the Nazis to America. Ley was a member of the German Rocket Society in Berlin, as was Wernher von Braun.[1]

Parsons and Forman probably also corresponded with Hermann Oberth, the father of German rocketry. Oberth had been born in Transylvania and then immigrated to Germany. Ley and von Braun owed much to him. They no doubt contacted Konstantin Tsiolkovsky, Oberth's peer in Russia. They may have also contacted the Frenchman Esnault-Pelterie, though no mention is made of him in the records. Esnault-Pelterie was contemporary with Oberth and Tsiolkovsky, and was just as well known in the field.

Forman later reminisced that they actually learned very little from the correspondence within this field, beyond the fact that nobody else had yet achieved much. Parsons and Forman eventually discontinued

sex and rockets

6

---

1. Ley helped popularize a number of scientific miscellany such as dinosaur survivals, space travel, and Atlantis. He had a long-running column in *Galaxy* Magazine. He also seems to be the one who informed the rest of the world of the Nazis' preoccupation with the occult. His books are relatively easy to find in used bookstores.

their letter-writing when they realized they were being pumped for information about their own work, without the others revealing anything about what they were doing, a problem that a later associate of the Pasadena pair, Frank Malina, would also experience when he went to visit Robert Goddard.

In 1934, John, Ruth, and Carrie moved to 620 St. John Ave., Pasadena, where Carrie is listed as homeowner, even though at 20 years of age John must have assumed the role of man of the house. John left his high school years employer Hercules Powder in 1934 to work for Halifax Explosives in the Mojave Desert. Ed Forman was also employed by Halifax, though possibly at a later date.

At this time Parsons bought a used car from a local dealership. The salesman was Robert B. Rypinski, who later worked for Jet Propulsion Laboratory (JPL). Rypinski liked Parsons immediately, and the two shared many interests, becoming good friends and remaining so for a number of years. A chance discovery at Rypinski's house a few years later would have great consequences for Parsons, but in the meantime the two enjoyed frequent weekends together, and Rypinksi later remembered that Parsons "burned with a warm, gem-like flame."

In the spring of 1935, John married Helen Northrup in the Church of the Little Flowers. The couple met at a church dance. Helen was the daughter of Burton A. and Olga Northrup, and worked as a secretary at her father's business, Northrup Business Adjustments. John and Helen bought themselves a home at 168 S. Terrace Drive, Pasadena, while Carrie Whiteside bought a new house for herself and Ruth Parsons at 723 Lincoln, possibly a smaller house just big enough for two widows.

In his memoirs Parsons cryptically referred to a "loss of family fortune" around this time, perhaps in connection with his grandfather's death. He wrote, "The early marriage to Helen served to break your family ties and effect a transference to her, away from a dangerous attachment to your mother. The experience at Halifax and Cal Tech served to strengthen your self reliance, scientific method and material powers. The influence of Tom Rose [reference uncertain] at this period, as that of Ed Forman in adolescence, was essential in developing the male center." Parsons also refers to ". . . Music, Lynn, Curtis, and Gloria, and the increasing restlessness." Parsons' love for classical music was great—as was his mother's—but the references to Lynn, Curtis, and Gloria, obvious early influences, remain uncertain.

Something else happened that autumn, something that would cure the restlessness and change the direction of Parsons' life forever. After seeing an article in the *Pasadena Evening Post* about a lecture given at the California Institute of Technology (Cal Tech or Caltech), Parsons and pal Ed Forman went to campus to talk to the speaker. The topic was the rocket experiments of the Austrian Eugen Sänger, and the lecture had been given by a graduate student named William Bollay, which is still on file in the JPL archives. Though the speech was written in 1935, it appears to have been presented several times—perhaps as late as 1939. It concludes with speculation on the possibility of "stratospheric passenger carriers," i.e., "spaceships."

NASA's Jet Propulsion Laboratory began in the 1920s and was known as the Guggenheim Aeronautical Laboratory, California Institute of Technology (GALCIT). GALCIT started as an aerodynamics research laboratory funded by a member of the famous Guggenheim family and administered by Caltech. In 1926, GALCIT came under the direction of the well-known Hungarian professor Theodore von Kármán (1881–1963).

Born in Budapest on May 11, 1881, von Kármán was descended from Rabbi Judah Loew ben Bezalel of Prague, and he often boasted of his ancestor's reputation for having created a golem, "an artificial human being in Hebrew folklore endowed with life."[2] Unmentioned in his autobiography, *The Wind and Beyond*, the golem appears in several secondary sources. Though not relevant to our discussion of GALCIT, the creation of the golem is a topic we will return to later when we discuss "magical children."

After graduating Göttingen University in Germany, von Kármán was awarded a fellowship there, and began to conduct research on aerodynamic drag in one of Europe's first wind tunnels, which he built for this purpose. He later moved to the position of Chair of Aeronautics at the Technische Hochschule in Aachen, Germany, where GALCIT's Clark Millikan found him in 1926. Clark Millikan was the son of Caltech president Robert Millikan and the head of the GAL-CIT lab when he recruited von Kármán away from Aachen.

Von Kármán's specialty was the new, wide-open field of aeronautics, and he eventually influenced a number of students who went on to great things in their own right. One of his pupils was a graduate student named Frank J. Malina, who was born October 2, 1912 in the small town of Brenham, Texas, northwest of Houston. In 1934,

---

2. Webster's.

Malina earned a degree in Mechanical Engineering from Texas A&M in nearby College Station and was working toward his Ph.D. at Caltech when Parsons and Forman presented themselves to William Bollay at the latter's lecture on Eugen Sänger's rocket experiments. For Malina, von Kármán became a father figure, much like the one Parsons was still seeking.

Although the older man did not actualize his father fixation, when Parsons was with von Kármán, he knew was in the presence of a great man. In turn, von Kármán called Parsons "a delightful screwball" who "loved to recite pagan poetry to the sky while stamping his feet"—a reference to Aleister Crowley's "Hymn to Pan," which Parsons loved to recite. At a party at the big house at 1003 S. Orange Grove Ave. where he would eventually live, Parsons stood in a balcony above the gathering and recited the Hymn from memory after being prompted by Andrew Haley, von Kármán's attorney. Aerojet employee Fritz Zwicky related that Parsons invoked Pan, the wild, horned god of fertility, before each rocket test. Parsons was probably not the only one present at such dangerous tests who said a prayer. His heterodoxy notwithstanding, von Kármán wrote in 1958 that Parsons was the third most important person in the development of rocketry in the United States—behind only himself and Frank Malina. Von Kármán praised Parsons' "rich talent for chemistry," and perhaps induced by Parsons' beliefs, von Kármán found it necessary to say he read John Symonds' *The Great Beast*, an early, somewhat sensationalistic biography of Aleister Crowley, the infamous "black magician" who exerted so much influence over Parsons.

After appearing at Bollay's lecture on Sänger, Parsons and Forman used the opportunity to ask Bollay about working at Caltech, where they could get the necessary funds for their experiments with rockets. Though unable to directly help Parsons and Forman, Bollay directed them to Frank Malina. Although Parsons and Forman held no degrees, Malina was able to spot their useful qualities right away. Forman was the expert mechanic while Parsons knew powder explosives backward and forward, even developing the practice of visiting industrial accidents to determine cause of explosions. The two men revealed their love of rocketry and developing ways of making them work. People remember Parsons as the theoretician and Forman as the mechanic, perfectly complementing one another. The pair were an inseparable team and an invaluable component for Malina, who later wrote that Parsons "lacked the discipline of formal training, [but] had an uninhibited fruitful imagination." The lack of discipline and uninhibited fruitful imagination would naturally spill over into other areas of Parsons' life.

Inspired by Parsons' and Forman's support, Malina prepared a dissertation on rocket propulsion. Targeting Clark Millikan to sponsor his doctorate, Millikan refused, an act that Malina resented from then on. Malina took his project down the Caltech hall to von Kármán, who immediately approved of it and provided his support. Von Kármán was well known for considering what others thought to be too kooky; after all, rockets were still viewed as science fiction by the public. The mere mention of rockets had people thinking of such impossible things as trips to the moon and rarely anything else. Von Kármán's allowed Parsons and Forman to use the lab at GALCIT despite their lack of affiliation with the school.

Malina later wrote of being influenced by reading Jules Verne's *From the Earth to the Moon* at the age of 12, as had Parsons and Forman. (Malina actually read it in Czech, when he lived in that country with his parents for a few years.) All three enjoyed the excitement of trial-and-error experimentation, though Malina also understood the importance of theoretical work, upon which von Kármán always insisted. Since Parsons and Forman were anxious to test rockets to prove brash theories, Malina best served his role by inducing them to work out their theoretical work. When experiments seemed to reach a dead end, Parsons would go to von Kármán, who'd perform a few quick calculations and say something like, "Yes, John, it is possible to achieve success in the direction you are heading, but first you must work out several dependant variables in the field." Fieldwork was Parsons' specialty; and for this very reason one is tempted to think von Kármán should have found him more important than Malina in his 1958 list of the most important people in aerospace.

Malina corresponded heavily with his parents in Texas when he was developing rocketry with Parsons, Forman and von Kármán. Significant portions of these letters are preserved in the JPL archives under the file, "Excerpts from Letters Written Home." Taken together with the memoirs Malina later wrote, these missives provide valuable insight and a complete picture into the early development of rockets in the United States.

The first mention of Parsons and Forman in Malina's documents comes on February 14, 1936. By March 30, Malina referred to the pair and himself as the "group." After reviewing the scant literature on the subject of rockets, the group decided that their first goal would be to develop a working motor. Stationary tests of motors, rather than launching test rockets, was the first priority. Other experimenters bypassed this important step, failing as a result. Von Kármán persuaded GALCIT to lease three acres of land from the city of Pasadena in the area known as the Arroyo Seco, which exists in the shadow of the San Gabriel Mountains, just above the dam called Devil's Gate. The acreage was the site of the new group's experiments. Today, NASA's Jet Propulsion Laboratory is situated there.

The great experiment started slowly. Malina writes on April 5 that Parsons and Forman take jobs at a powder company. Presumably they returned to Halifax. Even though rockets were their passion, there was no money in it—yet. On April 13, Malina wrote that he hadn't seen either of them for at least several days; Parsons finally phoned Malina on May 24, telling him that he almost had a rocket motor completed.

A month later, on June 18, Malina writes of Parsons testing with powder, a reference to a solid fuel called "ballistite," which is made by inserting a compressed black powder into the rocket motor so it will burn more slowly and evenly. The compression is accomplished by heating smokeless powder at first, then extruding it under pressure into long thin rods. Smokeless powder is a "double-base propellant" consisting of nitroglycerine and nitrocellulose, a formula known since the time of Alfred Nobel, the inventor of dynamite. This propellant was the fuel that eventually powered bazooka rockets and was not much different from the wax and aluminum used by Parsons and Forman in 1932. Ballistite was used in some of their tests prior to their work with GALCIT.

The work took off rapidly once the testing started. On June 29, Malina wrote, "Parsons and I drove all over Los Angeles—looking for high pressure tanks and meters. Didn't have any luck. Two instruments we need costs $60 a piece and we are trying to find them second hand. I am convinced it is a hopeless task. Will have to approach Kármán." The group's lack of funds reflects that GALCIT wasn't anxious to bankroll a project they felt was far-fetched. Malina approached Professor Irving P. Krick, who made a lot of money forecasting weather for movie studios. Though intrigued by the possibilities, Krick did not contribute. Parsons, Forman, and Malina were required to fund the project on their own.

On July 18, Malina wrote, "The early part of this week Jack Parsons and I covered much of Los Angeles looking for equipment. Our next lead points to Long Beach. Parsons is planning to start manufacturing explosives with another fellow [Forman]. Up to the

11

The Early Years: 1914–1936

present time he has been working for an explosives concern. Hope they make a go of it. I have found in Parsons and his wife [Helen] a pair of good intelligent friends." "Hope they make a go of it" almost sounds defeatist, but Malina persisted.

In the summer of 1936, Malina took the trouble to visit Robert Goddard (1882–1945) in Roswell, New Mexico. Goddard left Connecticut for Roswell years earlier to work on his own rocket project, about which he was very secretive. Goddard actually worked in Pasadena for a while during World War I, in the very Arroyo Seco where Parsons, Malina, and Forman were laboring. Malina visited Goddard to get ideas for his own research and to perhaps find a new position working for Goddard—who had funding—rather than at the cheap domain of Caltech.

At the invitation of Harry Guggenheim and von Kármán, who were interested in recruiting him, Goddard visited Caltech. Unwilling to leave Roswell, Goddard requested that Caltech send Malina to Roswell to visit his facility, which Malina did in September.

During Malina's visit, Goddard was polite on the surface, but displayed obvious tension. As Goddard showed him around, Malina realized his host didn't show anything of value. Malina knew right away that Goddard wanted another hand to do the hard work rather than a co-researcher. Malina returned to California disappointed. Goddard later refused a position at Caltech offered by Clark Millikan, probably understanding he would just be another scientist on a large campus, rather than the head of his own program. In his memoirs, von Kármán made some rather negative comments about Goddard's research suffering from self-imposed isolation.

Back at Caltech, "the group" was joined by three others: Apollo M.O. Smith (called "Amo" by his friends), Carlos C. Wood, and Rudolph Schott, bringing the total to six. Smith was a Caltech student like Malina, and regarded an eccentric since he constantly wore a pith helmet he modified by placing a small cooling fan on top. Wood and Schott were just a couple of guys from town who walked out to the test site and offered their assistance. Schott's red pickup truck became the group's standard means of transporting test apparatus. There was also associated with the group for a while an individual named Rockefeller ("Rocky"), but little mention of him exists in the records. Someone operated a motion picture camera during some of the tests; Rocky may well have been the camera operator.

In September, 1936, Malina got a new roommate: Martin Summerfield (1916–1996), a graduate student interested in rockets who arrived at Caltech from Brooklyn College in New York. Summerfield went on and made great advances in the field of liquid propellants; the Summerfield Burning Rate Law is named after him. Summerfield became fast friends with Malina, as the two had many things in common that Malina did not share with Parsons. Both Summerfield and Malina were graduate students, well-versed in theory, while Parsons held no degree and was entirely self-trained. A week after Summerfield moved in, Malina learned that he shared birthdays with Parsons, one of the last discoveries they would enjoy together as friends.

Parsons at left, and Ed Forman.

two

Parsons at Caltech: 1936-1939

$\mathbf{H}$alloween of 1936 produced the event which JPL still refers to as its birth. From Malina's letters, one gets the impression that this important date meant little except another series of tests ending in failure. Even if the day signified failure to Frank Malina, a photographer was present to get shots of Rudolph Schott, Amo Smith, Malina, Ed Forman, and John Parsons posing with testing apparatus. Though the photo is referred to by JPL staff as "the Nativity Scene," Carlos Wood, one of the researchers, failed to attend the apparently momentous gathering.

Once a year, on JPL's Open House for the public, the Nativity Scene is recreated with mannequins just behind the JPL Visitors' Center. For the 50th anniversary in 1986, JPL contemplated hiring live actors to portray the five founders. This event never materialized, but the Parsons mannequin and four others are stored at JPL today, stored for the next Open House when they'll be put on display. It seems ironic that this Nativity Scene took place on Halloween in 1936, containing the likeness of a man who signed an oath stating he was "the Antichrist." Photographs of the original scene and the JPL recreation are reproduced in the photo section of this volume. (It should be pointed out that the Nativity Scene celebrates the test of liquid fuel, though the group worked with both solid and liquid fuel at this time.)

The day after the Nativity Scene, an incident occurred that Malina thought significant to report: One of the fuel hoses pulled free, and the fuel spilling out the end ignited. The hose started twisting and turning, a flaming serpent from which they all ran for their lives. After they composed themselves, the group regretted not capturing the moment on film. Later tests fared somewhat better, but the group still measured success in how many *seconds* the rocket fired. By January 16, 1937, they were up to 44 seconds.

The test apparatus at Arroyo Seco was built with borrowed tanks and hoses, Forman later recalled. He machined the casing for the chamber himself and stated, "It was a hand-to-mouth operation where you rented machine time for $2 an hour and did the work yourself, in a day when wages were 25 cents an hour." That's half a day's wages for one hour of shop time. Forman's skill in this precise field is what gave him his excellent reputation as a mechanic. He continued to head the GALCIT/JPL mechanics department for as long as he stayed with the group.

The original schematic for the Nativity Scene test, is drawn on tracing paper by Malina, who signed both his and Parsons' names at the bottom. The schematics show oxygen flowing from one side, with methyl alcohol (the fuel) and nitrogen flowing from the other side. Water cooled the rocket during the burn. Thrust pushed down a spring that measured force. The deflection of the spring measured the force applied to it. A small diamond tip on the apparatus scratched a glass plate to mark the furthest point of deflection. The rocket and mount were protected by sandbags, with the tanks (and the experimenters) well away from it.

Five pages of Parsons' handwritten notes, which cover the period November 15, 1936 to January 17, 1937, begin:

The research is conducted with the view of acertaing [sic] the apliaction [sic] of the rocket to altitude exploration and other fields, the properties of various fuels and of metals at high temperatures. Rockets to be investigated are solid fuel rockets, utilizing explosives or combustibles and liquid rockets employing liquid explosives or liquid or gaseous oxygen and various combustibles.

Different motors and materials will be tried together with various methods of fuel injection. Relevant previous data will be compiled, together with records of all tests + calculations.

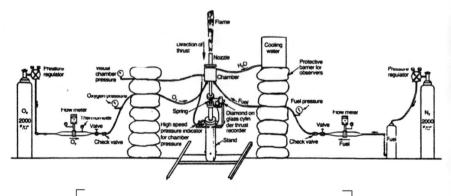

Schematic diagram of test setup for GALCIT rocket research drawn by Frank Malina in August, 1936.

Data from the first test—the actual Nativity Scene—are missing. The second test on November 15 employed methyl alcohol at various pressures as a fuel, ignited by a remote battery. All three trials on that second test day ended in failure. In his notes, Parsons remarked that he should switch from rubber tubing to copper tubing to prevent the tubing from burning up during future tests.

A third test, on November 28, yielded four burns of various duration, the best of which was 20 seconds. Parsons' notes outline the various materials used in these tests, as well as their procurement sources, as well as a record of the test taken January 16, 1937. Obviously these field notes are incomplete. The long periods of time between each test are due to von Kármán's insistence that the group analyze each burn before they start another.

While waiting, Parsons and Forman launched their own powder rockets. Malina wrote, "[T]heir attitude is symptomatic of the anxiety of pioneers of new technological developments. In order to obtain support for their dreams, they are under pressure to demonstrate them before they can be technically accomplished."

Parsons is mentioned in Malina's letters a couple of times during this period and the months following. For the record, Malina wrote on November 21, 1936 that Parsons had the flu the previous week. Though the first successful test of a solid-fuel rocket motor took place in January 1937, Malina didn't think much of it at the time, as it is not even mentioned.

The group left the *arroyo* next April and moved on-campus at Caltech, located right in Pasadena, where they worked out of one of the GALCIT lab buildings. Only von Kármán would have been daring enough to let these unsophisticated researchers work on-campus. In May, Hsue-shen Tsien, who had come from China on a scholarship funded by Boxer Rebellion reparations, began working with the group, sharing an office with Amo Smith. Weld Arnold, a meteorology student, contributed by presenting the group with $1000 in small bills wrapped in a newspaper. No one dared ask where he got them. A small fund was opened at Caltech, and the money deposited. Curiously, at the end of the war there was still $300 left in the account. Arnold became the group's unofficial photographer for a while, riding his bicycle at least 20 miles from Los Angeles every day.

Campus residents soon resented the group's presence. Testing was loud and violent. Immediately after their arrival on campus, the group met with their first disaster. In the lab they had mounted a rocket motor to a 50-foot pendulum. They measured the swing of the pendulum to calculate the thrust produced. The first motor tested exploded, filling the building with a cloud of methyl alcohol and nitrogen dioxide. A thin layer of rust formed on many pieces of valuable equipment throughout the lab. The other campus residents started referring to the group as "the Suicide Squad." Parsons would remember this event four years later, when he finally figured out a way to put the volatility of red fuming nitric acid (RFNA) to good use.

Von Kármán moved the group outside, adjacent to the lab, and had them rebuild the pendulum, this time making it five times stronger than thought necessary. Two years later the pendulum was destroyed again during an explosion, when a piece of steel was hurled into the wall where Malina had been standing just minutes earlier. Fortunately, he had been called away by von Kármán's secretary on some mundane matter concerning a typewriter. After this dangerous incident, back to the *arroyo* the group went.

On March 22 there is another brief mention of Parsons in Malina's letters, and on April 24 Malina related that Parsons was writing a paper "on the chemistry end of it." This paper was entitled "A Consideration of the Practicality of Various Substances as Fuels for Jet Propulsion." The finished paper is dated June 19, 1937, and is signed "J. Parsons, Halifax Explosives Company." Despite its origin, it was later classified by the government but has long been declassified and is on file at the JPL archives, the only paper in the archives bearing Parsons' name as the sole author. He was co-author on several other papers, but this one was his alone.

The paper begins:

> In considering the practicality of various fuels and oxidizers for rockets, certain criteria apply which are not met with in ordinary internal combustion motor problems.
>
> Since rocket performance is influenced by the ratio of fuel weight to total weight, and since the rocket must carry all the oxidizer necessary for combustion, the ratio of total weight of fuel and oxidizer to the available energy is of utmost importance. Since mass per unit flow is also important, a high specific gravity is preferred.
>
> In addition, ordinary considerations of safety, availability, cost and convenient physical state should not be neglected.

Parsons was saying that the fuel must be dense to pack a real punch, and be powerful enough to lift its own weight as well as that of the rocket and the cargo it may be carrying. This seemingly obvious statement is one that nevertheless must be made at the start of analysis. In the paper, Parsons presents five tables of various fuels with some algebraic calculations and chemical equations determining various properties of each. These calculations make it clear that Parsons was no amateur rocket hobbyist. He was, as everyone said, the theoretician of the group, even if he was an impatient theoretician. Parsons had obvious mathematical and scientific knowledge to back up his assertions. Malina specialized in differential calculus, which does not appear in the work of Parsons.

Parsons' first table looks at the explosive gases acetylene, butane, butyne, hydrogen, and methane. He dismisses acetylene as inherently dangerous, without carrying out the calculations of combustive properties. He further mentions potential problems with hydrogen and methane. Liquid oxygen is not even in the table, as Parsons eliminates it from calculations altogether as being too dangerous. He was right about this for decades. Only when the safe handling of liquid oxygen was finally perfected did it replace the liquid fuel combinations that Parsons himself would help perfect.

Table II contains the liquid hydrocarbons methyl alcohol, ethyl alcohol, propargyl, benzol, ethyl ether, and heptane. All had great availability, were cheap and easy to handle, but all had a low energy content.

Table III contains self-combustibles (explosives) such as gunpowder, etc., the energy content of which was low compared to gases and liquids, and which were difficult to handle. With a few precautions, Parsons added, they might be rendered useful. Parsons even mentioned that they might be "moulded or pressed into sticks," which was the seed of an idea that would later lead to success.

Table IV addresses metal organics and hybrids. Little was known about them, Parsons said, and they were costly to handle and difficult to prepare. One of them, trimethyl aluminum, is spontaneously inflammable in air. Parsons believed they were worthy of further investigation, though nothing seems to have come of it.

Table V is labeled "Various Elements" and contains figures for aluminum, boron, carbon, lithium, and magnesium. Parsons thought they may have some value when blended with other substances, for which aluminum was already being used in the field of explosives. Parsons further thought the energy obtained from such blends could be used indirectly to heat another substance, such as water.

There is also a sixth table, which lists not fuels but oxidizers, sub-

ASTRONAUTICS

Journal of the American Rocket Society

Number 41   July, 1938

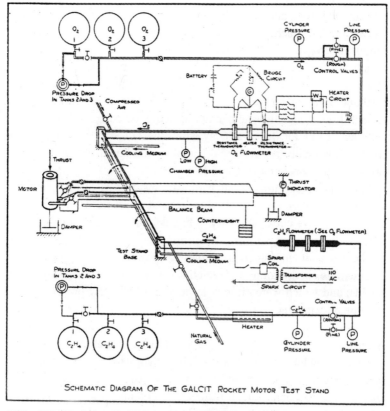

SCHEMATIC DIAGRAM OF THE GALCIT ROCKET MOTOR TEST STAND

The GALCIT Rocket Research Project — Plans and Program for Research at Cal. Tech. **Dry Fuel Experiences**—What can be done with powder rockets? **The Rocketor's Workshop**—Parachutes, valves.

The cover of *Astronautics* uses a schematic diagram of Parsons', Forman's and Malina's GALCIT liquid fuel research set-up.

stances introduced into a chemical process to speed combustion. Much experimentation remained to be done with oxidizers, Parsons concluded. The 13-page paper contains six appendices showing values for different materials obtained through actual experimentation by Parsons and others. These appendices represent the real-world follow-up to the theoretical calculations showed in the first part of the report. The appendices reflects not only the up-front calculations but also actual tests of fuel mixtures at Halifax. Documenting each step represents a lengthy but necessary process. No definite conclusions were reached, but Parsons always saw in each experiment the beginning of another. Each test led to new ideas for him, and he never stopped thinking.

Malina credits Parsons' paper with the development of red fuming nitric acid as a storable oxidizer. He also pointed out that Parsons first anticipated the use of boron hydride as a fuel in this paper, putting him ahead of his time. The key, as von Kármán said, was to make the fuel burn slowly. In armaments applications the fuel was burned as quickly as possible. Parsons and Forman had to unlearn this technique and find a new one.

When the term ended the next month, Malina paid Parsons a visit. On May 22—before the paper was actually finished, Malina wrote, "Antelope Valley, near New Hall—This weekend I accepted an invitation of Jack Parsons to spend at the house he has rented near the powder company for which he works. Jack's wife [Helen] is here which ensures good meals. We are about 40 miles from Pasadena in the foothills."

Antelope Valley is the current site of Edwards Air Force Base—a large valley—and it is uncertain if the powder company Halifax, for which Parsons labored, was anywhere near the base. Several explosives companies came from Antelope Valley, all conveniently remote from the city. John and Helen Parsons must not have lived there very long, for the Pasadena city directories show them living at 168 S. Terrace Drive from 1937 to 1940. Perhaps they retained the house at S. Terrace, which they owned, and rented the house intermittently in Antelope Valley until Parsons finished his paper in June.

While writing the paper, Parsons commuted back to Pasadena to do additional testing with GALCIT. That group achieved its best results yet in May, running a motor for longer than a minute. However, the graduate students finished their term and summer arrived and drifted away. Malina and Tsien focused on doctorate programs. Weld went to New York. Those who stayed behind collected their papers on rocketry into what they called "the Bible," copies of which exist in the JPL archives. Parsons' paper was among the half-dozen or so in the volume.

Around this time, Parsons and Malina started to write "a novel with an anti-war plot" that was also supposed to serve as a movie treatment. The manuscript is framed in anti-capitalist beliefs, with Malina documenting his own struggles with corporate culture and the coming war in Europe. Some writers have claimed the manuscript was some sort of sci-fi story about a flight to the moon, or about evil rocket scientists. This is not the case.

The original script is in the possession of Marjorie Malina, Frank's widow. It is untitled and bears no author's name, and is entirely in Malina's handwriting. Malina's memoirs make it clear that Parsons was a collaborator and that Malina worked on the manuscript at Parsons' house. Indeed, Malina expressed being nervous about being around the tetranitromethane in Parsons' kitchen—a chemical that Parsons was collecting though the army decided it was too dangerous to use due to its connection to several deaths. Because of its rarity, Parsons was stockpiling the stuff rather than disposing of it, and also had enough gunpowder hoarded "to blow up a city block"—this according to Ed Forman's first wife, who probably was not exaggerating. The gunpowder was in an open barrel on the back porch. After Parsons' death, Malina wrote that "Parsons' familiarity with explosives led to contempt."

The 38-page handwritten synopsis of the script is full of crossed-out passages and other editing marks, indicating that the two men brainstormed together as Malina set it all to paper. The story is about a group of rocket scientists—obviously based on themselves and their associates at Caltech—who are struggling to carry out pure research while other factions have more selfish aims for their work—anti-capitalist at almost every turn. The character based on Forman is a union organizer. The intellectual characters (and even their mechanics) are all philosophical heavies. The "bad guys" are all big industrial types and those who cater to them. The story is full of side stories involving love interests and the like. It is also eerily prophetic.

The character based on Parsons is named "Theophile Belvedere," whose description shows insight (and possibly a little humor) on Parsons' part. Belvedere is "a mystic who speaks for religion and the organized church." He is "extremely fanatical and is to used to add a sinister effect to the plot." His description is worth quoting verbatim, but it should be kept in mind that the manuscript was an obvious first draft never taken beyond this stage.

Theophile Belvedere is a tall slightly stooped, rosy cheeked man with a face whose lines continuously change from those of joy to those of misery. Shortly before the story opens he has been defrocked from the Franciscan order upon his own suggestion. In the monastery he has pursued a study of astronomy, a subject also of interest to the abbot. A small telescope had been built at the corner of the monastery enclosure where Belvedere spent many nights gazing at the stars. The monastery is located on a hill overlooking a small town of Spanish atmosphere. Once each year a fiesta is held in the town and for many years the monks have watched through niches in the enclosure the parade that took place on the closing night. On this night Belvedere, as usual, entered the space between the observatory and the corner of the enclosure. He is suddenly surprised by a young woman in pajamas who in her disarray clutches his arm. The next day Belvedere goes to the abbot and confesses his temptation and decides that he will leave the order. He learns that the young woman is the daughter of the abbot's brother who has been visiting the monastery. Belvedere returns to Rock [Pasadena] where he finds his fanatically religious mother being abused by her drunken husband. The family is on relief. Belvedere, having an M.S. degree in science, applies for a public school teaching position in the Rock High School. He is accepted and becomes a teacher of general science.

Near the end of the story, Belvedere accidentally blows himself up trying to stop one of his experiments—it should be noted that this story was written 15 years before Parsons died the same way, an eerie prophecy. Further, the character based on Tsien gets sent back to China under suspicion of communism and drops out of touch with the others, an incident that also later occurred. Many of those who remain are investigated for their anti-capitalistic political beliefs, and Malina's greatest fear—that their work would be used for wartime applications—also came true. In the story it is a rich investor who actually sells their secrets to the Nazis and Fascists.

Included with the manuscript is another movie treatment, some of which is typed on MGM letterhead. Further handwritten technical descriptions (and illustrations) were composed in Malina's hand. The typed portion is dated June 17, 1937 and entitled "Shadow of the Wing," bearing Malina's name as author. The treatment appears to be a different movie project entirely, one that an "M. Balcon" at MGM was evidently considering. "Shadow of the Wing" is the story of a mock bomber mission from Australia to London that goes awry. The hero is the pilot, who lands the plane despite all odds. Both stories never went beyond a preliminary stage, the first due to a sudden influx of funding for the rocket project, the second for reasons unknown. Lack of interest on MGM's part, perhaps?

On July 4, 1937, Malina wrote, "For our 'fourth,' Parsons and I are going to make some tests with a powder rocket motor," which sounds like a suitable way to celebrate both the Fourth of July and the completion of Parsons' paper just a few days earlier. On the 26th Malina wrote, "Parsons and I yesterday discussed the possibility of seeing Goddard again. Perhaps he and wife and I would drive to Roswell in his car, he to return while I go on to Texas . . ." They did not make the trip. The wording suggests that Parsons had visited Goddard previously, but such a trip is not recorded elsewhere.

As the months proceeded, Malina focused on his doctoral thesis, which he had been postponing for some time. Work on the thesis moved him closer to Summerfield and further from Parsons. Malina next refers to the rocket project a full five months later, on December 18. "Parsons wants to make some tests this weekend" was all that Malina wrote, causing one to wonder why he even mentioned it. Later that December Malina lectured the local Sigma Xi chapter on "Facts and Fancies of Rockets." And the group made the newspapers on January 26, 1938, when Malina and Smith traveled to New York to present a paper to the Institute of Aeronautical Sciences. Clark Millikan had convinced the school to put up $200 for the trip— Caltech's first direct financial support of the project. That day in January, articles appeared in the *New York Times* and the *Houston Chronicle*, as well as in the *Los Angeles Times*, *New York Herald-Tribune*, and *Time* magazine.

The story begins, "A scheme for shooting an exploratory rocket to a height of 967 miles above the earth was unfolded today before a convention of aeronautical engineers." Malina and Smith told the convention "the idea works in theory . . . whether it will work in fact depends on the efficiency of the rocket." They proposed a three-stage rocket with a maximum velocity of 11,000 miles per hour. As a result of the publicity, a New York stuntman wanted to ride a rocket up 1000 feet and parachute down at county fairs, and one Hollywood radio station wanted to broadcast the sound of a rocket motor firing.

On February 2, 1938, the Caltech student paper *California Tech* printed an article on rockets written by Malina with the help of Smith and Tsien. In April of 1938, the Associated Press released an item about the group's work that is worth quoting verbatim, as it is contains valuable information unrecorded in Malina's letters. It reads:

Frank J. Molina [sic] and three student-scientists [probably Parsons, Forman, and Smith] are working on a motor from which they hope to develop another which will take a rocket nearly 100 miles above the earth's surface.

They see it carrying instruments to obtain data useful in weather forecasting, records on cosmic radiation, facts valuable to astronomers and information for other scientific purposes.

This motor, set up at the Guggenheim School of Aeronautics, California Institute of Technology, is a combustion chamber which mixes and burns gaseous oxygen and ethelene [sic] at 5000 degrees Fahrenheit, a temperature about half that of the sun [!].

The flaming gas comes out of the "exhaust" at a speed of around 9000 feet a second. With a "step rocket," one with three motors, two of which would be released in flight, a speed of 11,000 feet a second might be reached, Molina said.

"After experiments with gases, we will next try liquids," said Molina, "for that is what the rocket will have to use. We can allow only seven-tenths of the total weight of the rocket for propellants.

"The design of the rocket will be highly important because of the difficulty in keeping one in a straight course. Experiments have shown rockets may be deflected in a change in air currents. A gyroscope may help meet this difficulty.

"Our aim is to devise a rocket which will carry scientific instruments to heights of about 500,000 feet, far above those reached by sounding balloons. The record for a sounding balloon, I believe, is 110,000 feet. We are working everything out by theory, so far as is possible."

Molina said the decrease with altitude in the earth's gravitational pull will be a favorable factor in building rockets to reach even greater heights. His reckoning is that this pull is one-tenth less 200 miles up than at the earth's surface, and that it decreases proportionately with altitude.

Soon after, Malina and the group abandoned step rockets altogether. The AP item spawned several more newspaper articles about the group's work, but Malina lamented all the fuss, as is evidenced by the conspicuous absence of rocket travel from the above quote. (The public still identified rockets with trips to the moon.) Malina did not appear in subsequent newspaper articles, but Parsons and Forman readily did, and were photographed repeatedly. They clearly saw this exposure as a way to gain attention—and perhaps some funding.

Parsons also seemed to enjoy the status his work brought and sometimes exaggerated his title when presenting himself to others. He would call himself "Engineer," a false title since he held no degree, though he actually had a more practical knowledge of explosives than many engineers who did have degrees. The occupations listed for Parsons in the Pasadena city directories simply came from whatever the homeowner told the compiler of the directories. Parsons started out calling himself a "chemist," and later on calling himself a "research assistant" at Caltech. A letter of recommendation he wrote for Robert Droz bears the signature block, "Project Engineer, Aeronautics Department." Two GALCIT organizational charts in the JPL archives do make one thing clear: Parsons was the sole individual in charge of the solid fuel program.

May 1938 found Parsons in the courtroom, named by Caltech as their best explosives expert when the prosecutor of a murder trial contacted the institute. The case for which he served as an expert witness was a murder by car bomb. The trial lasted months and is well-documented in the *Los Angeles Evening Herald and Express*. Parsons is mentioned in articles on May 6 and May 10, the latter of which has a photo of him.

The defendants in the case were Captain Earle E. Kynette and his two aides, Lieutenants Roy Allen and Fred Browne of the Los Angeles city police's "spy squad" who were accused of planting a pipe bomb in the car of another officer, Harry Raymond. Raymond was a vice investigator; and apparently the three crooked cops thought he was getting too close for comfort. When Raymond stepped on the starter switch, the bomb exploded, killing him. The murder took place on January 14 of that year.

After surveying the available evidence, Parsons prepared a mockup of the bomb for the jury to see. In the *Los Angeles Herald and Express* May 10 photo, Parsons is seen displaying his mockup to prosecutor Gene Williams. It is a six-inch piece of pipe, three inches in diameter, capped at both ends, with a pair of wires leading to it. Parsons stated that the original contained a pound of pressed powder and "jagged bits of metal." The bomb destroyed both the victim's car and the garage it was parked in.

After leaving the courtroom on May 6 Parsons went to the desert near Lancaster with a working model of the alleged pipe bomb,

GALCIT Project No. 1, July 1, 1941

(from contemporary memos and sources)

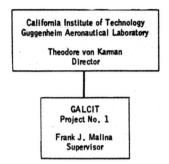

**California Institute of Technology
Guggenheim Aeronautical Laboratory**

Theodore von Karman
Director

**GALCIT
Project No. 1**

Frank J. Malina
Supervisor

Powder Group	Liquid Propulsion Group	Machine Shop	Computers
J. W. Parsons Res. Asst.	Martin Summerfield Res. Fellow	Ed Forman Res. Asst.	Richard Canright
Fred Miller Res. Asst.	B. M. Forman Res. Asst.	E. G. Crofut Res. Asst.	Barbara Canright
Clyde Miller Tech. Asst.	R. C. Terbeck Mechanic	Chas. Thore Machinist	
Art Richardson Mech. Helper		B. W. Morant Machinist	**Mechanic's Helpers (Part-Time)**

**Chem. Engineering
(Bruce Sage, CIT)**

E. W. Hough
Res. Asst.

J. M. Green
Res. Asst.

J. E. Booth
Machinist

Lawrence Karchner
Stockman

K. Anspach *
Draftsman

M. L. Lesser*

R. Latter*

M. M. Nyborg *

|*CIT Students|

Watchman

J. E. Booth (OT)

K. Anspach* (OT)

JPL reconstructs the GALCIT project's organizational chart of 1941
showing John Parsons in charge of its solid fuel program.

destroying an old car with it. Despite intense cross-examination, Parsons remained firm in his testimony that the bomb contained smokeless powder and not some other explosive. The *Los Angeles Times* speaks highly of him in this regard. He could not be shaken, remarkable for a 23-year-old.

Several police officers refused to testify against their former colleagues during the course of the lengthy trial, but the three were convicted nonetheless. A bomb threat was called in on the day of Parsons' testimony, the caller stating, "I am a friend of Kynette and a member of the police force, and you tell [special prosecutor] Joe Fainer if he doesn't lay off Kynette I'll bomb him the way Harry Raymond was bombed." Fainer was not bombed, but this incident may have had something to do with Parsons' death 14 years later.

The same month of the trial, May 1938, a technical article aimed at rocketeers appeared in *Astronautics: Journal of the American Rocket Society*, issue 41. Parsons was not mentioned. On July 15, the morning edition of the *Pasadena Star-News* printed a more sensational article, in which Parsons and Forman appear in a large photograph, Parsons in a dark suit, Forman in a cream-colored jacket with matching driver's cap. Forman smokes thoughtfully as both men lean on their elbows in front of their launch apparatus. A small, single-stage model rocket hovers just overhead—obviously inserted into the photo by means of double-exposure. The article gives some highlights of the pair's work in the Arroyo Seco. By this time Tsien had taken leave from the group, later returning to work on Rocket Project No. 1 at Caltech, while Parsons and the others worked at GALCIT in the *arroyo*.

The *Los Angeles Examiner* ran its own account of work in the *arroyo*. The article doesn't vary from the *Pasadena Star-News* article, except for having a different photo. This *L.A. Examiner* photo is one of the best early photos of Parsons and Forman around. Unlike the Pasadena photo, it was actually taken indoors. The caption could have read "Gentlemen Rocketeers." Both men wore dark jackets and ties, with hair slicked back and mustaches well-trimmed. Parsons stands on the left, holding a multi-stage rocket, while Forman kneels on the right, inspecting the spring-operated testing device.

Unlike Parsons, Malina did not appreciate publicity, feeling that the group hadn't accomplished anything worth publicizing. Nearly a year elapsed before Malina said anything more about Parsons in letters home, and one can almost feel the tension as the "good intelligent friends" drifted apart. Malina's letters were now full of references to roommate and fellow doctorate candidate Martin Summerfield. On October 24, 1938, Malina wrote, "A 'big shot' from the Army Ordnance division was here today. He told of the army's experience with rockets and thought there was little possibility of using them for military purposes. I silently rejoiced, however Parsons, who is about broke, was not so happy about it, as he hoped to get some funds for research from the army."

This source of funding became another contentious point, as Malina was against all military applications of his work. He was interested in civilian innovations only—namely, scientific applications that would benefit mankind, as well as possibly (eventually) an improved means of travel. Parsons was interested in the end result— working rockets—and wasn't concerned about how he got there. As it turned out, both Malina and the "big shot" were wrong—there *were* military applications for rockets just around the corner.

At one point Malina was invited to visit Ruben Fleet, President of the Consolidated Aircraft Company in San Diego, who gave Malina a tour and asked him about the possibility of rocket-assisted takeoffs of "big, heavy planes." Malina left, intrigued, but nothing came of the meeting until three years later, after Parsons had spent some more time experimenting. In fact, seaplanes were not fitted with JATOs until 1943 and they were liquid-fueled.

Malina also prepared a scientific paper for a contest in France that was sponsored by André Louis Hirsch, a banker with an above-average interest in rocketry. The contest was to award a cash prize to the best paper on current issues in the field. Malina won, but because of the war he did not learn of his prize until 1946—far too late for the winnings to help the project. Tsien appears to have helped Malina with the award-winning paper, though it bore Malina's name solely as author.

At this time, an interesting reversal of responsibility is recorded in Malina's letters home, in which he had written that Parsons and Forman "disappear for weeks or months sometimes with me trying to keep the project alive. They were working for the powder companies and testing their own rockets during these times." Malina took other time-consuming jobs, including wind-tunnel studies and a soil conservation project. Such outside endeavors increased tension in the group. Four months later, in a letter dated February 19, 1939, Malina wrote, "Parsons is doing some experiments with powder and is disgusted with me for not putting more time in to the research." The results of the powder experiments were written up by Parsons, who shared a byline with Forman in issue 43 of *Astronautics*. Certainly this byline was merely a courtesy, as the article is obviously Parsons' work.

The title of the article is "Experiments with Powder Motors for Rocket Propulsion by Successive Impulses." Like Parsons' previous paper, it was classified during the war, though the article was presumably still in circulation. The article begins with an editorial comment from the publisher to the effect that "the American Rocket Society believes the liquid fuel rocket motor has very definitely proven its superiority over powder motors . . ." This assertion would be proven wrong in two years' time.

The article, the technical analysis of which leaves little doubt that Parsons was the author, starts with a discussion of Goddard's work from 1919 forward and includes Goddard's early results with rockets using black powder as a fuel, a method by which he was able to achieve altitudes of 8000 feet, i.e., a mile-and-a-half up. Parsons then goes into a detailed explanation of his own test apparatus, including very exact specifications used to construct his rocket motors. Hercules black powder alone was used in the first series of tests, and different results were obtained for different degrees of compression (i.e., how densely the powder was packed into the rocket). Other powders were used in the remaining experiments, including smokeless varieties, and different types of wads were used at the bottom to hold the fuel in. Most charges were ignited by an electric wire run through this wadding and into the fuel source.

Parsons concludes the article with the assertion that powder was indeed efficient enough to pursue further. Indeed, he and Forman got rockets to reach velocities of 7150 feet per second (4875 miles per hour) in this series of tests, which approached what Goddard had achieved 20 years earlier. Parsons said they were working on an erosion-resistant insert of special steel as well as a satisfactory method of measuring chamber pressures. Erosion was often a problem with the throat nozzle—the part of the rocket from which the burning fuel leaves the rocket and pushes it up. In the article, Parsons thanked Malina, Tsien, a Mr. Spade of the Ludlum Steel Company, and a Mr. Henry N. Marsh of the Hercules Powder Company, which was Parsons' original employer from 1932. At the time the article was written, Parsons was employed by Halifax Explosives.

Around this time some money finally came through, and the school received a $10,000 grant to work on solid-fuel rockets, based on the group's progress. About this time, Fritz Zwicky, who had taken graduate courses under Einstein, scolded Malina for thinking that a rocket could ever fly in space, asking how the exhaust could push against a vacuum. What Zwicky didn't realize was that displacement of mass was all that was needed. On March 13 Malina wrote, "Parsons and Forman are to work full time and earn enough money to afford smoking ready-rolled cigarettes. Parsons' wife [Helen] will be happy that she is not the only breadwinner in the family." Parsons' good friend Rypinski related much the same thing, that Helen would "cry on his shoulder" that Parsons would only save his money for rockets, and not spend it on her.

This stroke of financial luck was the result of a visit by H.H. "Hap" Arnold, commanding general of the Army Air Corps. Arnold was a sharp individual who would work with von Kármán for many years after the war, and always on the lookout for some new scientific development to be used for military applications. Unlike the previous military "big shot" who visited, Arnold was intrigued by the possible uses for rockets. Ed Forman, for instance, recalled Arnold's suggestion that rockets might help airplanes take off while being as much as 50% over payload.

Arnold had worked with von Kármán before. Though Army Ordnance was against exploring the possibilities of rockets, Hap was less conventional, and had taken Malina and von Kármán to Washington the year previously on an unrelated matter. He knew talent when he saw it and convinced the National Academy of Sciences' Committee on Air Corps Research to fund the grant. Von Kármán and Robert Millikan were both members of the committee, which made Arnold's job much easier. There were actually several aeronautics projects being funded at this time, but the Massachusetts Institute of Technology (MIT) avoided the rocket project, opting to working on the problem of deicing aircraft windshields. "Kármán can take the Buck Rogers job" said the head of their aeronautics department. Kármán was glad he did and later called the project "one of the most fascinating periods of my career."

On April 18, 1939, a proposal was submitted to the Board of Directors at Caltech entitled, "Proposal for a Jet Propulsion Experimental Station at the Guggenheim Aeronautical Laboratory of the California Institute of Technology." The draft I have seen has the title "Chairman, Subcommittee for Jet Propulsion Research" below the signature block. Presumably this "Chairman" was von Kármán, though the work is probably Malina's. Two pages of summary are followed by an $80,000 cost estimate for the initial annual budget, with a footnote explaining that the figure does not include the cost for constructing the facility itself.

As to the construction, Forman later told a Lockheed company newsletter that he made an arrangement with a local bulldozer operator who worked for the city to grade the experimental station arena in the Arroyo Seco. The group itself fabricated the buildings from timbers and other items found in the *arroyo*, a "complex" that was a far cry from the 6000-employee facility JPL of today. In his memoir, von Kármán says he originally obtained the land, countering Forman's similar, and perhaps exaggerated, claim.

In the following months, Parsons and Forman are mentioned in passing in several Malina letters, and both earn a longer mention in his letter of August 21 when a large explosion hit the building they were working in on campus. The explosion occurred at 8:20 in the morning, "too early for Parsons and Forman to be at work," causing $10,000 in damage to the building—the entire value of the grant. The explosion caused an unrecognizable film to deposit itself on everything in the building, and when Parsons and Forman finally arrived, the Caltech staff were waiting for them with cleaning rags, expecting the two to clean it up. As had happened after the explosion of 1937, the group was soon working back in the *arroyo*.

On October 21, Parsons and Forman received invitations to a staff dinner at the Athenaeum, but old, social prejudices arose when they presented themselves at the door. "You two aren't Caltech staff. You're from town," they were told by the overzealous doorman, who wouldn't let them in despite their invitations. About this time Malina arrived and convinced the man the pair should be let in just this once, to save face for Caltech, claiming he would ensure that the mistake of inviting them would not be made again. The doorman was swayed, and the two were finally allowed to enter.

On November 26, 1939, the magazine supplement to the *Los Angeles Sunday Times* ran an article on Parsons, Forman and Malina featuring a photograph of the first two, stating that the three "are tired of explaining they are not trying to build a rocket ship for initiation of the first airline tours to the moon." Their goal, the article said, was the exploration of the properties of near space. No mention of Hap Arnold's project was made, but other scientists' ideas on accomplishing this exploratory feat were also discussed. The accompanying photo shows Forman at the controls of a liquid fuel test pit, which replaced the earlier open-air tests, as well as the old-fashioned sandbags still in heavy use. In the photo Parsons stands behind

Forman, taking notes. Later he had the idea of photographing the gauges rather than trying to write everything down during the short-duration burns, a policy that made it much easier to document the actual readings.

Around this time Parsons made an interesting discovery in Robert Rypinski's library, a discovery that would change the direction of Parsons' personal life as much as Bollay's lecture changed the direction of his professional life. When Parsons rummaged through Rypinski's library he found a copy of Aleister Crowley's *Konx Om Pax*, published in 1907, which Rypinski had bought years earlier. The discovery, Rypinski said, was to Parsons "like real water to a thirsty man." Rypinksi himself never had figured out the rather dense book, so he gave it to Parsons, who soon told him he had entered into correspondence with its author.

Although recorded in several places, including Nat Freedland's *The Occult Explosion* and Sybil Leek's *Diary of a Witch*, the story is untrue that Crowley had once been in Pasadena long enough to start a lodge for his mystical order, the Ordo Templi Orientis (OTO). In reality, Crowley did make a brief stopover in Los Angeles in 1915—and couldn't wait to leave. Not until 20 years later would there be an official representative of the OTO in the area, namely Wilfred Talbot Smith, at whose home Parsons was to present himself shortly after his discovery of Crowley. It seems more than coincidental that the only lodge of the OTO was located within a few miles of Parsons' home.

Some familiarity with the magus Crowley (1875–1947) will be assumed throughout the remainder of this book, though I will elaborate on the elements of his work that have a direct bearing upon the work of John Parsons. Readers wishing to learn about Crowley are referred to the works listed in the bibliography; however, a satisfactory biography of the powerful and enigmatic Crowley remains to be published.

Crowley's Los Angeles representative, Smith, was from Tonbridge, Kent, about 20 miles southeast of London. He started his magical career as a member of the original Agape Lodge in Vancouver, British Columbia—the first North American lodge of the OTO—of which "Frater Achad" (Charles Stansfeld Jones, 1885–1950) was the founder. Smith had met Crowley at the Agape Lodge in 1915, during the latter's second American tour, and had soon risen to a position of greater authority in the Lodge, as Achad (Hebrew for "Unity") fell into disfavor with Crowley and was eventually expelled for a variety of heresies. Smith moved to Los Angeles in 1930, and, upon his arrival, began working on reopening the Agape Lodge, sometimes referred to as Agape Lodge #2.

Smith's colleague was Regina Kahl, who served as his High Priestess of the Gnostic Mass. The two are said to have run the Agape Lodge very strictly, almost tyrannically. Separate photos of Kahl and Smith are reproduced in Crowley's OTO publication, *The Equinox*, vol. III, no. 10.

The Gnostic Mass was Crowley's replacement for the "corrupted" mass celebrated by the Roman Catholic and Eastern Orthodox churches. The text of the Mass, referred to as Liber XV, was written in Moscow in 1913. Partly inspired by the Russian Orthodox Mass, it is surprisingly Christian in its symbology, and there is nothing obscene about it despite what certain detractors may say. In fact, it is reminiscent of Wagner's *Parsifal* with its repeated references to "lance" and "Grail," which are its most suggestive elements. As in the Christian Mass, the Holy Spirit is invoked often. The most openly erotic element in the mass occurs when the priestess disrobes for part of the ceremony.

The Gnostic Mass is too long to reproduce here but may be found in its entirety in Crowley's book, *Magick*. It is also reprinted in section IV of *Gems from the Equinox*, edited by Israel Regardie, and *The Equinox* vol. III, no. 10, as well as various locations on the internet. It would have been interesting to see what Crowley and the OTO would have done with the Gnostic Library discovered at Nag Hammadi by Egyptian Bedouins in 1945, two years before Crowley's death. However, the library was not published until 1978; thus, the Mass was not influenced by any of its previously unknown texts.

Originally intended by Crowley as the central ceremony of the OTO, both public and private, the Gnostic Mass is a rite conducted today by the *Ecclesia Gnostica Catholica* ("ECG"—the Gnostic Catholic Church) and celebrated regularly in major cities around the world. Evidently, visitors are usually welcome, provided they are willing to partake of the gnostic eucharist. The EGC is a religious body whose history and structure overlap that of the OTO.

Parsons became involved with the OTO when an unknown scientific colleague took the rocketeer to a meeting at Smith's house in Hollywood, after which Parsons and his wife, Helen, began attending the various meetings of the lodge, as well as the weekly performance of the Gnostic Mass. The "Church of Thelema," which Smith had incorporated for this purpose, used the Gnostic Mass as a recruiting ground for the OTO.

In the OTO Parsons had found a new outlet for his romantic notions. By day he was a student of the physical sciences; by night, of the occult sciences. In *Analysis By A Master of the Temple* he wrote of his first impressions of Smith: "The alternate repulsion and attraction you felt the first year after meeting [Smith] were caused by a subconscious resistance against the ordeals ahead. Had you had these experiences before, without such resistance, you would have become hopelessly unbalanced." The 25-year-old Parsons eventually discovered in Smith what Malina had found in von Kármán: a father figure who could act as mentor to his hungry intellect, something Parsons had been searching for since the death of his grandfather eight years earlier—indeed, since he was old enough to hear the tales of how wicked his real father had been.

The Sign of Horus: SILENCE.

three

A Short History of the OTO

The *Ordo Templi Orientis* (Order of the Temple of the East) is a quasi-Masonic initiating body founded in Germany just after the turn of the century. Its German name is *Orientalischer Templer-Orden* (Oriental Order of Templars), and there is purportedly a secret meaning to the letters "OTO" as well. The occultic order's highest grades are said to involve working with "tantric" exercises, usually referred to as sex magic.

Publicly the Ordo Templi Orientis claims descent from some of the great heretical movements such as the Bavarian Illuminati, the Rosicrucians, the Albigensians and Cathars, the Knights Templar, and various early gnostic sects. These claims are very helpful, for they aid in placing the OTO within a proper historical context, as we can guess much about it from its spiritual forebears. However, it is also desirable to learn about the secular origins of the OTO as well.

The Order traces its modern origins to two men: Carl Kellner and Theodor Reuss (pronounced "Royce"). Kellner, born September 1, 1851, was a wealthy Austrian industrialist who had made a good bit of money as a paper chemist. Reuss was born June 28, 1855 in Augsburg, Germany, about 15 miles northwest of Munich. Both men were born not long after the German Revolution of 1848, and thus lived in a world of Prussian military expansion. Borders changed often during their lifetimes. At various points throughout the men's lives, Austria and Germany were intermittently a part of Prussia, then a major western power.

Reuss became a Mason in 1876, and was also a singer, journalist and possible spy for the Prussian police. It is alleged that he infiltrated the Socialist League founded by Karl Marx's daughter and her husband. It is interesting to note how many famous occultists are said to have had connections with intelligence organizations, the military, and the police, such as Reuss, Crowley, Parsons, John Dee, Grady McMurtry, Anton LaVey, Michael Aquino, to name a few.

Reuss was also working on a revival of the Bavarian Illuminati, dispersed nearly 100 years earlier, and was at the same time the Grand Master of the Swedenborgian Rite in Germany, as well as a Magus of the Societas Rosicruciana ("Rosicrucian Society").

Kellner was an initiate of the influential Hermetic Brotherhood of Light (HBL), founded by P.B. Randolph around 1870. The history of the HBL is not germane to our story, but its rites included sacred applications of sexual energy, and Crowley names the HBL in writing as the source of the OTO's "secret," which is sexual in nature. The reader desiring more information on the Hermetic Brotherhood of Light is directed to Allen Greenfield's published history of the order, listed in the bibliography herein.

Kellner was also a high-ranking Freemason and a student of the Eastern mysteries. In the 1890s, Kellner claimed to have met three adepts from the East. One was a Sufi, Soliman ben Aifa, and the other two were Hindu tantrikas, Bhima Sena Pratapa of Lahore, and Sri Mahatma Agamya Paramahamsa. After their meeting, Kellner alleged he had found a "Key" (German: *Schlüssel*) to "the Mysteries," the heart of esoteric rites.

The word KEY turns up so many times in the telling of this tale that it reminds one of the pulp publisher Ray Palmer, who always said he had a FACT which proved the validity of Richard Shaver's wild Dero tales. It's as if the word itself has a hidden meaning. Kellner's Key, of course, was sex magic; perhaps the implication was key-in-lock sexual symbolism.

In 1895, Kellner proposed to Reuss that they disseminate this new-found Key through an organized masonic rite. Kellner planned a reformation of the Hermetic Brotherhood of Light in Germany, a series of three degrees that would be open only to the highest-ranking masons. Reuss used his masonic connections to acquire the 90th and 96th degrees of the Ancient and Primitive Rite of Memphis and Mizraim, and the 33rd degree of the Ancient and Accepted Scottish Rite, from John Yarker, a masonic historian in England. Despite its initial association, the OTO eventually retreated from Masonry, beginning with Crowley, who abandoned any claim to "make" Masons.

One of the Kellner-Reuss Order's platforms was the Swedenborgian Rite, named for the Swedish mystic Immanuel Swedenborg, which was used for the first three "Craft" degrees of Freemasonry (Entered Apprentice, Fellowcraft, and Master Mason), with the other, higher degrees serving as a vehicle for dissemination of the Key. Things seem to have been finalized somewhat within the Order in 1902, at which time the Memphis-Mizraim degrees were acquired. Initiations began, but students who advanced were often shocked at the revelation of the Key; others reportedly found it absurd, and many left the as-yet unnamed order. Occultist Franz

Hartmann (1838–1912) was one early member who left, around the time the order began calling itself "OTO."

On June 7, 1905, Kellner, now known as Frater Renatus, died. Reuss, who had already taken the lead role, was fully in charge now, and it was apparently he who chose the name Ordo Templi Orientis, since the appellation evidently did not exist before 1905. As to the significance of the name, the east (Orientis), of course, is where the sun rises, and is also where Kellner found his Key.

Within this body of adepts, Reuss was known variously as "Merlin" and "Peregrinus," and it was he who set up the 10-degree structure of the OTO that remains in place today. He also wrote various rituals for each degree, but most of these are no longer in use, having been replaced by those of Crowley.

Several famous occultists were chartered by Reuss to operate OTO lodges, including Rudolf Steiner (1861–1925), founder of Anthroposophy, who was chartered for a German lodge in 1906, although some of his spiritual descendants prefer to ignore this fact today. Dr. Gerard Encausse (1865–1916), better known as Papus, was chartered in France in 1908. The absorption of the *Ecclesia Gnostica Catholica* formed another link between the Papus lineage and the modern OTO.

A Dr. Arnold Krumm-Heller (1879–1949), also known by the Aztec name Huiracocha, was chartered for all of Latin America, but he never took the Order any further there and it seems to have died out. The use of Aztec names is still a practice among well-to-do Mexicans today.

Aleister Crowley joined the OTO in 1910, thinking it was just one of many other Eastern masonic lodges. He seems to have collected degrees from initiating bodies like some people collect postage stamps, and had been initiated all the way to the 33rd degree of the Scottish Rite in Mexico some 10 years earlier. He had also been initiated into the 90th and 95th degrees of the Memphis-Mizraim Rite by the same John Yarker who had given the 90th and 96th degrees of that rite to Reuss. The OTO was just another order like any other—or so Crowley thought.

The famous story concerning Crowley's initiation into the higher mysteries of the order goes like this: Crowley's *Book of Lies* was published in 1912, at which time he was an honorary VII° member of the OTO (and rather disappointed about it at that). After reading the book, Reuss approached Crowley angrily, accusing the latter of having revealed the secret of the highest degree of the Order, i.e., the IX°.

Reuss stated that Crowley would be compelled to be initiated into that degree immediately, and thus sworn to secrecy.[3]

Crowley denied the allegation, so Reuss pointed out the offending passage to him. Crowley would say that he instantaneously knew the answer to all the mysteries, the mysteries of the OTO and of many other spiritual traditions as well: He had the Key.

It is unclear what chapter of Crowley's book contained the passage that had riled Reuss. Robert Anton Wilson, popular author and writer of our introduction, says in *Cosmic Trigger* that it was chapter 69, but the most likely candidate appears to be chapter 36, the Star Sapphire, which is named in Crowley's *De Arte Magica* as containing the secret of the OTO. In reading some of the other chapters (15, e.g.) in *The Book of Lies*, it is difficult to believe that Crowley did not at least suspect the Key before his meeting with Reuss.

Regardless, Crowley was given the IX° in 1912, and the entire written corpus of the Order was at his disposal. He would soon rewrite almost everything within it to bring it into line with his own magical discoveries. On April 21, 1912, Crowley was given the X° and authority over the entire British Isles. His own magical record says he learned the Key in June of that year, in actuality a reference to when he translated the documents from German into English. In 1916, Crowley appointed Charles Stansfeld Jones, whom we have already met as Frater Achad, to be his Viceroy to North America. Jones' X° name was Parzival. On May 10, 1921, Reuss chartered Jones as Head of the OTO for North America, but Crowley overturned this action after succeeding Reuss.

Too many other charters and degrees were granted by the OTO to relate here. One of interest, although not part of our story, was to H. Spencer Lewis, founder of the Ancient and Mystical Order of the Rosy Cross (A.M.O.R.C.), i.e., "the Rosicrucians." Lewis was given a document referred to as a "Gage of Amity" in 1921, and his mail-order mystery school San Jose, California, still thrives today, evidently without possessing the Key.

In 1917, Crowley rewrote the OTO degrees again, especially the lower ones, removing most of the masonic material and replacing it with *thelema* (explained below). Reuss was in agreement, but other lodges would not be. In 1920, Reuss translated Crowley's Gnostic Mass into German and began to translate *Liber AL* as well, until he had a stroke in the spring of that year. Crowley then assumed an acting role as head of the OTO until November 27, 1921, at which time

---

3. Some sources say it was 1913, which means there is a discrepancy in Crowley's account. Perhaps Reuss saw the book while it was still in manuscript form.

he proclaimed himself "Outer Head of the Order." Jones and another X° initiate, Heinrich Tranker of the German *Pansophia* group, confirmed his position. Reuss died on October 28, 1923.

There were other orders that, although not a part of the OTO, were officially associated with it, many of which were not prepared to accept *thelema* when it was finally revealed to them by Crowley at a German conference in 1925. Readers interested in the histories of the various orders and breakaway groups are referred to *The Equinox*, vol. III, no. 10, and the various online histories of the Order.

As noted, in 1914 the Agape Lodge had been founded in Vancouver by Jones, AKA Achad/Parzival, under Crowley's authority. Crowley visited the lodge in 1915, at which time he met Wilfred Smith, who had been a charter member of the Agape Lodge. The two got along well at that point.

Fifteen years later, in 1930, Crowley sent Smith to Los Angeles with the express intent of opening another lodge, also to be called Agape Lodge. The lodge was incorporated April 4, 1934, and its first meeting was held on September 21, 1935 in Hollywood. Smith was appointed as "Head" for the United States, for which office he bore the X° name "Ramaka."

In 1941, Grady McMurtry (October 18, 1918–July 12, 1985) was first initiated into the OTO by Wilfred Smith at Agape Lodge No. 2. In 1943, Crowley granted McMurtry the IX° and the magical motto of "Hymenaeus Alpha," in England, where the latter was stationed during the war. McMurtry worked with Army Ordnance during World War II, served in Korea and retired a major. Today he is better remembered as the second Caliph of the OTO, while Karl Germer was the first Caliph, though he never used that term. The third Caliph, Hymenaeus Beta, has been Outer Head of the Order since McMurtry's death in 1985.

The grades of the Ordo Templi Orientis have rather involved names and echo the grades of various masonic rites, as well as those of the Bavarian Illuminati. They are:

0. Minerval
I. Man & Brother
II. Magician
III. Master Magician
IV. Companion of the Royal Arch of Enoch
V. Sovereign Prince of Rose Croix, Knight of the Pelican & Eagle
VI. Illustrious Knight Templar of the Order of Kadosh & Supreme Companion of the Holy Grail

VII. Very Illustrious Sovereign Grand Inspector General
VIII. Perfect Pontiff of the Illuminati, Epopt of the Illuminati
IX.   Initiate of the Sanctuary of the Gnosis
X.   Rex Summus Sanctissimus, Supreme & Most Holy King

The first three grades are open to all who request them and corre-spond roughly to the "nursery" grades of the Illuminati. The five lower grades correspond to the "chakras," i.e., yogic/tantric energy centers, as well as to the "naked-eye" planets. Higher degrees are by invitation only. Most people are surprised to learn the VII° requires a vow of chastity. There is also an XI° that is not part of the formal structure but was developed by Crowley.

As noted, Crowley rewrote the OTO degrees, replacing the masonic material with what he called "thelema." Thelema is the Greek for "will," a word important in the work of Aleister Crowley for several reasons. In 1904, Crowley "received" The Book of the Law, techni-cally called *Liber AL vel Legis*, through the mediumship of his first wife, Rose Kelly, while the couple was in Cairo celebrating their hon-eymoon. The book was allegedly dictated by a discarnate entity call-ing himself Aiwass, also spelled Aiwaz before Crowley changed it for numerological reasons.

One of the precepts contained in *The Book of the Law* (abbreviated "AL") is, "Do what thou wilt shall be the whole of the law" (see AL III:13). Its oft-cited complement is, "Love is the law, love under will." These two precepts are standard salutations for members of the OTO even today. The words for "will" and "love" in Greek—*thelema* (θελημα) and *agape* (αγαπη), respectively—each have numerical val-ues of 93, a number important in Crowley's system of magick.

These phrases carry with them a great duty to live deliberately, to find one's True Will *and then do it* and nothing else. Outsiders often interpret them as invitations to "free love," but that definition is not necessarily so. However, the word *agape* is a reference not only to "charitable love" but also to the "love feasts" of the second-century Christians, especially as interpreted by the Christian Gnostics, which did include a sexual meaning. The Agape Lodge was not called "Agape" for nothing.

A Rosicrucian order, the Golden Dawn—used as the basis for Crowley's "Astrum × Argenteum" magickal grading system—was modeled more after the mystery schools of the ancients, with the pur-pose of taking the candidate for initiation through a series of mysti-cal exercises and ritual ceremonies.

Around 1887, a manuscript in cipher was found in a bookstore by a Dr. Woodman and/or Woodford. Woodman was a colleague of Dr. William Wynn Westcott, who in turn was acquainted with Theodor Reuss. Woodman and Westcott called on Samuel "MacGregor" Mathers to help them decipher it.

The manuscript consisted of rituals and analyses of the Tarot cards, as well as the address of a Fräulein Sprengel in Nuremberg, Germany. Upon being contacted by them, Anna Sprengel, as *"Sapiens Dominabitur Astris"* [Wise Mistress of the Stars?], sent the three men a charter for a new lodge in England: the Isis-Urania Lodge of the Hermetic Order of the Golden Dawn, which opened on March 20, 1888. All three were chartered at the $7° = 4°$ degree, "Adeptus Exemptus," and soon opened other lodges around the British Isles. The Golden Dawn seems to have had a surprisingly large network.

According to the foundation myth, Sprengel died soon after, and her remaining German colleagues allegedly withdrew all support from the English lodge; however, as it turns out, they never really existed. The English were on their own for now, but they felt assured that they had already received sufficient information to place them in contact with the mysterious "Secret Chiefs" of the Order.

Subsequently Woodman died, and in 1897 Westcott stepped down. Mathers began claiming to have made contact with three of the Secret Chiefs, a doubtful assertion. Mathers also soon started to work on his greatest achievement, the translation of *The Book of the Sacred Magic of Abramelin the Mage*, which he had found in manuscript in a Paris library, the *Bibliotheque l'Arsenal*. This document explains how one may attain to the "Knowledge and Conversation of the Holy Guardian Angel."

Crowley was initiated into the Order of the Golden Dawn on November 18, 1898, at the age of 23. This was his first initiation, and he took it with all seriousness. Many famous writers were also members of the Golden Dawn: Arthur Edward Waite, William Butler Yeats, and Arthur Machen, to name a few. Oscar Wilde's wife Constance was a member, as was Yeats' mistress Florence Farr, an actress who was also the mistress of George Bernard Shaw.

The degree system of the Golden Dawn was later adapted by Crowley for the A∴A∴ and consisted of three different schools or orders: the grades 1 through 4 in the Order of the Golden Dawn proper; the grades 5 through 7 in the Order of the Rosy Cross (a Rosicrucian reference); and the grades 8 through 10 in the Order of the Silver Star.

The grades from 0 to 10 respectively are:

Probationer 0°=0°
Neophyte 1°=10°
Zelator 2°=9°
Practicus 3°=8°
Philosophus 4°=7°
Adeptus Minor 5°=6°
Adeptus Major 6°=5°
Adeptus Exemptus 7°=4°
Magister Templi 8°=3°
Magus 9°=2°
Ipsissimus 10°=1°

Crowley advanced through the lower grades promptly, and was overall quite pleased with the Order, becoming an "adept," as he moved from the lower grades into the Order of the Rosy Cross.

The idea of the progression through grades in the Golden Dawn was seen more as a teaching tool, somewhat like the Scottish Rite degrees of the Freemasons. A broad, religious order modeled after the Rosicrucians, the Golden Dawn, and subsequently Crowley's A∴A∴, are designed to bring the student to full spiritual potential in all areas.

The OTO, on the other hand, was conceived as a specialized rite to convey the Key that Kellner had discovered in the East. It then grew into a quasi-masonic initiating body, though the lower grades were initially granted honorarily to Masons in good standing with other lodges, and would subsequently be "de-masonized" by Crowley. Unlike the OTO, the focus of the Golden Dawn was not sexual in nature, although Crowley later used sex magic for the purposes of his own continued self-initiation.

As early as 1899, there was already dissent in the Golden Dawn, and in 1900 Arthur E. Waite left to found his own order. Another member broke away later to form the *Stella Matutina* ("Morning Star"). In addition, Mathers had been caught in his lie with Westcott regarding the existence of the Germans, and all the inner turmoil broke up the remaining order quite quickly, a development Crowley attributed to occult forces coming down on Mathers in retribution for his having publishing the Abramelin book. The other members were angry for Mathers having initiated Crowley into the 5° = 6° degree, Adeptus Minor, for a variety of reasons. The two had to left the country to do this initiation, traveling to Mathers' home in Paris, where

Mathers conferred the grade upon Crowley, during January 1900.

Crowley initially supported Mathers but could not do so forever, as Mathers slid further and further into madness. A lawsuit ensued, and Mathers declared in court that he was one of the mysterious "Secret Chiefs," an affair Crowley parodied quite humorously. The parody is reproduced in *The Aleister Crowley Scrapbook* by Sandy Robertson.

Crowley pursued his Golden Dawn work independently, later admitting other members under the aegis of the A∴A∴, but he would eventually openly claim all of the 10 degrees of the Order.

It was into this strange, esoteric and occult world that John Parsons stepped that fateful day when he received from Rypinski his first Crowley composition. This enigmatic fusion of "sex and rockets" was to prove a fascinating development in the history of the aerospace industry in America.

The Parsons invention, the solid fuel JATO cannister, now displayed at the Smithsonian.

four

Parsons' Double Life: 1940–1942

In 1940, the editor of *Astronautics* magazine compiled quotes from famous people under the heading "What They Think About Rockets," a few of which are worth excerpting here, as they indicate that, like John Parsons, even some of the "big thinkers" were looking to the stars. For example, the Secretary of the Smithsonian Institution, Dr. C.G. Abbot, stated:

> A few hundred thousand dollars invested today in the scientific development of rockets would pay the nation dividends amounting to hundreds of millions of dollars in the next two decades.

World-renowned pilot Charles Lindbergh opined:

> The rocket offers the only known possibility of sending instruments to altitudes above those reached by sounding balloons. Observations taken outside of the earth's atmosphere or even in the higher levels of the atmosphere, would be of immense value in the study of such subjects as astronomy, meteorology and terrestrial magnetism.

And Dr. John O. Stewart, Associate Professor of Astronomical Physics, Princeton University, declared:

> With rockets speeds of 1000 miles per hour are possible by 1950. By 2050 a rocket trip to the moon at 25,000 miles per hour is not impossible.

Despite such open-mindedness in the world at large, within the GALCIT group, all was not well, and Malina found reason to complain about Parsons and Forman again in a letter of April 7, 1940. The complaint had nothing to do with Parsons' newfound interest in the occult, which Forman seems to have shared to a lesser degree. Malina had his own unorthodoxies, including communism. Malina's mind was on more mundane matters. He wrote, "Need a good physicist.

Forman and Parsons are all right for some types of work, sometimes they are like inventors, in the worst sense of the word." This instance is the very last time Parsons is mentioned in any of Malina's letters home, except when his name appears with the others on a list of Aerojet founders. The break between the two was complete, although Parsons may not have realized it. Parsons remained with Forman, but Malina was with Summerfield, who joined the group that July. Later, Forman's widow would relate that her husband and Parsons thought Malina was unnecessarily "cold and arrogant" toward them.

In August 1940, *Popular Mechanics* devoted six pages to the work of Parsons and Forman in an article entitled, "Seeking Power for Space Rockets," which is informative and well-illustrated. Malina is also mentioned but not pictured. A shorter article, "New Experiments with Rockets," appeared the following month in *Popular Science* and is also well-illustrated but ends with a discussion of the work of Robert Goddard and the potential military applications for rockets. They are reproduced in the pages that follow. Only Parsons and Forman are featured, which speaks well to their level of involvement at this time. While Malina was head of the project in name by virtue of his status at Caltech, Parsons and Forman were the ones doing the dirty work.

Also in 1940, the United States started sending ammunition and supplies to England, embargoing Japan. President Franklin Delano Roosevelt and his Congress increased defense spending 800%, from $1.9 billion to $17 billion. Von Kármán began making frequent trips to Washington, D.C, trips that would continue throughout the war. The city of Pasadena had 13,300 people working in the aircraft industry that year, a figure that may sound like a lot, but by the next year— after the United States entered the war—it had increased to 113,000. In order to recruit so many workers, Boy Scouts were hired to distribute job applications door-to-door.

In that year, von Kármán and Malina demonstrated on paper the feasibility of long-duration burns in a confined space such as a rocket motor casing, a procedure that von Kármán later listed as the first critical step in the development of rockets in the United States. As a result, the National Academy of Sciences immediately doubled the GALCIT group's budget for 1941, to $22,000. This action infuriated Goddard, working alone in Roswell, as he didn't appreciate the young upstarts getting all the funding and attention. His decades of work were indeed unappreciated by the world, mainly due to self-imposed isolation. Malina, Parsons and Forman shared the byline on

BLITZKRIEG!

POPULAR
MECHANICS
MAG

WRITTEN SO

USED TRADE MARK GREAT BRITAIN No. 40428

AUG.
25 CENTS

SEE PAGE 210

SEEKING POWER

Small test rocket is loaded into firing stand, upper left, to trace its characteristic path. Above, putting powder charge in rocket. Diagram shows man's altitude records and his hopes for the rocket

Stratosphere, 200 miles

Range of aurora borealis: 43 to 200 miles above earth

Proposed "step" rocket should reach 500,000 ft.; would have three motors, two of which would detach when charge was spent

Instruments carried by rocket to be returned to earth by parachute

Sounding balloon: record height 110,000 ft.

Free balloon with human passenger; record height 72,394 ft.

Mt. Everest, 29,141 ft.

Airplane: record height 56,046 ft.

Troposphere 5 miles above earth

EARTH

G UARDED by sandbags, a man sits before a panel on which are rows of gauges. As he turns valves, needles of the gauges spin and gyrate. From behind the sandbags comes a hiss, a puff of smoke.

The man relaxes, the gauges come to rest. If it were not for the tiers of protecting sandbags, it would seem undramatic, almost unimportant. Yet in those few seconds all the fires of hell have been raging in the little cylinder behind the sandbags. Terrifically explosive gases have just reached a temperature half that of the sun and a velocity of 3,600 miles per hour—and one more experiment has been added to the long list by which men have sought to gain knowledge which will enable them to conquer outer space.

Scientists are hard-headed men. They do not speculate on traveling to the moon every time they see a sky rocket. They say simply:

"We are experimenting with fuels for

for SPACE ROCKETS

rockets. We've found out a few things. It may be that in the reasonably near future science will succeed in sending a rocket higher than any man-made contrivance ever traveled before. Perhaps such a rocket might reach an altitude of 500,000 feet.

"If a rocket could be shot that high, it could carry recording instruments which would gather information of the greatest importance. A rocket to the moon. Men still dream of that. But science deals with facts. Still, the dream is perhaps a little bit nearer realization."

Behind that simple statement is another chapter in man's struggle to escape the chains of gravity which bind him to one planet.

Three years ago it was decided to study rocket motors at California Institute of Technology. Although many rocket experiments had been conducted throughout the world, no complete and systematic investigation of motors has been available. Yet it is just those

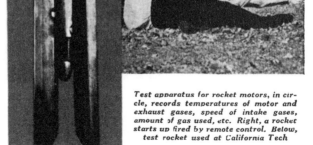

Test apparatus for rocket motors, in circle, records temperatures of motor and exhaust gases, speed of intake gases, amount of gas used, etc. Right, a rocket starts up fired by remote control. Below, test rocket used at California Tech

century. Immediately, the question of their possible military importance arose. But no one devised a successful military rocket until 1805, when William Congreve perfected one—and in so doing helped write the American national anthem.

For it was the Congreve rockets fired by the British forces attacking Fort McHenry that inspired Francis Scott Key to write the lines of the Star Spangled Banner, "and the rockets' red glare." Congreve rockets were also used with telling effect against Napoleon at Waterloo. Both incendiary and explosive charges were carried by these rockets. Not until modern artillery was developed did interest in military rockets wane.

However, the military potentialities of rockets have again come under serious consideration. With nations searching for new weapons, rockets were bound to have their day once more.

Major James R. Randolph of the U. S. Army recently set forth the advantages of military rockets. They are cheap, as no elaborate gun barrel or firing mechanism is needed. Rockets are fired from

very problems of a powerful enough fuel and a long-life combustion chamber that are the stumbling blocks which are holding back rocket flights.

So three experimenters at California Tech., Frank J. Malina, John W. Parsons, and Edward Forman, decided to build a rocket which did not fly, a rocket which moved but a few fractions of an inch, but which told those vital facts about what goes on when a charge is fired.

As a background for their work, they had the long history of rocket experimentation, going back to the days of early Chinese culture when rockets were first used for fireworks displays. The western world did not begin to construct rockets until about the fourteenth

To determine stability, a flying model is fired with powder by remote control, top. Center, recoil of spring gauges strength of powder fuels. Behind the sandbags (bottom) California Institute of Technology scientists test rocket motors and explosive fuel—mixture of oxygen and ethylene—developing 5,000-degree heat and gas velocities of 3,600 miles per hour

simple tubes. They are easy to transport. The tubes may be set up in a few moments, and a terrific fire concentration achieved suddenly, without the elaborate preparations which make artillery concentrations obvious to the foe.

But whatever the military significance of the rocket, its most dramatic and intriguing potentiality is that of conquering space. Although many older writers of fantasy speculated on space rockets, the first really practical experimentation in America was done by Prof. R. H. Goddard, beginning in 1909.

In 1918 Goddard published a set of calculations which he believed established the possibility of a rocket flight to the moon. If such a rocket could be constructed, he proposed that a small charge of flash powder be carried, and exploded when the rocket struck the moon. The flash would be visible to the earth's large telescopes.

Ten years later Goddard fired some experimental altitude rockets which attained a height of about two miles and a vertical

(Continued to page 118A)

Heavy barricade of stones is laid to protect operators before firing a rocket with its highly explosive charge (top). Dials in center show the fury of the thrust of a rocket motor in operation, its fuel consumption, temperature of motor and exhaust, and intake velocity. Three tanks of ethylene gas, shown at bottom, are on a delicate balance accurate to one-tenth ounce

Seeking Power for Space Rockets

(Continued from page 213)

climbing speed of 700 miles per hour, far greater than the fastest airplane. Since that time, Goddard has continued his experiments in perfecting rocket design. Recently he incorporated a gyroscope to stabilize his rockets during flight.

However, the old problem of a sufficiently powerful fuel and a sufficiently durable firing chamber still remained. Certain experiments seem to favor the use of powder explosives, but in general, liquid fuels seem to offer the best prospects. A combination of liquid oxygen and gasoline has proved very efficient.

Rockets powered by such fuels have been used by the American and German rocket societies. A British society has made speculative plans for space travel should the day ever arrive when fuel and construction problems are licked. This society has designed space suits, and has even made tentative arrangements to secure human beings who would be willing to take the terrific gamble should the conquest of space ever be technically possible.

These problems of fuel and combustion chamber the California Tech. scientists have set out to study—and they have made such advancement that they talk of a sounding rocket which might reach a height of half a million feet.

The first problem faced was to design a highly accurate testing machine. Such a device must be able to register thrust, temperature, pressure of gases, amount of fuel used, and the efficiency of the combustion.

For experimental purposes gaseous combustibles are used instead of liquid. The propellant now being experimented with is a mixture of ethylene and oxygen. These gases are kept under pressures of 1,200 and 2,000 pounds to the square inch. Operators control the flow of gas by means of valves. The gauges which record the performance of the rocket motor are photographed to give a permanent record.

The rocket motor is a single steel cylinder about eighteen inches long and six in diameter. It is lined with carbon to guard against the terrific heat when the motor is operated. A temperature of 5,000 degrees Fahrenheit is sometimes reached—almost half that of the sun's corona.

Rocket motor, tanks of ethylene and oxygen, and connecting tubes are mounted on a torsion balance so delicate that it will register forces of only one-tenth of an ounce. When the motor is fired, motor, lines, and braces move as a single unit. The thrust is then registered by a dial on the control panel.

Because of the terrifically explosive character of all fuels used, the control panel and operator are protected from the firing chamber by sandbags. Once a nozzle blew out during a test, and the resulting roar was heard for blocks.

Nozzles for the rocket motor are made from such substances as pure carbon, stainless steel, and copper alloys. Experiments have shown that few substances will stand the extreme heat and pressure of the exhaust gases. Velocities of 6,000 feet per second, or better than 3,600 miles per hour, have been recorded. Often after one minute in the firing chamber, a nozzle, which a moment before was a beautifully machined piece of metal, will be charred, distorted, and blacked, looking as if it had been subjected to the eternal fires.

Rocket scientists have calculated that a velocity of seven miles per second, or approximately 25,000 miles per hour, would be necessary for a rocket to escape the earth's gravity. They further believe that 6,000 tons of fuel would be necessary to carry ten tons of pay load. The California men do not speculate on space travel. However, they do say that their experiments indicate that with a "step" rocket (one having three motors, two of which would be released during flight), a velocity of 11,000 feet per second might be reached. This would carry the rocket to a height of 500,000 feet, five times the record height for a sounding balloon. Physical information gathered by such a rocket would be of incalculable value.

Meanwhile, the motor behind the sandbags hisses and thrusts and the needles on the dials continue to write their record of vital facts. And another significant step is being taken in man's struggle to conquer space.

❡ If you will send stamped, self-addressed envelope to our Bureau of Information, you will be given the name and address of the manufacturer of or dealer in any article described in this magazine.

their feasibility paper, entitled, "Air Corps Jet Propulsion Research, Final Report for 1939–40," a copy of which is on file in the JPL archives.

At this time, Parsons received recognition and accolades not only in the aerospace industry but also in his personal life. One of the people in Parsons' new esoteric circle of friends was the actress Jane Wolfe, who had appeared in the silent films, *The Woman Next Door* (1919), *Men, Women and Money* (1919), and *Behold My Wife* (1920). Wolfe, who had chosen the magical name Soror Estai, had been with Crowley at Cefalu (his "Abbey of Thelema" in Italy) before coming back to California and the Agape Lodge, when Mussolini closed the Abbey. After her return she does not appear in any of the film guides. Adding to the Parsons' legend, Wolfe recorded her first impression of him in her "magical record" for December 1940:

> Unknown to me, John Whiteside Parsons, a newcomer, began astral travels. This knowledge decided Regina [Kahl] to undertake similar work. All of which I learned after making my own decision. So the time must be propitious.
>
> Incidentally, I take Jack Parsons to be the child who "shall behold them all" [i.e., the Mysteries of *The Book of the Law*. See AL I:54-56, below].
>
> 26 years of age, 6′2″, vital, potentially bisexual at the very least, University of the State of California and Cal Tech., now engaged in Cal Tech chemical laboratories developing "bigger and better" explosives for Uncle Sam. Travels under sealed orders from the government. Writes poetry—"sensuous only," he says. Lover of music, which he seems to know thoroughly. I see him as the real successor of Therion [Crowley]. Passionate; and has made the vilest analyses result in a species of exaltation after the event. Has had mystical experiences which gave him a sense of equality all round, although he is hierarchical in feeling and in the established order.

The passage in Crowley's *The Book of the Law* to which Wolfe refers (AL I:54-56) reads, "Change not as much as the style of a letter; for behold! Thou, o prophet, shalt not behold all these mysteries hidden therein. The child of thy bowels, he shall behold them. Expect him not from the East, nor from the West; for from no expected house cometh that child." At 26, Parsons was still a "child" in the eyes of the older members, at least in the spiritual sense, regarded by Wolfe as this "chosen one," so to speak.

Parsons' "mystical experiences," if they were recorded then, have since been lost and are unknown. For sake of comparison to Wolfe's portrayal, Parsons' FBI file describes him as 6'1", 185 pounds, with brown hair and brown eyes, medium build, and fair complexion. The remark "potentially bisexual at the very least" may refer to his admitted attraction to Smith, as well as to another unique characteristic: at least two former work associates have said that Parsons sweated profusely, which caused strong body odor that he tried to mask with heavy cologne. A man who wore a lot of cologne at the same time that he displayed an above-average interest in another man may have inadvertently given the impression of bisexuality. Parsons himself once expressed a latent homosexuality, and Aleister Crowley, Parsons' new idol, was well known for his bisexuality.

Like many other Agape Lodge members, Wolfe was also in the A∴A∴. Crowley had initiated her at Cefalu as a Probationer 0° = 0° on June 11, 1921, and had further recognized her as a Neophyte 1° = 10° in May 1940, after she had written him to lament her long term as a Probationer.

Wolfe was not the last to identify Parsons' potential. After more than a year of attending meetings and the Gnostic Mass, John and Helen Parsons joined the Agape Lodge on February 15, 1941, when they simultaneously joined the A∴A∴. Just a few weeks after they joined, in March 1941, Smith wrote to Crowley, "I think I have at long last a really excellent man, John Parsons. And starting next Tuesday he begins a course of talks with a view to enlarging our scope. He has an excellent mind and much better intellect than myself . . . John Parsons is going to be valuable."

Parsons became "Frater T.O.P.A.N." and was known as "Frater 210" for short. His wife became "Soror Grimaud." The initials in Parsons' magical motto stood for *Thelemum Obtentum Procedero Amoris Nuptiae*, Latin for "the obtainment of *thelema*—Will—through the nuptials of love." The initials T.O.P.A.N. were also a declaration of Parsons' dedication: To Pan. In Hebrew the enumeration for T.O.P.A.N. is $400 + 70 + 80 + 1 + 50 = 601$. Parsons counted it as I.O.P.A.N., giving the more desirable sum 210, with "Io Pan" being Greek for "Hail Pan." Indeed, Crowley's "Hymn to Pan," which Parsons had memorized and often recited, begins, "Io Pan! Io Pan Pan!"

The numbers 1 through 20 add to 210. In the book 777 Crowley also speaks of certain numbers important to each of the *sephiroth* (spheres) of the kabbalistic Tree of Life. The first has the value 1, the second $1 + 2 = 3$, the third $1 + 2 + 3 = 6$, and so on; there are 10 altogether. Although Crowley does not say so, a little quick math will show these 10 values add to 210. In 777 Crowley calls the meaning of 210 "too holy" to divulge, an allusion to the "N.O.X. formula." N.O.X., Latin for "night," is akin to "L.V.X." or "Lux"—light. Both are portrayed during simple rituals of Crowley's that came from the Golden Dawn.

Coincidentally, the interstate highway running through Pasadena which makes a 90-degree turn due north of the beginning of South Orange Grove Ave., heading straight to JPL, is numbered 210, as if some cosmic force numbered the highway in Parsons' honor.

Helen's chosen name, Grimaud, is a French name that may refer to a character in one of Lord Bulwer-Lytton's novels who acted as a "magical servitor." Bulwer-Lytton is probably most famous for having started a novel with the phrase, "It was a dark and stormy night."

Eventually, Parsons came to view Smith as the father he always wanted, and the two stayed in touch throughout their lives, despite the many problems between them and with other members of the lodge. While many members of the Agape Lodge drifted apart, Parsons and Smith continually came back to each other, and, although Parsons called Crowley "Father" in his many letters to him, the immediate presence of Smith was much more powerful.

In addition, Parsons' interest in science fiction continued into adulthood, and he attended many of the weekly meetings of the Los Angeles Science Fantasy Society (LASFS), which met Thursday evenings. LASFS started as chapter 4 of the Science Fiction League, one of many fan clubs begun in 1934 when Hugo Gernsback's magazine *Wonder Stories* announced the new program. All closed but chapter 4, which remained a vital concern due to the work of one man—Forrest J. Ackerman. Ackerman has said that he remembers meeting Parsons once, though others insist he must have met him on many occasions. Helen Parsons Smith remembers at least one meeting.

In 1940, Ackerman's group became the independent LASFS, which, as home base for Los Angeles-area fans and writers, was quite active. JPL archivist John Bluth heard that many science fiction people frequented Parsons' house, but it was less common for Parsons to go to the LASFS. He was thus probably not a member, just an attendee.

At one of the Thursday meetings in 1941, Parsons met one of his favorite authors, Jack Williamson, who records this meeting in *Wonder's Child*, his autobiography. Williamson had written *Darker Than You Think*, which first appeared in the magazine *Unknown* in 1940, and was expanded considerably in 1948 for the book edition.

In *Wonder's Child*, Williamson wrote, "He [Parsons] had read my novel *Darker Than You Think*, which deals with the supernatural. I was astonished to discover he had a far less skeptical interest in such things than I." Nonetheless, it was Williamson's favorite story as well, and he identified with the main character, Will Barbee, who is horrified to discover he is really a werewolf, but gradually learns to accept his newfound powers.

Williamson subsequently went to Parsons' house for one of the Sunday afternoon meetings of fans and writers that Parsons sponsored every week. He recorded the event in *Wonder's Child*:

> I met John Parsons. An odd enigma to me, he was a rocket engineer with unexpected leanings toward the occult. He wanted to meet me because I'd written *Darker Than You Think*—a good many people have taken it more seriously than I ever did; witches now and then have taken me for a fellow Wiccan.
>
> Parsons belonged to the OTO, an underground order founded, I think, by the satanist Aleister Crowley. One night Cleve Cartmill and I were allowed to climb after him into an attic to attend a secret meeting. The ritual was disappointingly tame. There was no nude virgin on the altar. Satan was not invoked.
>
> Yet the priest impressed me. He was a lean, dynamic little man with bright, light blue eyes, driven by a virulent hatred of God. Talking to him after the ceremony, I found that he was the son of a British clergyman who must have been the real target of that savage animosity.

From the above description it sounds as if Williamson got to meet Wilfred Smith.

Darker Than You Think is the story of hereditary werewolves who have discovered their true bestial nature and seek to revive the old ways and the old gods. They accomplish this revival under the leadership of the "Child of Night," who is the result of a magical prodigious birth, finding him in the character of Will Barbee. Williamson's first science fiction treatment of werewolves (a novel approach at the time) had been in 1932, when he wrote the short story, "Wolves of Darkness."

The connection to Wicca and neo-paganism is obvious, as is the parallel to Parsons' magical "Babalon Working," which will be the subject of chapters 7 and 8. *Darker Than You Think* is even listed under "Religion and Myths" in *The Visual Encyclopedia of Science Fiction*. Williamson's book evidently influenced Parsons' writing,

"You must be strong, Will, to take such a shape!"

Edd Cartier's illustration for the 1948 Fantasy Press edition of *Darker Than You Think,* Jack Williamson's sci-fi novel John Parsons found extraordinarily inspirational.

such as follows, which sounds like a fair synopsis of *Darker Than You Think*:

> To go deep you must reject each phenomenon, each illumination, each ecstasy, going ever downward, until you reach the last avatars of the symbols that are also the racial archetypes.
>
> In this sacrifice to the abysmal gods is the apotheosis that transmutes them to the beauty and power that is your eternity, and the redemption of mankind.

Several other authors visited Parsons, including A.E. Van Vogt, as well as regulars like writer Alva Rogers and science fiction illustrator Lou Goldstone. Another possible visitor was E. Hoffman Price, a would-be writer who knew most of the people in the circle of H.P. Lovecraft, the famous fantasy and horror writer, as well as in much of science fiction fandom. Price later bragged of having introduced occult ideas to Lovecraft, whose treatments of Theosophical elements are well documented in his letters to Price, thus revealing that some of the material did indeed originate with the latter.

Parsons also met a young Ray Bradbury, or, rather, Bradbury met Parsons. As Bradbury told me, "I only met him once, when I was a teenager and he came to lecture at the Los Angeles Science Fantasy Society in the late thirties . . . I was merely part of a small audience of about 20 or 30 who were fascinated with his ideas about the future."

One other person who Parsons met at the LASFS was Grady McMurtry, who later became Frater Hymenaeus Alpha and was Karl Germer's successor as Outer Head of the OTO, running the Order until his death in 1985.

Much has been made of a connection between Robert Heinlein and Parsons, and it has been said that Heinlein was the first person to whom Parsons introduced his second wife, Cameron. Parsons is also thought to have corresponded with Heinlein after his leaving Hollywood; unfortunately, Mrs. Heinlein destroyed all of her husband's correspondence from the period before they were married. However, Mrs. Heinlein and L. Sprague de Camp have maintained that Heinlein did not know Parsons, although Cameron asserted their meeting occurred and was later covered up. Claims that Heinlein's *Stranger in a Strange Land* was influenced by Parsons and *thelema* are left to the reader's judgement.

POPULAR SCIENCE
MONTHLY
Mechanics & Handicraft

SEPTEMBER
15¢

Can We Defend Our Coasts? PAGE 94

NEW EXPERIMENTS WITH ROCKETS

PROTECTED against deadly explosions by a wall of sandbags and heavy timbers, two young California Institute of Technology scientists feed explosive gases under pressure into the motor of a rocket. At the touch of a button, a leaping spark ignites the mixture, and with a roar, a sheet of flame, and a cloud of smoke, the gases go into action. Operating a camera, one of the researchers photographs a battery of instrument dials that reveal such vital facts as the thrust of the motor and the weight and pressure of the gases surging through pipes from metered chambers.

But the rocket itself, instead of soaring into the heavens, remains rooted on the ground, since it is

anchored in place and pointed earthward. For Edward S. Forman and John W. Parsons, the California rocket researchers, are mainly interested for the present in studying the action of various fuels for stratosphere - stabbing rocket ships, and the effect of their intense heat on various types of nozzles.

This question of rocket-motor nozzles is one of the major problems now facing rocket experimenters, who are constantly devising new improvements and new methods to take the rocket out of the realm of fantasy and into the field of practical use. Booster motors to assist rocket take-offs, gyroscopes to guide flights along straight paths, water-cooled nozzles, range finders to record altitudes and speeds, automatic

parachutes that return the rockets safely to earth—these are some of the devices that are now being tested and brought to perfection by laboratory experiments on a dozen fronts.

North of Roswell, N. M., for instance, rockets wobble skyward from a sixty-foot tower, and then straighten out into a true vertical path, soaring up two miles into the air at a speed of more than 700 miles an hour. At the top of their flight, they hang in air a split second, then tumble over and float gently down to earth as their parachutes automatically belly out. The gyroscopic mechanism that straightens out the initial take-off wobble is a development engineered by Dr. Robert H. Goddard, rocket pioneer. Stabilizing vanes attached to the rocket are automatically controlled by the gases of the

By ROBERT E MARTIN

John W. Parsons preparing an experimental rocket motor for a test. At the left, gases burning at 3,000 degrees centigrade shoot out of a tiny nozzle. The general view at the far left shows the sandbagged outdoor laboratory that is used by Parsons and his associate, Edward S. Forman

exhaust stream, moving the rocket back into line when it wanders ten degrees away from a vertical path.

But actually how close is rocket science to practical exploration of the stratosphere at an altitude of, say, fifty miles? Studies at the California Institute of Technology lead investigators to believe that with the exhaust velocity of 7,000 feet a second obtained by Goddard's rockets, powder rockets could now be built capable of rising 100,000 feet. In fact, under some conditions, they believe a gas-propelled, eighty-five pound rocket, exhausting its burned fuel through a nozzle at the rate of 12,000 feet a second, could rise under power to an altitude of fifty miles, and then continue, "coasting," straight up for another 175 miles.

For more than three decades scientists have sought ways to explore the atmosphere at great heights. Today their thoughts are turning to levels where rockets would fly through a vacuum, and celestial observations might be made without interference from city lights, haze, clouds, or air molecules of lower altitudes. One well-known astronomer even went so far as to suggest the possibility of a complete astronomical observatory, raised a thousand miles above the earth by one set of rocket motors, and maintained at that level by another.

Of more immediate practical application is the proposal that rockets take over the duties of heavy artillery in laying down a concentrated bombardment of an intensity not reached even with dive-bombing airplanes and the latest type of field and railway guns. Major James R. Randolph, of the U S. Army Ordnance Reserve, recently declared that rockets could easily equal the performances of long-range guns firing shells as far as seventy miles.

These long-range cannon fire a projectile eight inches in diameter. "Instead of firing shots of moderate caliber at long intervals," said Major Randolph, "a rocket plant could fire the equivalent of twenty-four-inch shells as fast as desired."

Projectiles envisaged by this officer would weigh four tons. Thousands of them, set off simultaneously or in volleys, might lay down in a few minutes a withering barrage that present artillery could equal only over a long period of time.

Armor-piercing rockets, Randolph further proposed, could be carried by submarines, while on land, the rocket shells could be transported in ordinary motor trucks bearing no resemblance to artillery weapons now easily identified by enemy planes.

Popular Science, in its September 1940 issue, plays up Parsons, Malina and Forman's explosive experiments in the Arroyo Seco. The magazine's caption mistakenly says that a Caltech photographer is Parsons, and neglects to mention the identity of a lone figure in a white shirt. He's John Parsons.

An essay in *Rapid Eye #3* entitled "Whence Came the Stranger" seems to document a definite relationship between Heinlein and Parsons. In this essay, Adam Rostoker wrote, "Parsons and Heinlein were quite close friends. They may have met at the Los Angeles Science Fiction Fan Club [Science Fantasy Society], which maintained a reading room . . . [They] were certainly seen there together." In a footnote he related that Marjorie Cameron, Parsons' second wife, was the source of this information: "Heinlein was the first person Parsons ever introduced her to. She didn't care for Heinlein too much; he was 'too slick, too Hollywood. But Jack and he were good friends.'" Adam Rostoker is the same "Adam Walks-Between-Worlds" of the Church of All Worlds which was inspired by Heinlein's *Stranger in a Strange Land*. He may have published a similar article in that organization's *Green Egg* magazine.

Williamson documents science writer and member of the German Rocket Society Willy Ley's occasional presence at meetings of the Mañana Literary Society, an informal science fiction discussion group which met at Heinlein's house, so Parsons may have met his old correspondent there—assuming he was in fact a part of Heinlein's circle.

Meanwhile, in Parsons' other life, the GALCIT group realized its first big success in August 1941. Parsons had come to realize that the rocket motors, now called jet-assisted take-offs (JATOs) to avoid the charged term "rocket," had to be used almost immediately, as they could not be stored for long periods of time or in extremes of temperature. He and Forman would get up very early and prepare the JATOs, nap a little, then meet the others at March Field. Von Kármán wrote, "He [Parsons] used a paper-lined cylinder into which he pressed a black-powder propellant of his own composition in one-inch layers." In August, the group was ready to test Parsons' JATOs on actual aircraft, the first time this type of rocket had ever been used.

The fuel used was called GALCIT-27, implying 26 failures before it. The airplane chosen was a hobby plane called the "Ercoupe," chosen because it was small, light and hard to stall. The pilot was Captain Homer A. Boushey, Jr. of the Army Air Corps, a graduate student of von Kármán's. Also present was another graduate student, Homer Joe Stewart, to whom was addressed a signed copy of Frank Malina's memoirs in the possession of the JPL archives.

The GALCIT-27 event was recorded on color film, a copy of which resides in the Library of Congress. The silent original, along with some outtakes, is in the JPL archives. Both the original and the outtakes feature Parsons sporting a goatee and small mustache.

By this time Weld Arnold had been replaced as the group's photographer by George Emerson, an Englishman, after whose arrival the quality of still photographs improved dramatically. Emerson stayed with JPL for 40 years as the lab's chief photographer, while Weld went to New York and, in the 1950s, ended up on the Board of Trustees at the University of Nevada, where Malina found him. The two corresponded until Weld's death in 1961.

Parsons was right about using the JATOs immediately, and, on August 6, 1941, one week after some nerve-wracking static tests in which the JATOs "exploded like the Fourth" 12 of the rockets were mounted under the wings of the Ercoupe. The JATOs each delivered 28 pounds of thrust for 12 seconds—336 pounds thrust total. The group had never seen a plane climb so steeply. The film clearly shows the plane leveling off immediately when the JATOs' fuel supply was exhausted. The JATOs were a success, and Parsons was to credit.

Some of the footage was shot from the air, in Clark Millikan's small plane. The ground footage showing the Ercoupe taking off alongside Millikan's plane reveals quite dramatically the difference the JATOs made: Takeoff distance was reduced over 30%. During one of the tests a nozzle shot off the end of a JATO, bounced off the runway, and tore a hole in the plane's fuselage near the tail. "At least it wasn't a big hole," one of the group joked. Undaunted, the pilot Boushey continued flying. The tests also continued, running until August 12.

The JATOs were envisioned for use wherever short runways were constructed. If the Army Air Corps were in some remote locale with rough terrain or lots of trees, a short runway would save the labor and expense of a lot of men. The second use was for quick getaways in the air. If an enemy plane came up behind a pilot who had JATOs, the latter could ignite the rockets and get out of the enemy's line of fire. Footage of this sort of maneuver is also included in the August 1941 film. Hap Arnold's original idea to utilize the JATOs to help overloaded aircraft take off was not a part of the tests, though it was put to use during the war.

On August 23, the propeller was then removed from the Ercoupe to demonstrate flight under rocket power only, the hole covered with three safety banners the group found at the site. One banner in particular amused them: "Ask yourself: what about tomorrow if I meet with an accident today?" To gain sufficient speed to get it off the ground, the Ercoupe was towed by a rope connected to Rudolph Schott's red pickup truck. As the truck accelerated to 25 mph,

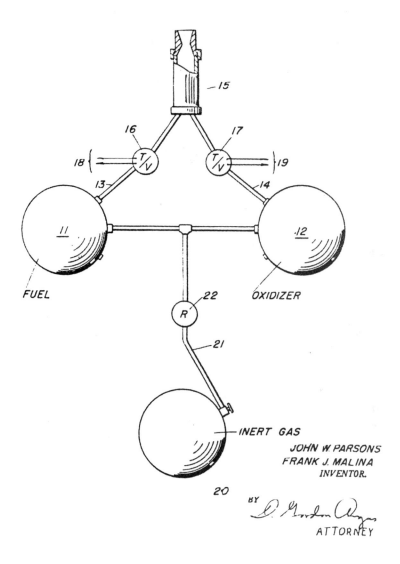

FUEL

OXIDIZER

INERT GAS

JOHN W. PARSONS
FRANK J. MALINA
INVENTOR.

BY

ATTORNEY

Three patents for liquid fuel discoveries were finally awarded
Parsons and Malina a full two years after Parsons died.

1

2

2,693,077

REACTION MOTOR OPERABLE BY LIQUID PRO-PELLANTS AND METHOD OF OPERATING IT

Frank J. Malina and John W. Parsons, Pasadena, Calif., assignors, by mesne assignments, to Aerojet-General Corporation, Azusa, Calif., a corporation of Ohio

Original application May 8, 1943, Serial No. 486,236, now Patent No. 2,573,471, dated October 30, 1951. Divided and this application September 1, 1950, Serial No. 182,742

2 Claims. (Cl. 60—35.4)

Our invention relates to jet propulsion and more particularly to propellants which are useful in connection therewith.

This is a division of my copending application Serial No. 486,236, filed May 8, 1943, now U. S. Patent 2,573,471.

While our invention is capable of use in connection with the propulsion of a wide variety of different devices and vehicles, since it finds particular utility in the propulsion of aircraft, its advantages are described with relation to such use, it being understood that our invention is, however, not limited to such use.

Prior to our invention special means were always required to ignite the propellants. For example, when liquid oxygen is used as an oxidizer and gasoline is used as a fuel, some auxiliary ignition means must always be provided to initiate combustion of the propellants. This is objectionable because it requires either a spark plug or other ignitor or means for heating the walls of the combustion chamber above the ignition point of the propellant mixture making this system complex and dependent upon the operation of such ignition system.

While spontaneous combustion is obtained with our preferred combinations of propellants which is especially effective when operating in accordance with our preferred method it will be understood that the propellants we have discovered offer advantages even when operating under other conditions.

The present invention relates to fuels, and oxidizers and their combination as propellants and their method of injection into a jet motor. Among the objects of our invention are: to provide more efficient and effective propellants for jet propulsion systems; to provide an oxidizing agent which is easily combustible with a suitable fuel and which has a large amount of oxygen available for burning a fuel; to provide propellants, that is, fuels and oxidizers, which are spontaneously combustible; to provide a method for utilizing such propellants to give smooth combustion and to eliminate danger of explosion; to obviate the difficulties attendant upon the use of liquified gases; to eliminate the need of an auxiliary ignition system to ignite the propellants.

Oxidizers

As a result of a thorough investigation of the various oxidizing agents which may be used as propellants we prefer to employ nitric acid. Since water tends to retard combustion of the acid with any fuel, the nitric acid should be substantially free of water. Thus, white fuming nitric acid, which normally contains less than about 2% of water by weight, is to be preferred to weaker solutions of nitric acid. However, we have found that more dilute solutions of nitric acid may be utilized provided that nitrogen dioxide is dissolved in the nitric acid; which is a way of increasing the concentration of an otherwise more dilute solution. Preferably the nitric acid should contain at least about 5% NO₂ but preferably at least about 15 to 20% NO₂. Such a solution of nitrogen dioxide is known as red fuming nitric acid and almost all red fuming nitric acid which is commercially available in this country contains between about 5% and 20% nitrogen dioxide by weight and less than about 5% water by weight. Specifications for nitric acid, obtain-

able commercially as red fuming nitric acid, are as follows:

Chemical composition:
HNO₃	90.5% by wt. min.
Water	2.5% by wt. max.
NO₂	7.25% by wt. max.—6.50% by wt. min.

Physical properties:
Density	1.5 min.—1.55 max. @ 70° F.
Melting point	—50° F. max.
Color, etc	Orange to dark red—fumes vigorously when exposed to air.

Specifications for nitric acid, obtainable commercially as white fuming nitric acid, are as follows:

Chemical composition:
Nitric acid	97.5% by wt. min.
Water	2.0% by wt. max.
NO₂ content	0.5% by wt. max.

Physical properties:
Density	1.46 min.—1.52 max. @ 68° F.
Melting point	—45° F.
Color, etc	Straw yellow to water white; fumes vigorously when exposed to air.

The term "white fuming nitric acid" as used herein means a nitric acid containing a maximum of about 2% water by weight.

The term "red fuming nitric acid" as used herein means a nitric acid containing at least about 5% NO₂ and a maximum of about 5% water, by weight.

Nitric acid of all types containing at least 80% HNO₃ is useful as an oxidizer. We have also found that liquid nitrogen dioxide is a very satisfactory oxidizer.

To eliminate the requirement for providing the jet motor with special igniting means, we employ nitric acid and preferably red fuming nitric acid, substantially free of water, as an oxidizer.

Fuels

We have discovered a family of fuels which are spontaneously combustible with the oxidizing agents herein above mentioned and which are satisfactory for jet propulsion provided that the propellants are supplied to the combustion chamber under suitable operating conditions. These operating conditions are discussed more in detail hereinbelow.

We have found that the four groups of compounds listed below may be utilized as fuels. These groups are listed in the order of their effectiveness.

Group I.—Liquid organic compounds containing a least one amine radical, such as,

A. Aniline, orthotoluidine, and methylamine.

B. Liquid hydrocarbons, containing large percentage of such amine substituted organic compounds.

Group II.—Highly unsaturated hydrocarbons: Liquid hydrocarbons of the acetylene type and containing a large fraction of unsaturated (double and triple) carbon bonds, or both, for example, divinyl acetylene, dipropargyl, and propargyl alcohol.

Group III.—Liquid substances containing the element having the properties of lithium (Li), beryllium (Be), boron (B), aluminum (Al), magnesium (Mg), phosphorus (P), potassium (K), and sodium (Na). With the exception of phosphorus all of the foregoing element are particularly useful in fuels because they generate large amounts of heat during combustion, and phosphorus is particularly useful because it has a low ignition temperature.

A. Liquid hydrides of those elements.

B. Liquid organo-metallic compounds containing one or more of such elements.

C. Liquid fuels containing one or more such element.

D. Liquid fuels containing one or more such element in suspension.

3

Group IV.—Organic compounds having the properties of:

1. Pyrole
2. Pyridine
3. Pinene
4. Terpene
5. Pinole
6. Terpinol
7. Hydrazine
8. Ozonides
9. Carbon disulphide containing phosphorus.

All the above identified substances are spontaneously combustible with the oxidizers hereinbefore discussed and re independently useful with other oxidizers where means or ignition is provided.

Of all of these fuels we prefer to employ the amine substituted hydrocarbons. Aniline, for example, not only has the advantage of being spontaneously combustible with the oxidizers hereinbefore mentioned but is less hazardous than gasoline in the presence of air. While aniline is toxic it has the great advantage of being relatively inexpensive, even though more expensive than gasoline, and of being commercially available in large quantities.

Method of operation

The above mentioned oxidizers and fuels may be used together as pairs of spontaneously combustible propellants at atmospheric temperature and pressure. However, if desired these oxidizers and fuels may be used with other fuels (such as gasoline) or other oxidizers (such as liquid oxygen) respectively.

So far as we know we are the first to achieve spontaneous combustion in jet propulsion systems at the temperature and pressure of the medium surrounding the jet motor and while other fuels and oxidizers might be utilized to accomplish such spontaneous combustion we refer to use the fuels and oxidizers hereinbefore mentioned.

Certain difficulties are encountered when utilizing these propellants for propulsion. Unless the propellants are applied to the jet motor under the proper conditions the motor is liable to fail completely, to pulsate in its operation, or to explode, even though the propellants are supplied at uniform rates.

These difficulties may be eliminated and certainly smoothness of operation secured by so relating the rates of injection of fuel and oxidizer to the size of the jet chamber and the inherent ignition properties of the mixture that explosion of the combustible mixture is avoided during the initial combustion; and subsequent injection occurs at rates conducive to the combustion of the continuously supplied propellants so as to avoid the accumulation in the jet chamber of any substantial amount of the unburned propellants. To achieve this result, we initially inject propellants into the combustion chamber at rates such that the amount of propellants injected prior the initiation of combustion is less than about 20% of the volume of the combustion chamber.

After combustion has been initiated, the propellants may be injected at a greater rate than they are injected initially inasmuch as the time interval between their injection and combustion is reduced because of the higher temperature and pressure of the mixture resulting from prior combustion and the heating of the walls of the combustion chamber by the products of combustion.

In the drawing the figure shows a jet motor system including tanks and conduits for supplying propellants to the motor.

The fuels and oxidizers hereinbefore described are advantageously employed in the propulsion of an aircraft providing the fuel and oxidizer in separate containers 11 and 12 respectively connected in any suitable manner by pipes 13 and 14 to a jet or combustion chamber. Throttle valves 16 and 17 energized by electrical circuits 18 and 19 are provided in said pipes to control the rates supply of the fuel and oxidizer respectively to the combustion chamber 15. A receptacle 20 is connected by a conduit 21 having a pressure regulator 22 therein to the

4

receptacles 11 and 12 and is provided with a gas under pressure, preferably a gas inert with respect to either propellant. Preferably the container for the fuel and the container for the oxidizer are connected to a source of pressure adapted to force the contents of such containers into the jet or combustion chamber at controlled rates determined by the degree of opening of the valves in said pipes.

The practice of the method of our invention contemplates so relating the rates of injection of the oxidizer and of the fuel to the combustion or jet chamber to their inherent combustion properties and the size and temperature of the chamber that smooth non-explosive combustion occurs initially and throughout the entire operation while providing the desired quantity of propulsive power. Our invention is particularly advantageous when the combustion chamber is initially at atmospheric temperature, or at the temperature of any other medium in which the motor is to operate, as we are able to achieve combustion initially without auxiliary ignition or preheating of the chamber or the propellants.

If the propellants are supplied at such initial rates, then, when the propellants are initially injected into the jet motor, the initially burned propellants soon fill the combustion chamber with high temperature gases and vapors which heat the incoming propellants thereby vaporizing them and reducing the ignition time lag. Then the subsequently injected propellants burn spontaneously without any substantial accumulation of propellants in the liquid phase.

As an example, applied to a combustion chamber having a length of about 10 inches and a cross sectional area of about 7 square inches, highly concentrated nitric acid and aniline operate very satisfactorily when they are injected into the combustion chamber initially and prior to combustion at the rates of 3.6 lbs. per second and 2.4 lbs. per second respectively.

While these propellants and method of use and the apparatus for their use in propelling aircraft or other devices, which are hereinbefore described, are fully capable of providing the advantages primarily stated, it will be recognized by those skilled in the art that various modifications and alterations may be made therein while still providing such advantages, and our invention is therefore to be understood as not limited to the specific embodiments hereinbefore described but as including all modifications and variations thereof coming within the scope of the claims which follow.

We claim as our invention:

1. The method of developing thrust which comprises ejecting from a reaction chamber the gaseous products produced by the spontaneous combustion of a compound selected from the group consisting of hydrazine and carbon disulphide containing phosphorus, and acid selected from the group consisting of red fuming nitric acid and white fuming nitric acid.

2. The method of developing thrust which comprises ejecting from a reaction chamber the gaseous products produced by the spontaneous combustion of hydrazine and acid from the group consisting of red fuming nitric acid and white fuming nitric acid.

References Cited in the file of this patent
UNITED STATES PATENTS

Number	Name	Date
2,573,471	Malina et al.	Oct. 30, 1951

FOREIGN PATENTS

Number	Country	Date
405,645	Great Britain	Jan. 29, 1934
576,227	Great Britain	Dec. 3, 1937

OTHER REFERENCES

Mellor: "A Comprehensive Treatise on Inorganic and Theoretical Chemistry," vol. VIII, page 313. Pub. 1928 by Longmans, Green & Co., New York and London. Copy in Division 59.

Boushey held the rope in his hand as long as he could, then dropped it and ignited the JATOs. It worked, and the success of the overall Ercoupe flight test earned the group a contract with the Navy. Parsons' and Malina's written report on the Ercoupe tests is in the JPL archives.

An oft-reproduced photo from the Ercoupe tests hints at the change in relationship between Parsons and Malina. Von Kármán is shown writing on the wing of the Ercoupe (suggesting the shot was staged), while Clyde Miller, Clark Millikan, Martin Summerfield, Frank Malina, and Homer Boushey look on. This photo is usually referred to as the "technical group." Why was Summerfield there? His specialty was liquid-fuel rockets, and this was a solid fuel test. And where was Parsons? He was always referred to as the "theoretician," with Forman being the mechanic. Parsons is in a separate photo, with the "flight test crew": Fred Miller (an "explosives technician"), Ed Forman, Malina, Boushey, and a couple of Air Force mechanics. If the technical crew photo had been a candid photo rather than a publicity photo, Parsons would have appeared; Summerfield would not. A large group photo from the same tests includes Helen Parsons, John's first wife. (See photo section.)

It is reported that patents exist in Parsons' name on solid-fuel JATOs and that he shares them with Mark M. Mills, one of his assistants. Frank Malina wrote that only Parsons would have thought of abandoning black powder and smokeless powder for more exotic solid fuels, which was way out of Malina's and Hsue-shen Tsien's league. It was also Parsons' idea to pour in one-inch thick layers, from the bottom up, to control the burn rate, a process that had not been done before.

It has been said that Parsons held a total of seven patents altogether, but the three I was able to find were for liquid-fuel rockets, not solid. On display in the Smithsonian Institution's National Air and Space Museum in Washington, D.C., is a specimen of an early solid-fuel JATO. The unit's spark plug is not for ignition but for an insulated pathway into the fuel mixture; rather than going to the expense of constructing something new, the group just had Forman drill and thread a hole the size of a spark plug into the end of the JATO. The plug already had a built-in porcelain insulator surrounding the conductor, and wires were attached to either end of it, so electricity could be directed safely inside the casing to ignite the mixture.

In early November 1941 one of their "boys," as Malina put it, got drunk and stole a car at gunpoint from a young couple:

He was a mechanic working with Jack, and it seems that he had gone to Parsons' house. They'd had a seance—what they were doing I don't know—anyway [he] had a gun and he found a car on the street that was parked nearby. There was a couple necking in it. He forced them out at the point of the gun, took the car, drove to Hollywood, evidently not quite knowing what he was going to do. And then, after a certain amount of time, he drove back to Pasadena. When he arrived at the flagpole by the Colorado [Ave.] bridge, the police were waiting for him.

Malina continued:

I went to the jail to talk to the fellow and asked him what exactly made him do a stupid thing like that. Well, he was very vague and I couldn't get anything out of Parsons or Forman as to why this had happened . . . It then became quite evident that whatever it was that Parsons and Forman were playing with had certain worrisome aspects.

Hypnosis, perhaps? Forman never did join the Agape Lodge, but Parsons and he were very close and may easily have been sharing Parsons' occult endeavors. The individual was released into Malina's custody, and the whole incident was kept quiet, simply because of the work going on at the school. War was imminent (the attack on Pearl Harbor was only a month away); there was no need to disrupt Caltech's work with an embarrassing detail like this.

Meanwhile, at the lodge Parsons was becoming increasingly influential. In March of 1942, Jane Wolfe wrote to Crowley:

I believe Jack Parsons—who is devoted to Wilfred [Smith]—to be the coming leader, with Wilfred in advisory capacity. I hope you two get together some day, although your present activities in England seem to have postponed the date of your coming to us [which never happened]. Jack, by the way, comes in through some inner experiences, but mostly, perhaps, through the world of science. That is, he was "sold on the Book of the Law" because it foretold Einstein, Heisenberg—whose work is not permitted in Russia—the quantum field folks, whose work is along the "factor infinite and unknown" lines [see *Liber 49*, v. 36], etc. You two would have a whale of a lot to talk over. He and Helen are lock, stock and barrel for the Order.

That same year, Parsons also made an intuitive leap that changed the future of rocket motor technology. There are apocryphal stories concerning the inspiration for his idea, but Parsons seems to have taken the truth with him to the grave. 40 years later Homer Boushey told an International Association of Aeronautics and Astronautics (IAAA) group in Oslo that the idea had come to Parsons while watching some roofers apply hot asphalt. Frank Malina said that Parsons knew of "Greek Fire," a mixture of pitch and other elements which the ancient Greeks used as flaming projectiles, hurling them at enemy ships during wars. However, Helen Parsons told an interviewer the idea had originated with her.

As early as 1928, Parsons and Forman had used glue as a binder to hold their black powder and aluminum oxide in their little rocket motors. In 1942 Parsons had the idea to use liquid asphalt for this purpose. The asphalt was heated, then the fuel and the oxidizer were mixed in, and the mixture was poured directly into the casing rather than an intermediate molding and allowed to cool. Dubbed GALCIT-53, the mixture did not shrink and crack as had earlier mixtures.[4] The new JATOs could be stored indefinitely, at either extreme of temperature, without the threat of explosion during use—and they could now be mass-produced. After Parsons left Aerojet, it was discovered that a hollow could be created in the center of the hardened fuel to provide increased surface area and thus an increased burning rate. At first they used a simple cylindrical shape, then later a star shape to further increase the surface area. This method was used in the Minuteman and Polaris missiles.

Mark M. Mills and Fred S. Miller assisted Parsons with his work on the GALCIT-53 JATOs, which delivered 200 pounds of thrust for eight seconds—a 476% improvement over GALCIT-27. Parsons invented the method of pouring the heated, liquefied propellant, which involved priming the empty casing first with a little bit of the liquefied solution, letting it cool just enough to start to harden, and then pouring the remainder of the fuel inside. This method is still used today on the solid fuel boosters used on the Space Shuttle.

Parsons also had the equally monumental idea to start using potassium perchlorate as an oxidizer, instead of aluminum and others. Successful variations on this idea included use of ammonium perchlorate for the same purpose. Potassium perchlorate was actually listed in the paper Parsons wrote at Antelope Valley for Halifax in

---

4. The next year, GALCIT-61c replaced GALCIT-53 as the fuel of choice.

1937, but he did not comment on its potential at the time. What brought him back to it in 1942 is unknown.

These breakthroughs led to the formation of the Aerojet Corporation on March 19, 1942, now one of the world's largest manufacturers of rockets. The founders were von Kármán, Malina, Summerfield, Parsons, Forman, and von Kármán's attorney Andrew Haley. Parsons and Forman had the idea to get a sponsor or form a corporation; Malina was the one who proposed the idea to von Kármán. Each put in $200, though Haley actually loaned all but von Kármán their share. Haley ended up putting in $2500, with the understanding that the others would pay him back later. The five assigned all future patents to the company, and Malina and Haley came up with the name Aerojet. Parsons and Forman immediately left GALCIT for Aerojet. The group still worked on projects together, with Aerojet employees selling their services as consultants to GALCIT. The company grew quickly.

Haley seems to have been a hands-on kind of guy, as his interesting book, *Rocketry and Space Exploration*, contains several photos of him working directly with various manufacturing efforts at Aerojet. Often he worked in the office by day and in the plant by night.

The group's next big success was with liquid JATOs. Parsons was still trying to find a way to use red fuming nitric acid (RFNA) as an oxidizer with fuels such as gasoline and benzene. RFNA was the chemical that had caused the large explosion—and the big mess—when the Suicide Squad was just getting started at Caltech. Current tests resulted in motors that burned but produced uneven burning which led to throbbing, caused by late ignition: The fuel did not begin burning immediately on contact with RFNA. Martin Summerfield's "instability of burning" law is still used to describe this phenomenon.

On a trip east, an acquaintance of Malina's suggested using aniline to help control the burn rate of the mixture and reduce the throbbing. On the train ride home, Malina suddenly realized that RFNA and aniline ought to be self-igniting without the gasoline or benzene. He wired Summerfield back in Pasadena, who arranged a test with engineer Walter Powell and others. The event was recorded on film: a small crucible sits on the ground, while a hand reaches in, holding a long pole at the end of which is another small crucible. When the contents of one were poured into the other, the mixture did indeed ignite into a huge flame, and the group was on their way to the perfection of liquid-fuel rockets.

With the help of attorney D. Gordon Angus, Parsons and Malina filed three patents on May 8, 1943 for various elements of this process. Parsons' name is on these patents because he insisted on working with RFNA despite what others said about the fuel, a fact documented by Malina in his oral histories with JPL. Ironically, two of the three patents were not granted until after Parsons' death in 1952. The patent numbers are 2,573,471 ("Reaction Motor Operable by Liquid Propellants and Method of Operating It," patented October 30, 1951); 2,693,077 (a division of patent 2,573,471, patented November 2, 1954, but with seemingly little if any difference from the first patent); and 2,774,214 ("Rocket Propulsion Method," patented December 18, 1956, which is basically the same proposal submitted under a different category).

The group's acid-aniline mix was used as late as the Titan missile, at which time it was abandoned in favor of liquid oxygen, which had had finally been made manageable. [In an odd "coincidence," the Great Beast Aleister Crowley referred to himself as "Teitan," which is the original Greek spelling of "Titan," because it adds to 666 in Greek *gematria*, a form of numerology.]

The flight test of the new liquid fuel occurred on April 15, 1942 at Muroc Field in Antelope Valley, site of today's Edwards Air Force Base. Liquid JATOs were the first Aerojet project. A Douglas A-20A was flown first to the Burbank airport for preparations, then to the test field for the liquid JATO tests. The plane weighed 20,000 pounds, as much as several Ercoupes combined. Major Paul H. Dane of the Army Air Corps was the test pilot. Beverly Forman, Ed's cousin, sat in back of the plane. His job was to release the fuel mixture at the appropriate time. Two 1000-pound thrust JATOs were mounted under the A-20A's wings, each with a 25-second burn time. They were designed by Summerfield with the assistance of Walter B. Powell and Edward G. Croft, and had five times the power of GALCIT-53, although solid fuel maintained its value.

A long, silent color film (three reels) exists of this event as well, located in the Library of Congress, as well as in the JPL archives. One excellent shot shows von Kármán, Malina, and Parsons walking side-by-side down the runway, discussing some issue about the tests: the three men who made rocketry viable—the great man, von Kármán, on one side, his protégé Malina in the middle, acting as go-between, and the man of the world, John Parsons, on the other side. These same three men later appeared in the same order on von Kármán's list of the top 10 people who had made American rocketry a possibility, occupying the first three positions.

Take-off distance was again reduced in excess of 30%. At the end of the tests, Malina said, "We now have something that really works and we should be able to help give the Fascists hell!" Von Kármán called the development "the beginning of practical rocketry in the United States." The success of the A20-A test earned the group another budget increase—from $125,000 in 1942 to several times that amount for the coming year, an incredible amount for the work of a few men. However, it was only one area into which the military was channeling large amounts of money in preparation for the war. Designated XLR-1-AJ-1, over 100 slightly modified liquid JATO units were sold by Aerojet for use on Boeing B36 bombers during the war. Smaller units were also used to help launch Corsairs from aircraft carriers; it is unclear whether they used liquid or solid fuel.

Observing the tests was Alfred Loedding, sent by the Army Air Corps from Wright Field. Loedding's later claim to fame was as the military's first UFO investigator in 1947: he started Project Sign, which sought to explain away all UFO reports and was the precursor to the Air Force's better-known Project Blue Book.

At Aerojet Parsons mostly worked in solid fuels and was the Project Engineer in charge of the Solid Fuels Department, although he wasn't actually a degreed engineer. Forman supervised the mechanics' shop and often went to the *arroyo* at GALCIT to perform static tests of his improved motors. Malina was working mostly with liquids at this time, which was his friend Summerfield's specialty. When he would visit the *arroyo* for tests, he would work out of his car.

Aerojet's first contract was for a solid JATO for the Navy Bureau of Aeronautics, and their second was a liquid JATO for the Aircraft Laboratory at Wright Field that was used on the Douglas Havoc Attack Bomber. The original Aerojet offices were located on E. Colorado Ave. in Pasadena, but they soon moved to 285 W. Colorado Ave., the site of a former juice vendor. Test and production facilities moved to Azusa the following year, about 40 miles east of Los Angeles. A picture of the groundbreaking appears in Haley's *Rocketry and Space Exploration*. The Defense Plan Corporation paid $149,000 to build the plant after some of von Kármán's friends in Washington got involved. Aerojet's third contract was with the Air Force, which committed $256,000 for solid-fuel JATOs.

The new work at Aerojet provided plenty of opportunity for evening and weekend work, and uncompensated overtime was a fact of life. The expanded group became rather close as a result; sack lunches were shared under a large oak tree. There was also a little tension. One time a mechanic cut off Malina's tie during a visit from Caltech by the latter, because he thought the tie was too formal.

One of the project's engineers from Aerojet, Walt Powell, had a glider he liked to fly, as it helped him relieve some of the stress. He did this so often that it became a distraction to the group, so Malina took it away and had it locked up. Powell chased Malina with an ax when he discovered what had happened.

GALCIT lost many young men to the draft. Project No. 1, however, the official rocket project at Caltech, had a top priority; thus, its men were exempt. The project in the *arroyo* rated further down the scale. Aerojet had the same problem, at the same time it was trying to expand to meet the new demand for its product. Hap Arnold himself had to intervene when Andrew Haley was drafted. Haley was back to Aerojet within a week, where he replaced von Kármán as the company's president, and worked hard, demanding that his employees work even harder. They often took pay cuts when he felt the company couldn't afford the payroll. Haley went on to become president of the International Aeronautical Federation. He traveled widely, and his book is full of pictures of himself with dignitaries like the Pope.

Newcomers to Aerojet were often shocked by the uneducated and inexperienced staff the company had to hire just to have some bodies around to do the work. A company photo taken when Aerojet was only one year old shows well over 100 people. Experienced engineers were not interested in rockets, so they had to rely on young inexperienced engineers fresh out of college. Von Kármán later said this arrangement worked out to their advantage, as they didn't have to untrain anybody. Amo Smith came back from Douglas Aircraft to work at Aerojet with his old classmates, and Fritz Zwicky also joined the company. Zwicky later designed the experimental "terrapulse" vehicle, which was intended for drilling deep into the earth toward its center. To my knowledge, it was never built.

Zwicky claimed that when Aerojet first was able to purchase some nitromethane, Parsons stole it and ran some of his own tests on it right there on Aerojet grounds. Zwicky also claimed that Parsons used to talk all sorts of occult doctrine with the Aerojet secretaries in order to get them into bed. Apparently, it worked, although Parsons was considered a handsome enough guy that he didn't need much "smooth talk."

Unwilling to pass up any lead, Parsons was sent to New York in May of 1942 to observe the work of a man named Maynor, who had written Caltech to tell them about his own rocket project. A two-page

May 5 42

Dear Frank.

Yesterday I witnessed one of Maynor's tests.

His apparatus is crude & he works under considerable disadvantage, but his motor worked after a fashion. While everything is fresh in my mind I will try to describe. Drawing on back.

At the start, his valves were leaking, & there was a considerable fume. He began insertion at 60 #, & opened his valve slightly. Ignition was quiet and immediate, with a cloud of acid & a slight flame. As he opened up, the acid cleared & the flame increased. There was nowhere near the noise of ours, & the jet was not as concentrated

In a two-page letter to Frank Malina in May 1942, John Parsons describes the stunning inadequacies of another rocket project he was sent to New York City to check out.

or intense. This continued for about 15 sec. Then, as he tried to shut off, the valve stuck, + acid, benzene, fire, etc, raised hell in general. There was no great damage, but that was the end of the test.

His measuring apparatus is primitive, and I believe his records are meaningless. He is absolutely foolhardy placing himself + all observers on top of the apparatus, with no protection.

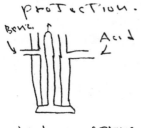

Benz.
Acid

Valve - spring loaded.

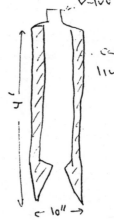

Valve

carbon liner

4"

← 10" →

Wt. - 100 # +
Claimed Thust.
1000 # doubtful.

Spring Scales

Tanks

Motor

Flexible
Tank support

Ballance

Not much — but he claims to hold 6 secret patents. See you next week.
Jack.

handwritten note on file in the JPL archives written by Parsons to Malina from the Hotel Governor Clinton, New York City, on May 5, describes the situation. Maynor's liquid fuel rocket was unsatisfactory mechanically, to say the least, and his procedures were unsafe. Parsons told Malina that Maynor endangered himself and the spectators. Maynor claimed 1000 pounds of thrust had been generated, but Parsons found his measuring apparatus and recordkeeping procedures questionable. Maynor told Parsons that he held six "secret" patents. Nonetheless, there was nothing further worth investigating here. The second page of Parsons' note includes a few hand-drawn sketches of Maynor's setup.

On August 30, 1942, Parsons and Mark M. Mills submitted "Progress Report on the Development of 200-lb.-Thrust Solid-Propellant Jet Units for the Bureau of Aeronautics, Navy Department, Progress Report No. 1-1." Multiple 200-pound units were to be used together for a single take-off. Despite the fact that Parsons was at Aerojet at this time, this report is on file in the JPL archives. On October 16, 1942, Parsons and Mills submitted "The Development of an Asphalt-Base Solid Propellant, Report No. 1-15." The photo of Parsons in a trench coat was taken around this time, on the occasion of a return to the *arroyo* from Aerojet for some tests. The photo may have been for the 200-pound units in the August report, or it may have been at the new Aerojet site in Azusa. (See photo section.)

After Parsons and Forman went to Aerojet, GALCIT's next project was a rocket car. Malina and Summerfield had received a military contract to test the "Hydrobomb," which was a euphemistically-named torpedo. In order to test the hydrodynamic properties of the Hydrobomb, the group constructed a 500-foot long "towing channel"—basically a long, shallow pit of water. The rocket car was built on a track above the pit, and the Hydrobomb was mounted on the underside of the rocket car, with liquid JATOs used to propel it 500 feet at 40 mph, a speed comparable to what it would experience underwater. Pressure gauges were mounted to the Hydrobomb to measure the effects of its motion through the water. Humorously, the track ended right at the project director's home.

The project had problems, however, caused by acoustic instabilities in the design of the JATOs. Acoustics was a yet-to-be-discovered field and thus was not recognized as the problem. The rocket car finally self-destructed in a huge blaze during one of the tests, and the project was abandoned. The dramatic demise of the rocket car was captured on color film. In 1942, author William A.H. White, who wrote science fiction as Anthony Boucher and mysteries as H.H. Holmes (the name of an infamous Chicago murderer), penned and had published a crossover murder mystery/science fiction novel about the rocket car called *Rocket to the Morgue*. It was written and published in 1942, and later reprinted under White's "Boucher" pseudonym. The novel clearly portrays John Parsons as one of the main characters. White later founded and edited *The Magazine of Science Fiction and Fantasy*, as well as writing several stories and novels in both genres. He was popular science fiction writer Philip K. Dick's editor for years.

In *Rocket to the Morgue*, Parsons is the character Hugo Chantrelle, to whom White often simply refers as "the goatee." Ed Forman is his assistant "Gribble," and Robert Heinlein is "Austin Carter." Science fiction writer and future founder of the Church of Scientology L. Ron Hubbard is "D. Vance Wimple," while John W. Campbell is "Don Stewart," and Jack Williamson is "Joe Henderson." In the "Afterword" of the 1951 edition, White says that Heinlein's Mañana Literary Society "existed in fact precisely as it is depicted in this book . . . I've managed to capture a moment that has some interest as a historical footnote to popular culture. This is the way it was in Southern California just before the war, when science fiction was being given its present form." Because of this assertion, we must pay close attention to the fact that Austin Carter (Heinlein) and Hugo Chantrelle (Parsons) spend a lot of time together in the book, including some meetings at the former's house. And it should also be noted that the book was written a few years before Parsons actually met L. Ron Hubbard.

White described Chantrelle as:

[A]n eccentric scientist. In working hours at the California Institute of Technology he was an uninspired routine laboratory man; but on his own time he devoted himself to those peripheral aspects of science which the scientific purist damns as mumbo-jumbo, those new alchemies and astrologies out of which the race may in time construct unsurmised wonders of chemistry and astronomy.

The rocketry of Pendray, the time-dreams of Dunne, the extra sensory perception of Rhine, the sea serpents of Gould, all these held his interests far more than any research conducted by the Institute. He was inevitably a member of the Fortean Society of America, and had his own file of unbelievable incidents eventually to be published as a supplement to the works of Charles Fort. It must be added in his favor that his scientific training automatically preserved him from the errors of the Master [Fort]. His file was carefully authenticated, and often embellished with first-hand reports.

The entire book is worth reading for nothing else than the characterization of Parsons as Chantrelle. While it is obviously a literary portrayal rather than a biographical sketch, *Rocket to the Morgue* certainly depicts the author's impression of Parsons. White's statement about Parsons being a member of the Fortean Society, for instance, may not be factual, but certainly Parsons was interested in "Forteana," the bizarre scientific anomalies found around the globe for millennia and chronicled by the indefatigable Fort.

White's reference to "the time-dreams of Dunne" was repeated elsewhere in the book and concerns J.W. Dunne's *An Experiment With Time*, an odd little volume first published in 1927. Dunne's hypothesis, which he supports with lengthy descriptions of his own dreams, is that dreams may often foretell future events. He goes to great lengths to support this with a philosophical discussion of the nature of time. Austin Carter (Heinlein) was also quite interested in Dunne's book, according to White's dramatization, in which Chantrelle spends much of the time describing his premonitions of the murder and other ominous events, brought on by his "Extra Sensory Perception," which he repeats often, or his equally mystical "awareness of past phases of seriotemporal existence."

Chantrelle mentions *Starmaker* author Olaf Stapleton as well as Fowler Foulkes as two science fiction writers who had impressed him, possibly favorites of Parsons' as well.[5] Chantrelle also says that "one of the greatest services science fiction can render to science" is to lead the public gradually into accepting implausible concepts as fantastic, evidently referring to Parsons' public acceptance of his own rockets, if this was indeed a comment of his.

White's account of the rocket car is a bit garbled, but the incidental material he documents surrounding the science fiction writers in Southern California at the time is invaluable to any historian. Based on his description, it is clear he never visited GALCIT to witness a test of the rocket car, nor did he seem to understand exactly how it was configured. He does make it an interesting plot device, however: it is the murder weapon. Perhaps he heard of the rocket car project directly from Parsons, though Parsons' involvement (if any) with the

---

5. Cameron said that E.R. Eddison was Parsons' favorite science fiction author. Parsons read Eddison's *The Worm Ouroboros* to her.

project was incidental, possibly exaggerated by him, or he may have been there in some less-than-official capacity. According to Alva Rogers, White/Boucher visited Parsons' house frequently enough to get much of his material from Parsons himself.

It is appropriate that Parsons was fascinated by and involved in not only rocket science but also science fiction, since the latter is an inspiration for the former, providing ideas about where humanity and the future are headed that can be acted upon and brought to fruition. Science fiction and fantasy also bridge the two seemingly disparate worlds that Parsons occupied, i.e., the aerospace industry and the occult. The combination is not so strange, however, as numerous scientists, engineers, researchers and other professionals also have had spiritual and religious lives. What is surprising to the average person, however, is that Parsons was apparently so unorthodox and rebellious, but this "delightful screwball," as von Kármán called Parsons, was never content with the conventional, ordinary and mundane. In both sides of his double life, he would always shoot for the moon.

The Return to South Orange Grove Ave.: 1942–1945

On June 26, 1942, John and Helen Parsons moved from 168 S. Terrace Drive into the old Arthur Fleming mansion at 1003 S. Orange Grove Ave., just blocks from where he had grown up at 537 S. Orange Grove Ave. Fleming Mansion was an expensive and exclusive part of Pasadena, called, as noted, "Millionaire's Mile," with palm trees lining the streets and flowering magnolias adorning the yards. There was also a smaller coach house on the grounds, at 1003½ S. Orange Grove Ave., where Wilfred Smith lived. Life in Pasadena in the early '40s is accurately portrayed in James Cain's novel *Mildred Pierce*, which was made into the film starring Joan Crawford.

According to writer Iris Chang, Parsons had a mannequin dressed in a tuxedo on his front porch, upon which he placed a sign saying, "The Resident." Next to the mannequin was a bucket for the mailman to place all mail so addressed.

Built by its namesake out of redwood around the turn of the century, the house was modeled after the Norwegian homes of the time.[6] There were 10 bedrooms on three floors in the main house, with several more bedrooms in the coach house behind it. A small domed portico supported by six concrete columns stood in the backyard. Parsons converted the estate buildings into approximately 19 apartments. The house was razed in the late 1940s to make room for an apartment complex.

Fleming, the original owner of the mansion, was a noted philanthropist and Nobel Prize winner who had made a good deal of money in the Canadian logging industry. He had donated over $5 million to Caltech alone and was the Chairman of its Board of Directors. He also owned what would become Yosemite after he sold the acreage to the government at half-price for the purpose of establishing a park, rather than selling out to commercial interests who were vying for the land.

83

---

6. From information on file in the Pasadena Centennial Room of the Pasadena Central Library.

The Return to South Orange Grove Ave.: 1942–1945

Fleming had arrived in Pasadena decades earlier, soon after which his wife died. Fleming himself died on August 11, 1940, and the big old house stood vacant until an attorney named John M. Dean and his wife Dorothy bought the place in 1942. Parsons leased the house from Dean, and the Agape Lodge relocated to "the Parsonage," as it came to be called. Dean does not show up on the membership rosters from that period, but he must have been privy and sympathetic to the lodge's activities, as he and his wife resided in the house along with Parsons and the others, according to the 1947 city directory.

Parsons' bedroom upstairs, which was the largest room, doubled as a temple. There was the obligatory copy (handcrafted) of the Stele of Revealing, an Egyptian tablet that had inspired Crowley during his trip in 1904 to Cairo, where it was object number 666 in the Museum of Antiquities.[7] Crowley's translation of the stele appears in *Liber AL*, a section of which, AL III:10, requires a copy for ritual purposes. The Parsonage also contained a beautiful library with wood paneling, a large signed portrait of Crowley, hundreds of books on occult matters, and the numerous letters exchanged between Crowley and Parsons. The living room contained an expensive, modern hi-fi system— Parsons loved to play classical music at very high volume.

Parsons lived next to the estate of the late Lilly Anheuser Busch, widow of brewer Adolphus Busch, and the house backed up onto the famous Busch Sunken Gardens, which were beautiful and huge, at least 34 acres in size, by early accounts. By Parsons' time there were 11 acres left, which is still quite sizable for a well-maintained park in a residential area. One photo of Lilly shows her painting a landscape scene in the gardens, surrounded by concrete yard gnomes. Her estate was also the site of public Easter egg hunts for the city's children. The city briefly considered making the gardens into a park after her death, but the land was sold and subdivided in the late 1950s.

Parsons shocked his conservative neighbors when he started renting out rooms to less-than-desirable tenants. The frequent visitors, noisy parties, and questionable goings-on raised many eyebrows. One visitor wrote that "two women in diaphanous gowns would dance around a pot of fire, surrounded by coffins topped with candles . . . all I could think at the time was that if those robes caught on fire the whole house would go up like a tinderbox." He also said that an opera singer and several astrologers lived in the house. It is amusing

---

7. It was Crowley's wife, Rose Kelley, however, who had picked out the stele—in a trance.

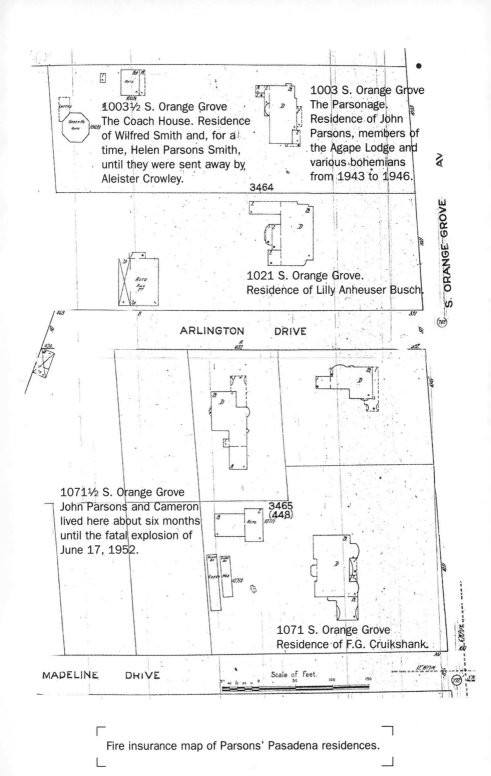

1003½ S. Orange Grove
The Coach House. Residence
of Wilfred Smith and, for a
time, Helen Parsons Smith,
until they were sent away by
Aleister Crowley.

1003 S. Orange Grove
The Parsonage.
Residence of John
Parsons, members of
the Agape Lodge and
various bohemians
from 1943 to 1946.

1021 S. Orange Grove.
Residence of Lilly Anheuser Busch.

ARLINGTON   DRIVE

1071½ S. Orange Grove
John Parsons and Cameron
lived here about six months
until the fatal explosion of
June 17, 1952.

1071 S. Orange Grove
Residence of F.G. Cruikshank.

MADELINE   DRIVE

Scale of feet.

Fire insurance map of Parsons' Pasadena residences.

to ponder the contrast to the previous owner's habits and what Lilly Busch and her friends thought about all this.

One of the longtime residents of the Parsonage was Alva Rogers, who became associated with the house after attending several science fiction meetings there. During these meetings Rogers soon fell in love with a young artist who roomed there, and visited whenever he could, prior to moving in. In a 1962 fanzine article entitled "Darkhouse," Rogers wrote:

> In the ads placed in the local paper Jack specified that only bohemians, artists, musicians, atheists, anarchists, or other exotic types need apply for rooms—any mundane soul would be unceremoniously rejected. This ad, needless to say, caused quite a flap in Pasadena when it appeared . . .
>
> There was a fine selection of hand-picked tenants, characters all. A few examples: The professional fortune teller and seer who always wore appropriate dresses and decorated her apartment with symbols and artifacts of arcane lore; a lady, well past middle-age but still strikingly beautiful, who claimed to have been at various times the mistress of half the famous men in France; a man who had been a renowned organist for most of the great movie palaces of the silent era.[8]
>
> Jack's library (a large wood paneled room graced with a comfortable leather couch and a couple of leather chairs) was lined with books devoted almost exclusively to the occult, and to the published works of Aleister Crowley. Dominating the room was a large photo-portrait of Crowley affectionately inscribed to Jack. He also had a voluminous correspondence with Crowley in the library, some of which he showed me. I remember in particular one letter from Crowley which praised and encouraged him for the fine work he was doing in America, and also casually thanked him for his latest donation and intimated that more would be shortly needed. Jack admitted that he was one of Crowley's main sources of money in America.

The financial arrangements Rogers mentioned were as follows: Parsons would forward the money to Karl Germer in New York, who would send it on to Crowley in England. Germer (January 22, 1885–October 25, 1962) was known in the OTO as "Frater Saturnus."

---

8. It was later said that this man founded the gay rights movement.

These financial arrangements lasted until Crowley's death in 1947. Again, to quote Rogers:

> Jack was the antithesis of the common image of the Black Magician; in fact he bore little resemblance to his revered Master, Aleister Crowley, either in looks or in his personal conduct. He was a good looking man in his early or mid thirties, urbane and sophisticated, and possessed a fine sense of humor . . . I always found Jack's insistence that he believed in and practiced magic hard to reconcile with his educational and cultural background. At first I thought it was all fun and games, a kick he was on for its shock value to his respectable friends; but after seeing his correspondence with Crowley, and the evidence of the frequent remittances to Crowley, I had to give him the benefit of the doubt.

The association becomes easier to reconcile when one considers Crowley's own view of magic, presented in *Liber O vel Manus et Sagittae*: "In this book it is spoken of the Sephiroth, and the Paths, of Spirits and Conjurations; of Gods, Spheres, Planes, and many other things which may or may not exist.

"It is immaterial whether they exist or not. By doing certain things certain results follow; students are most earnestly warned against attributing objective reality or philosophic validity to any of them."

Despite Parsons' outward appearance, he was the subject of regular public attention and rumors that he was the leader of a "black magic cult," rumors denied by his scientific associates, many of whom were regulars at the house, if not members of one or the other orders. As early as 1941, Parsons was investigated (at his previous residence), but no arrests were made. Rather than any occult activities, this investigation concerned some explosives he was storing at the house, either the tetranitromethane Malina mentioned, or the gunpowder Forman's first wife talked about, or both.

In 1942, local police came to 1003 S. Orange Grove to investigate an alleged backyard ceremony wherein a pregnant woman had reportedly jumped nude through a fire nine times. The police made it clear that they thought the claim absurd and that they were only investigating because it was their duty. Parsons easily assured them of his community standing: he was an important rocket scientist with a professional reputation to uphold. Ironically, the ceremony probably took place as described.

A 16-year-old boy reported Parsons to the police, claiming that three of Parsons' followers had forcibly sodomized him during a "Black Mass" at the house. Again the police investigated but found Parsons' "cult" to be little more than "an organization dedicated to religious and philosophical speculation, with respectable members such as a Pasadena bank president, doctors, lawyers, and Hollywood actors." The actor John Carradine, for example, read one of Crowley's poems at the inauguration of Agape Lodge No. 2 in 1935.

In September 1942, the Pasadena police received an anonymous tip via a letter sent by an ex-member of the Agape Lodge bearing the signature "A Real Soldier" and postmarked San Antonio, Texas that accused Parsons of "black magic and sex orgies." Once again, Parsons was cleared of all charges. An anonymous letter was also sent in October 1944.

Local papers are said to have revived these stories during slow news periods, but I was unable to find any of the articles. The police always stood by their original findings whenever further accusations arose. Too many cries of "Wolf!" made them turn a blind eye. Although rape was not going on, plenty of other unusual (but legal) things were, and the neighbors just had to learn to live with it.

The Pasadena branch of the OTO had its other troubles, some of which were caused by Parsons' and Crowley's financial go-between, Karl Germer. Germer had arrived in the United States from a German concentration camp and settled in New York. His stated goal was to work on building up the OTO in his new country; in actuality he did the opposite. Germer took a paranoid dislike to Wilfred Smith, perhaps because he saw him as a competitor for the lead position, and began a smear campaign, constantly writing Crowley about Smith's activities in the worst possible light.

Wilfred Smith had a reputation as a womanizer which equaled that of Crowley, who viewed his own succession of "Scarlet Women" as a necessary magical aid. Smith's affairs, however, seemed to be an opportunity for Germer to deride him. Over 200 letters exchanged between Crowley and Smith during this period have been preserved, letters that evidently document the slow but steady deterioration of the relationship between Crowley and Smith.

Like Parsons, Lodge Master Wilfred Smith was a good-looking man with a charming personality and a strong love of women. One of Smith's lovers was Helen Parsons, John's wife, who bore Smith a son in 1943. Germer convinced Crowley that this affair was the last straw with Smith, who was now a detriment to the work of the OTO, particularly with a child to rear.

Ironically, considering the "Great Beast's" own salacious reputation, Crowley wrote Smith that he was giving the OTO "the reputation of being that slimy abomination 'a love cult.' Already in 1915 in Vancouver, all I knew of you was that you were running a mother and her daughter in double harness—since then one scandal has followed another."

Crowley himself was no stranger to scandal. In fact, he himself had had a number of children by different women. This "black magician," as he came to be considered in his native England, eventually committed many blasphemies against Christianity, which, after his wretched childhood, he set out to destroy and replace with "Crowleyanity" and his "Law of Thelema," which he truly hoped would sweep the world.

Married to Rose Kelley, whose brother Gerald would become the Knighted President of London's Royal Academy, Crowley lived a leisurely life because of a large sum of money his father left him. He was an imposing figure and the beneficiary of numerous unusual adventures. One night of his and Rose's honeymoon, for example, was spent in the so-called King's Chamber of the Great Pyramid, during which Crowley worked ceremonial magic.

Crowley was not content to be monogamous, however, and he had a voracious sexual appetite for both women and men. In fact, the "Key" to the OTO was sex magick. Crowley's sex rites, however, were not to be taken lightly or casually, as he himself thought them to be very serious and powerful magic.

Crowley's ritual sex partners were often prostitutes and men he'd picked up in Turkish bath houses. Even with the women the Great Beast often insisted on having anal intercourse, so convinced was he of its magical qualities. One of his sexual partners and first disciples was Victor Neuburg, an orthodox Jew who had become agnostic and with whom Crowley played the passive recipient. Neuburg, who was in love with the Great Beast, was also the victim of Crowley's sadism, enduring beatings, including one across the butt with nettles.

In his practices he also used his "Scarlet Women," including a young girl named Leah Hirsig, to whom Crowley had taken a fancy in the spring of 1918. Leah did not serve as the Scarlet Woman, however, until 1920, at Crowley's Abbey of Thelema at Cefalu, Sicily, which he and Leah called the "College of the Holy Ghost" and which was "sexually free." At one point at the Abbey, a male goat was supposed to copulate with Leah, but he "failed to perform" and was sacrificed, splattering Leah with his blood.

One scandal that nearly torpedoed Crowley was the death of a young acolyte who had engaged in a ritual of drug-taking and drinking the blood of a sacrificed cat. The incident was the source of sensational headlines in London: "New Sinister Revelations of Aleister Crowley. Varsity Lad's Death. Enticed to 'Abbey'. Dreadful Ordeal of A Young Wife. Crowley's Plans," as well as "Young Wife's Story of Crowley's Abbey. Scenes of Horror. Drugs Magic and Vile Practices." Crowley was accused not only of sexual deviation but also of cannibalism. Because of such bad publicity, Crowley ironically riled Italy's fascist dictator, Mussolini, no angel himself, and was subsequently tossed out of that country and his abbey.

The German branches of the OTO were closed because of the Nazis, who also arrested and tortured Crowley's main advocate and money-supplier, Karl Germer, one of whose friends, Martha Küntzel, became an ardent admirer of Hitler and "regularly bombarded Crowley with letters loaded with praises of Hitler."

Adding to his scandals, at one point Crowley tried to make money selling "Elixir of Life Pills" that were supposed to enhance virility. Those who took them probably never realized they were composed of a "neutral base combined with Crowley's own semen." They were probably energized by some sort of sex magick.

Thus, it is clear that Crowley's excoriation of Smith was based not on any so-called morals but was merely an excuse for him to blast Smith. In reality, when Crowley heard that Smith had legally incorporated the Church of Thelema, he mistakenly took it to mean that Smith intended to raise his new son to replace Crowley. Germer played no little part in this deception.

Crowley removed Smith through an ingenious means. First, he drew up a horoscope for Smith based on the unusual circumstance of his birth. Smith's horoscope had a complex of eight planets, which one could easily interpret as if Smith were an avatar of some god. This complex was something Crowley had found in only one other instance, that of Shakespeare. He called it "one of the most astonishingly fortunate figures that Frater 666 [Crowley] has ever set up in his whole life!" and printed the horoscope, intended only for Smith, under the title, "Is Smith A God?" The 12-page document was also titled *Liber Apotheosis* or *Liber 132.*

Crowley wrote:

The simple, the astounding truth, flooded the mind of Frater 666 with light. It explains all obscurities; it reconciles all contradictions. We have all of us throughout been kindled by a single misapprehension, precisely as if a Staff of Astronomers mistaking a planet for a star, observed its motion, and so found nothing but irritating, bewildering, inexplicable attacks upon the "Laws of Nature."

All becomes clear on recognizing the fundamental mistake: Wilfred T. Smith, Frater 132, is not a man at all; he is the Incarnation of some God!

He hoped Smith's ego was big enough to fall for it yet he also secretly wondered if it weren't somehow true, as his belief in astrology required it to be true no matter how paradoxical he personally found it to be. The members of the lodge started referring to Smith as "the Unknown God," a reference to the New Testament verse of Acts 17:23, which reads:

For as I [Paul] passed along, and observed the objects of your worship, I found also an altar with this inscription, 'To an unknown god.' What therefore you worship as unknown, this I proclaim to you.

It has not been documented whether Smith ever claimed "Knowledge & Conversation of the Holy Guardian Angel," which was a part of the A∴A∴'s 5° = 6° rite.

"Is Smith A God?" continues:

The word "god" implies a fact; it is no question of convenience as when the Ephesians called Barnabas "Jupiter" and Paul "Mercury." [Acts 14]

The incarnation of a god is an exceedingly rare event to become known, although frequent enough when he makes it secretly "to take his pleasure on the earth among the legions of the living." It being known, it is important to ascertain his purpose, especially as (in the present case) the material envelope has been so perfectly constructed that he is himself not fully aware of it.

One must distinguish such cases very sharply indeed from that phenomenon—in these days so common as to constitute an appreciable percentage of the population as to exercise noticeable influence upon society—of the incarnation of elementals.

Nor is a god here to be confounded with a daimon or angel,

even although his function wholly or in part prove to be that of an angel or messenger (cf. *The Book of the Law I*, 7: there is no reason to suppose that Aiwaz is, or is not, a living man).

By "god" is to be understood a complete macrocosmic individual as contrasted with human-elementals who incarnate partial-planetary or zodiacal-intelligences of higher or lower rank in the Yetziratic Hierarchies; such are salamanders, undines, sylphs and gnomes in human form.

It is of the first importance for those who would reap full benefit from the sojourn of such a King on this planet that they should understand his nature; they ought to know his name! To determine his identity is a task of notable magnitude . . .

It must therefore be his primary task to recognize himself. With this end in view he must first of all withdraw completely from further occasion of contamination; and he must devise for himself . . . a true method of self-realization.

It is not necessary that the god should have incarnated at (or before) the birth of Wilfred T. Smith. A quite possibly significant moment might have been the Summer Solstice of 1916, or during the Winter of 1906 when terrific forces were set in motion by the Chiefs of the Order.

The "child" (i.e. the "god") might well have been begotten by the Paris Working (January, 1914) or as the result of some of the immense Enochian invocations: in the latter case the name of the god required might be found on the Watch Towers of the Universe [the Enochian Tablets], his nature determined by analysis of the squares concerned. Another possibility suggested by the place of residence of Frater 132 is that one of the aboriginal "Red Indian" gods may have seized the opportunity somehow afforded by Frater 132's state at the moment . . .

Frater 132 has to realize and proclaim his identity and function very much as Frater 666 regards himself in the light of what is spoken of him in *The Book of the Law*. He ought to be able to say simply: I am Apu-t or Kebeshnut or Thoum-aesh-neith, or as may be the case. It will not serve the present purpose to accept Asar [Osiris], or Ra, or one of the universal gods such as of whom all men are in a sense incarnations.

Crowley then sent Smith on a "Grand Magical Retirement" to find the god within himself. Unknown to her, Helen was going to accompany him, but it is unclear where their son went during this time. The

High Priestess of the Agape Lodge, Regina Kahl, was quite ill and spent much of this period in the hospital. Her last attendance of a lodge meeting occurred in November 1942. After his "retirement," Smith often tried to go back to the house, according to Grady McMurtry (later Hymenaeus Alpha X°), but he was not welcome there.

At this time, Parsons was corresponding with McMurtry, who was stationed in Europe on military duty. McMurtry often sent Parsons poems he had written, usually of a mystical nature. Parsons encouraged McMurtry to contact Crowley while he was in England, an act that led to Crowley initiating McMurtry all the way to the X° of the OTO. To Parsons' surprise, McMurtry returned to the United States a few short years later as his superior in the Order. With Smith having left, Parsons was Acting Head of the Lodge at this time.

Smith's retirement took place at a turkey farm outside of Pasadena belonging to a member of the lodge named Roy Leffingwell. In his quest to find the god within himself, Smith had to build a small altar from rocks he found the site. He also had to tattoo the "Mark of the Beast" on his forehead or right palm and (if desired) over his heart and his *mons veneris* (sic). Everything that happened to him during the retreat was to be carefully recorded and forwarded to Germer, the "Outer Head" of the OTO. Eventually, Smith was told by Leffingwell to leave the farm.

While Smith thus floundered, Parsons had plenty of money for his occult activities, as, by the summer of 1943, Aerojet was doing $650,000 in business. In June of that year, Parsons and von Kármán were invited to Norfolk, Virginia, where they turned their attention to aircraft carriers because JATOs were unable to keep up with the bigger bombers and the ease with which runways were now being constructed. Two of von Kármán's former students were now a captain and an admiral in the Navy, and the Hungarian and Parsons were invited to demonstrate their JATOs for the Secretary of the Navy and his admirals. This test took place on the USS *Charger*, which was docked at Norfolk. Parsons outfitted a Grumman airplane with solid-fuel JATOs, but when the plane took off it covered the Secretary and his admirals with a cloud of yellow smoke that left a nasty residue. A few of the officers got mad, but the Secretary merely told them to find a way to get rid of the smoke and they would have a contract. This incident led to the development of Aeroplex, Aerojet's brand name for smokeless powder.

Also in 1943 Parsons divorced Helen, having struck up a relationship with her younger sister (they may have been half-sisters),

Sara Elizabeth Northrup, AKA "Betty." Another version of events says that Parsons took up with Betty before this, when Helen was out of town. Parsons told his old friend Rypinski, "I got rid of my wife [Helen] by witchcraft." Born April 8, 1925, Betty was tall (5'9"), slender, with blondish brown hair. Like Helen before her, Betty acted as Parsons' priestess at the Gnostic Mass, the pair fulfilling the roles left vacant by Smith and Kahl. Parsons' devotion was such that the Mass was held every single day. Betty was also Parsons' partner in the performance of sex magick—the "magic" of inducing altered states through prolonged sexual ecstasy. Kahl, on the other hand, was a lesbian.

At Parsons' urging the 18-year-old Betty left the University of Southern California (USC). Parsons was 11 years her senior, and her parents were not at all happy about the arrangement. Parsons later noted the implied element of adultery and incest in this relationship with his wife's sister was most appealing. (The breaking of taboos is a typical "tantric" practice, but it may also be that Parsons felt stung by his wife's "betrayal" with Smith.) Parsons and Betty lived as a couple, although they never did marry.

Interestingly, Parsons encouraged Betty to take other lovers, as he did, because he perceived himself above the petty jealousies felt by normal men. For a time, this sentiment was true, and their various affairs seem to have strengthened their feelings for each other, paradoxical as that may sound. At the end of the day, they always had one another to turn to.

Of their relationship, Alva Rogers wrote:

Betty, who had been living with Jack for a number of years, complemented him admirably. She was young, blonde, very attractive, full of joie de vivre, thoughtful, humorous, generous, and all that. She assisted Jack in the OTO and seemed to possess the same devotion to it and to Crowley as did Jack . . . The rapport between Jack and Betty, the strong affection, if not love, they had for each other, despite their frequent separate sextracurricular activities, seemed pretty permanent and shatterproof.

As Parsons was fond of Crowley, so was the magus in turn impressed by Parsons, although he worried about the young man's loyalty to Smith, in whom Crowley could only see trouble. Soon after Smith departed, Parsons sent an offer of retirement to Crowley, as he thought Crowley was treating Smith unfairly and therefore didn't feel right about taking his place. Crowley did not accept the offer and, in July 1943, wrote a letter to lodge member Max Schneider: "As to Jack: I think he is perfectly alright at the bottom of everything; but he is very young, and he has at present nothing like the strength to deal with matters within his jurisdiction objectively." (Schneider and his wife had a small cabin on Mount Palomar that the members of the lodge often used for short retreats.)

Although quite reckless in his personal life, Crowley was a decent judge of character, and his opinion of Jack was good, if somewhat guarded, consistently documented in his letters to other members. In December of 1943, Crowley wrote to the actress Jane Wolfe, who had earlier alerted him to Parsons' potential as "the child":

Jack is the Objective (Smith is out, an affaire classée: anybody who communicates with him in any way is out also; and that is that, and the best plan is to sponge the whole slate clean, and get to work to build up Thelema on sound principles. And no more of this brothel-building: let's use marble, not rotten old boards!) Jack's trouble is his weakness, and his romantic side—the poet—is at present a hindrance. He gets a kick from some magazine trash, or an 'occult' novel (if only he knew how they were concocted!) and dashes off in wild pursuit. He must learn that the sparkle of champagne is based on sound wine; pumping carbonic acid into urine is not the same thing.

I wish to God I had him for six months—even three, with a hustle—to train in Will, in discipline. He must understand that fine and fiery flashes of Spirit come from the organization of Matter, from the drilling of every function of every bodily organ until it has become so regular as to be automatic, and carried on by itself deep down in the Unconscious. It is the steadiness of one's Heart that enables one to endure the rapture of great passion; one doesn't want the vital functions to be excitable.

In February 1944, he wrote to the Burlingames (also lodge members):

. . . I am very glad indeed of your offer to co-operate practically in any way possible. I have left Jack Parsons in charge; he is quite all right in essence, but very young and easily swayed by passing influences. I shall look to you to help in keeping him up to the mark.

In contrast, three Aerojet memos written by Parsons in August of 1944 clearly show him in charge of his program there, working on smokeless powder with aluminum perchlorate as an oxidizer. Despite others' failures with these materials, Parsons practically insisted on moving ahead with his own experiments. He also attended a solid fuel conference during the summer and fall of 1944, of which his typed notes are now in the JPL archives.

Obviously, Parsons liked to be in charge and not under authority, in both his professional and personal lives. Sometime that year Parsons made an interesting statement in a letter sent to McMurtry: "I am a little sour on the OTO inasmuch as by experience I doubt the value of membership coming in except via previous experience and individual training of the A∴A∴ sort. It seems to me the early grades (which are all we have here) are too free in admitting non-descripts and too lax in that they do not provide a definite program of training and qualifications. The better people I have met always seem to come via an interest in A∴A∴ aspects." This instance is not the first time Parsons questioned his association with the OTO, nor would it be his last. He had a long history of bucking authority; the OTO soon became one more "authority" trying to tell him what to do.

While he concerned with formal training and qualifications in his "spiritual" life, Parsons had no need for it in his aerospace occupation. Indeed, he thrived without such academic accomplishment and credentials, as did the business and science he helped found. In 1944, GALCIT changed its name to the Jet Propulsion Laboratory (JPL), a term coined in a memorandum written by von Kármán, Malina, and Tsien on November 20, 1943. At that time their budget was an astounding $650,000, and approximately 80 people worked there, though Summerfield was still operating out of his car. Malina was soon named Director of JPL, a position he held until 1946, although he is usually referred to as the second Director, von Kármán by default being the first. It seems that Malina was retreating from his anti-capitalist stance, also expressing to his parents just a little over a year earlier that "we are getting to be more and more like capitalists." However, Malina and his first wife were long-standing members of the local communist "cell," which certainly had much to do with his getting out of the rocket business after the end of the war.

Despite the impressive budget, the JPL facilities were still rather primitive. Eugene Pierce, a local architect, took a job as an administrative assistant around this time. Of his first trip to the *arroyo* he said, "I took one look at those half-a-dozen nondescript, corrugated-metal and redwood-tie and stone buildings and thought, my God!—what have I gotten myself into? There's no future for an architect here." Inside, the buildings things were no better. The corridors were extremely narrow, and Pierce shared an 8-by-10 office with Malina and secretary Dorothy Lewis, with whom JPL historians were able to conduct an oral history interview in 1972. In the interview, Lewis told them that Parsons "was the clown of the group. He loved to play jokes. That was all right." Dorothy's office overlooked the liquid fuel test pit. Conversation halted whenever a test was run.

Malina and Summerfield launched a small series of rockets called the "Private" in 1944, when Malina paused long enough to realize that they now had the means to carry out the original goal of the early GALCIT group. Constructed of little more than JATOs to which fins and a nose cone were attached, the Privates successfully carried meteorological equipment high into the atmosphere—for the purposes of pure research rather than military applications. This completed goal made Malina happy. The Private A was launched from Leach Spring, at Camp Irwin near Barstow, California, an army base in the Mojave Desert.

The following year, however, found Malina working with missiles meant to be fired into enemy territory. The project ORDCIT—"America's first long range missile and space exploration program"—was formed for this purpose, in the same *arroyo* where GALCIT was located. Two of the missiles developed, the solid-fuel Sergeant and the liquid-fuel Corporal, were never deployed, but the later Regulus missile was. The Regulus was developed by others for deployment in western Europe during the Cold War. These small, mobile missiles were launched from the backs of trucks and, as with the other early missiles, were simply made from large solid-fuel JATOs with a few minor modifications to make them fly.

It is another odd "coincidence" that the term "Regulus," a star in the constellation Leo, appears in the work of Aleister Crowley, appearing in the title of Crowley's *Liber V vel Reguli* in its plural form. Reproduced in Regardie's *Gems from the Equinox*, *Liber V* is "the Ritual of the Mark of the Beast: an incantation proper to invoke the Energies of the Aeon of Horus, adapted for the daily use of the Magician of whatever grade." The "Mark of the Beast," of course, is what Smith was supposed to tattoo on himself during his retreat.

On March 11, 1945, Parsons wrote to McMurtry that he was "trying to get out from under [the OTO] and more into A∴A∴ work which suits me far better and in which I think I can do more." However, he was not quite ready to leave the OTO at this time, and its apparent influence on his life would continue.

Despite his occult leanings, Parsons enjoyed respectability in his professional work. On March 15 the *Saturday Evening Post* ran an article called "JATOs Get 'Em Up," highlighting the very successful use of solid-fuel JATOs, with mention of Parsons, Forman, Malina and Summerfield as the developers, under the direction of von Kármán. The article discusses the different wartime applications for which JATOs were currently being used, including on the Navy's PB-2Y seaplanes and the small Corsairs that were launched from aircraft carriers. Because of the JATOs, which helped them launch without the advantage of a long, smooth stretch of water, Catalan Flying Boats were able to land in the choppy waters of the South Pacific, undeterred by 18-foot swells, to carry out a rescue mission. Another dramatic rescue was made in Southern California when a Martin Mariner was forced down in a small lake: the Mariner needed a full mile to take off, but the lake was only 3000 feet at its greatest width, so JATOs were mounted under the plane's wings, allowing it to get back into the air safely.

Another one of the JPL group, Charles Bartley[9], made an improvement to Parsons' original asphalt binder in 1945. To replace the asphalt, Bartley created a polysulfide compound, for which the word "thiokol" was coined, from the Greek words for "sulphur" and "glue." Called "Thiokol LP-2," the compound is a polymer, which means an artificial compound with a very repetitive molecular structure consisting of long molecules joined together endlessly. The regular molecular structure is what gives polymers their desirable qualities.

The compound name can also be found in "Morton-Thiokol," a well-recognized aerospace manufacturing firm today. As late as the Korean War, solid-fuel JATOs were used on Sabre Jet fighters, which would jettison the canisters after use, such that the Korean jungles must be full of them. Solid-fuel rockets launched the Polaris missiles, a name correlating to "Pole Star," the moniker Parsons used in writing to refer to Smith. Solid fuel, of course, is also what launches the Space Shuttle, of which Morton-Thiokol was the manufacturer until the Challenger disaster, after which Aerojet got the contract.

In 1945, Betty's sentiment was recorded by Jane Wolfe who shared

---

9. Bartley would later work with Parsons on special effects for the film industry.

some other concerns about Parsons' private life in a letter to Karl Germer:

> There is something strange going on, quite apart from [Wilfred] Smith. There is always Betty [Northrup], remember, who hates Smith. But our own Jack is enamored with Witchcraft, the hounfort, voodoo. From the start he always wanted to evoke something—no matter what, I am inclined to think, as long as he got a result.
>
> According to Meeka [Aldrich] yesterday, he has had a result—an elemental he doesn't know what to do with. From that statement of hers, it must bother him—somewhat at least.

Parsons' ardent thrill-seeking was, of course, not just professional but personal, and he once wrote that one of the rituals he used was "liable to produce dangerous side phenomena and sometimes permanent haunting in an area where it is repeated." Wolfe's "witchcraft" reference is to one of Parsons' projects, called "The Witchcraft," which, along with "The Gnosis," was his attempt to devise a religious system of his own that addressed fields Crowley seems to have stayed out of. The surviving papers concerning The Gnosis and the Witchcraft are reproduced in the book *Freedom Is A Two-Edged Sword.*

The elementals or spirits Parsons was invoking evidently disturbed the other Parsonage residents. One still-living and active member of the OTO and the A∴A∴ today, Phyllis Seckler ("Soror Meral," initiated by Wolfe into the A∴A∴), recorded:

> Meeka also reported to Jane that another two persons always had to do a lot of banishing in the house. They were sensitive and knew that there was something alien and inimical was there [sic]. When I had been there during the summer of 1944, I also knew there were troublesome spirits about, especially on the third floor. It got I couldn't stand being up there, and a friend of mine couldn't even climb the stairs that far, as the hair on the back of her neck began to prickle and she got thoroughly frightened.

The "Meeka" referred to was Meeka Aldrich, who pledged the grade of Minerval in August 1945 and was granted the I° of the OTO on August 25. Like Helen Parsons had for a while, she served as the treasurer of Agape Lodge in September, though she shared that office with another during the following month. Meeka kept active in the lodge after that, and was the one who found places for the lodge to meet from late 1946 into 1948.

As the war ended, the founders of Aerojet started looking for a way to make the firm viable, because its future was suddenly very uncertain. It is ironic that Parsons' work, despite its anti-military beginnings and goal, had become the backbone of military operations, so much so that his company was virtually dependent on war. How he was able to reconcile his profession with his personal life, which, while hedonistic, he ostensibly viewed as spiritual, is a quirk of the human mind in general, as millions of others have been able to do the same.

Fortunately, the firm was able to convince General Tire to invest in it. If it succeeded, fine; if not, General Tire was big enough to absorb the loss as a tax write-off. With the purchase, Aerojet became Aerojet General, today known as GenCorp Aerojet. Once General Tire bought in, it decided it wanted the whole pie but none of the old-timers hanging around, so it sent its people out to strong-arm Aerojet's founders into relinquishing their stock. All sold out but Malina, who happened to be in London at the time and who later wrote that sunspot activity disrupted the telegraph transmission, such that he never got the offer. The solar storm proved a boon, however, as he became a millionaire as a result. In the '60s, von Kármán calculated that if he himself had held onto his stock he would have been worth $12 million.

But it was hard to resist the offer Aerojet General was making. The war was ending, the future was uncertain, the group had achieved what they intended to achieve with rockets, and now Aerojet was offering them $50,000 apiece for their stock. Charles Bartley remembers Parsons and Forman coming into his office at JPL quite excited, bragging how they had managed to get out of the company while they were still ahead. The war was over, they told him, and rockets were finished. The field had no future. They were going to start a chain of laundromats with their money and become rich men. It is difficult to understand how the two obviously passionate men could have given up their youthful goals about rockets so easily, particularly since they still hadn't launched anything into space.

In fact, Parsons had actually sold out before the war ended and intended to continue his hazardous passions. In a letter dated December 14, 1944 to Grady McMurtry, Parsons wrote that he had "sold out at Aerojet, purchased 1003 [S. Orange Grove Ave.], and am starting a new company engaged in chemical research." Evidently interested in other dangerous pursuits, he added that he was trying to get the ex-High Priestess Regina Kahl to return to the lodge. In apparent response to a question from McMurtry as to whether he could send Parsons anything from Europe, Parsons replied "a witch, young, red headed . . ." His letters to McMurtry are full of references to Europe being "witch country."

The "lady-killer" Parsons did not confine his sexual largesse to his private world, however. Indeed, both he and Forman were well-known around the Aerojet office as well, and the office managers cringed when they saw the randy pair come in because both men seemed to be working their way through the secretarial pool. Each had had affairs with several women there, according to those who knew them then, and their relationships with these women interfered with the secretaries' work to the point of disruption. But they were the founders, and their presence had to be tolerated until they sold out and left. Zwicky claimed that Haley had actually convinced Parsons to sell out prior to the General Tire buyout, simply because of his problems at the office, but von Kármán and others disagree with Zwicky on this count. Parsons told Rypinski that he left because Aerojet was less interested in research and more interested in production and sales. However, Parsons did not get back into research after he left.

Parsons and Forman formed Adastra Research, a small explosives company that was investigated for "espionage" when the two were caught with a large quantity of "x-nitrate," a powerful explosive. It was determined that the compound had been procured for experimental reasons, and the charges were dropped. Parsons then went to work for the Vulcan Powder Company in Pasadena, where he would remain for the next two years.

Back in New Mexico, Robert Goddard had his own problems. At the end of the war, he fell into a depression, became ill, and died before the year was out. Certainly his failure with rockets—and Caltech's success—was a contributing factor.

In late August of 1945, Lou Goldstone brought L. Ron Hubbard over to meet Parsons, who liked Hubbard immediately. As noted, Hubbard had been the model for D. Vance Wimple in White's *Rocket to the Morgue.* He told a lot of war stories which, though hard to believe, were well-liked by most, and he fit right in with the unusual assortment of people who lived there.

Hubbard had just come from the Oak Knoll Naval Hospital in San Francisco and complained of various ailments including rheumatism, arthritis, hemorrhoids, conjunctivitis, and aches in his side, shoulder, stomach, and knee. After several hospital visits, Hubbard was given a medical discharge from the Navy and began receiving financial benefits when he told them he could no longer practice his livelihood of being a writer.

The Parsons circle included not only a circuit connecting Hubbard and Crowley but also one linking Crowley to Lovecraft, whom Hubbard had met through Lovecraft biographer Frank Belknap Long. (Writers have tried for years to link Lovecraft and Crowley in one way or another, but this is a direct connection that has not yet been explored.) In addition, Hubbard and Parsons associated with people in Pasadena who had met Clark Ashton Smith, one of Lovecraft's regular correspondents, as well as of Crowley's "inner circle." Lovecraft's "The Colour Out of Space" had appeared in the September 1927 issue of *Amazing Stories*, the publication Ed Forman had written about, so Parsons had probably read it. He may also have read *Weird Tales*, which regularly featured the work of Lovecraft in the teens and twenties. Judging by Crowley's remark in December 1943 in his letter to Jane Wolfe, this was simply the sort of "magazine trash" Parsons was reading.

Parsons had begun his magical work with Betty, Helen's younger sister, after Helen had left with Smith. His encouragement of an open relationship, which demonstrated his evolution beyond petty human jealousy, was to backfire on him, however, as Betty readily agreed to take up other lovers and ended up with Hubbard. The relationship was to be a source of extreme aggravation for Parsons, who suddenly had more than he could bear.

Hubbard charmed Parsonage resident Alva Rogers, who, like Hubbard, was a redhead. Indeed, Hubbard confided his belief that all redheads descended from the Neanderthal rather than pure *Homo sapiens*. "Needless to say," Rogers wrote, "I was fascinated." The redhead-Neanderthal connection is interesting to keep in mind when reading Williamson's *Darker Than You Think*, the story of werewolves who return to their atavistic state. Rogers further wrote:

> It all began on an otherwise undistinguished day in the late fall of 1945 when we got word that L. Ron Hubbard was planning to wait out his terminal leave from the Navy at "The Parsonage" . . . Short visits by such pro authors as Jack Williamson, Edmond Hamilton, Tony Boucher, and other were fairly frequent; but Ron was planning on an extended stay.

Ron arrived on a Sunday, driving an oldish Packard and hauling a house trailer which he parked on the grounds behind the house. He originally intended staying in the trailer, but within a few days someone moved out of the house and he moved in.

I liked Ron from the first. He was of medium build, red headed, wore horned rim glasses, and had a tremendously engaging personality. For several weeks he dominated the scene with his wit and inexhaustible fund of anecdotes. About the only thing he seemed to take seriously and be prideful of was his membership in the Explorers Club (of which he was the youngest member) which he had received after leading an expedition into the wilds of South America, or some such godforsaken place. Ron showed us scars on his body which he claimed were made by aboriginal arrows on this expedition . . . Unfortunately, Ron's reputation for spinning tall tales (both off and on the printed page) made for a certain degree of skepticism in the minds of his audience. At any rate, he told one hell of a good story . . .

Ron was a persuasive and unscrupulous charmer, not only in a social group, but with the ladies. He was so persuasive and charmingly unscrupulous that within a matter of a few weeks he brought the entire House of Parsons down around poor Jack's ears. He did this by the simple expedient of taking over Jack's girl for extended periods of time . . . Ron was supposedly his best friend, and this was more than Jack was willing to tolerate . . .

A reporter named Nieson Himmel also lived in the house, sharing a room with Hubbard, after the latter moved out of his trailer and into the house. Himmel wrote:

Parsons was a superb chemist. He had this big old house up in Pasadena, among some huge old mansions. It was built by some rich people at the turn of the century. The coach houses were still back there . . . His specialty was explosives. He was a follower of Aleister Crowley. He used to have meetings there. I knew him through science fiction, we had meetings of the science fiction society out there. They used to have these meetings come down the stairs in black robes. There were two pyramid sort of things where they held their services. He converted the place into apartments, about 19 of them. He put an ad in the paper, "Apartments for rent. (This was at the end of the war when no one could find a place to live.) Must not believe in God."

There was an Englishman [Wilfred Smith] living in the coach house who was one of the original Crowley followers. Parsons made no secret that he was a follower. There were woodcuts in Crowley books and Parsons had some of the originals. There were two crowds out there—science fiction and Crowley . . .

Parsons was living with a beautiful girl called Betty Northrup who I understand came from a rich family. She was beautiful, just lovely. This girl did not get married. Hubbard came in, he was irresistible to women, swept girls off their feet. There were other girls living there with guys and he went through them one by one. Finally he fastened onto Betty. Parsons was desperately in love, but could not countenance marriage because of his beliefs. The atmosphere became very tense. You would sit at the table and the hostility between Hubbard and Parsons was tangible . . . Betty was not her name, Sara was her name. Everyone knew her as Betty, beautiful, sweet as nice could be, she had dropped out of school to be with Parsons . . .

There was a bunch of people there, 18–20 in the big house and 5–6 in the coach house. When he broke it up into apartments, I think there were about 19 of them. The atmosphere became so tense . . . Lou Goldstone, an artist, was living there and he was my entree to the place . . .

I think Lou Goldstone introduced Hubbard to the house. Although I think Parsons was an early science fiction fan.

Lou said he stumbled into a couple of meetings. I presume it was a black mass. People talked about it quite openly . . .

Betty was beautiful—the most gorgeous, intelligent, sweet, wonderful person. I was so much in love with her, but I knew she was a woman I could never have . . . Betty was a raving beauty.

Alva Rogers was my first roomer, then Ron.

Himmel went on to a long career in crime writing and personally knew several mob bosses, including Bugsy Siegel and Mickey Cohen. He died in March 1999 at the age of 77.

Concerning Parsons' growing resentment towards the Hubbard-Betty affair, Rogers wrote:

Although the three of them [Parsons, Hubbard, and Betty] continued to maintain a surface show of unchanged amicability, it was obvious that Jack was feeling the pangs of a hitherto unfelt passion.

> As events progressed, Jack found it increasingly difficult to keep
> his mind on anything but the torrid affair going on between Ron and
> Betty and the atmosphere around the house became supercharged
> with tension . . . In the end, Jack reacted as any ordinary man
> would under similar circumstances.

In September 1945, Hubbard was declared unfit for service due to an ulcer and left the Parsonage to go to the hospital for a while to strengthen his disability claim. To his credit, Hubbard was sending what little he had to his wife and children, who were still living with his parents in Washington state.

In early December, Hubbard was "mustered out" of the Navy. The very next day he applied to the VA for his pension, claiming a sprained left knee, malaria, and other maladies. He told them he was a writer, that his income had been $650 per month before the war, and that now it was zero. Then he hopped into his Packard and pulled his small trailer to the Pasadena, returning to the Parsonage and resuming his affair with Betty.

Alva Rogers was one who realized the true pain hidden beneath Parsons' cavalier front. He wrote of an accidental peek caught one night through the cracked-open door:

> As events progressed, Jack found it increasingly difficult to keep
> his mind on anything else . . . the atmosphere around the house
> became supercharged with tension; Jack began to show more and
> more strain, and the effort to disguise his metamorphosis from an
> emotionless Crowleyite 'superman' to a jealousy-ridden human
> being became hopeless . . .
>
> The final, desperate act on Jack's part to reverse events and
> salvage something of the past from the ruin that stared him in the
> face occurred in the still, early hours of a bleak morning in
> December. Our room was just across the hall from Jack's apart-
> ment, the largest in the house, which also doubled as a temple, or
> whatever, of the OTO. We were brought out of a sound sleep by
> some weird and disturbing noises seemingly coming from Jack's
> room which sounded for all the world as though someone were
> dying or at the very least were deathly ill. We went out into the hall
> to investigate the source of the noises and found that they came
> from Jack's partially open door. Perhaps we should have turned
> around and gone back to bed at this point, but we didn't. The
> noise—which, by this time, we could tell was a sort of chant—drew

us inexorably to the door which we pushed open a little further in order to better see what was going on. What we saw I'll never forget, although I find it hard to describe in any detail. The room, in which I had been before, was decorated in a manner typical to any occultist's lair, with all the symbols and appurtenances essential to the proper practice of black magic. It was dimly lit and smoky from incense; Jack was draped in a black robe and stood with his back to us, his arms outstretched, in the center of a pentagram before some sort of altar affair on which several indistinguishable items stood.

His voice, which was actually not very loud, rose and fell in a rhythmic chant of gibberish which was delivered with such passionate intensity that its meaning was frighteningly obvious. After this brief and uninvited glimpse into the blackest and most secret center of a tortured man's soul, we quietly withdrew and returned to our room, where we spent the balance of the night discussing in whispers what we had just witnessed . . .

The ritual seems to have worked, at least temporarily. After Hubbard's return, Parsons wrote in his diary, "I have been suffered to pass through an ordeal of human love and jealousy . . . I have found a staunch companion and comrade in Ron . . . Ron and I are to continue with our plans for the Order." They did so a few days later, on January 4, 1946. Parsons wrote to Crowley around this time:

Most Beloved Father,

About three months ago I met Capt. L. Ron Hubbard, a writer and explorer of whom I had known for some time . . . He is a gentleman; he has red hair, green eyes, is honest and intelligent, and we have become great friends. He moved in with me about two months ago, and although Betty and I are still friendly, she has transferred her sexual affections to him.

Although Ron has no formal training in Magick, he has an extraordinary amount of experience and understanding in the field. From some of his experiences I deduce he is in direct touch with some higher intelligence, possibly his Guardian Angel. He describes his Angel as a beautiful winged woman with red hair whom he calls the Empress, and who has guided him through his life and saved him many times . . . Recently, he says, because of some danger, she has called the Archangel Michael to guard us . . . Last night after invoking, I called him in, and he described Isis nude on the left, and a faint figure of past, partly mistaken operations on the right, and a rosewood box with a string of green beads, a string of pearls with a black cross suspended, and a rose . . . He is the most thelemic person I have ever met and is in complete accord with our own principles. He is also interested in establishing the New Aeon but for cogent reasons I have not introduced him to the Lodge.

We are pooling our resources in a partnership that will act as a limited company to control our business ventures. I think I have made a great gain, and as Betty and I are the best of friends there is little loss. I cared for her deeply but I have no desire to control her emotions, and I can, I hope, control my own.

I need a magical partner. I have many experiments in mind . . . The next time I tie up with a woman it will be on my own terms.

Thy son, John.

Even at 30, Parsons was still young enough and immature enough to be quite impressionable and vulnerable, despite the fact that he had gone through repeated upheavals during his short life. He was a romantic, a poet—not a businessman. Hubbard made a big impression on him, so much so that Parsons forgot his obligation and violated his oath to the Order, revealing to Hubbard the secrets of the highest grades of the OTO—grades which Parsons himself may not have actually held but merely had access to some of the documents associated with them. However, two of his letters refer to himself as holding this grade, so the matter is unclear. He may have been exaggerating again.

With the war ended and the business buyout, it seems Parsons had a lot of time on his hands and threw himself into the magical work, possibly also as a distraction from and remedy for his painful experience with Betty and Hubbard. The "magical partner" Parsons envisioned was to be his partner in a "working" of sexual magic— probably not a IX°, but one of his own devising that fell well outside the system of the OTO. Parsons was known to invoke spirits called elementals, so-called because of their association with the four elements of the ancients: Earth, Air, Water, Fire. The classical symbols associated with each are usually gnomes, sylphs, mermaids, and salamanders, respectively. These are, of course, just symbols, such that modern replacements for each could be found: For example, UFOs, perhaps, would be a good replacement for sylphs.

According to Crowley, to summon an elemental requires a large

amount of magical energy, the kind said to be generated by an VIII°
working, the VIII° being a solo sexual rite, i.e., masturbation. As
Parsons once wrote, "The invocation of lesser forces (spirit, angel,
demon, elemental) is exact, since love doesn't usually enter in so
much, in one sense [it is] far more dangerous than invocation of
Gods. In the higher work you are actually wooing the god—it is an
act of art. In the lower you are compelling—it is an act of science."
(Whether Parsons actually followed the rites of the VIII° of the OTO is
known only to initiates.)

There are several ways to go about doing what Parsons was
attempting, and he wrote:

> The primary methods are: 1. Goetia *Daemonic*, 2. Planetary
> *Clavicle of Solomon*, 3. Enochian *Elemental and Aires*, 4. Solar
> *Guardian Angel*. I have found the Enochian the best (although com-
> plicated). The Tarot corresponds to the Enochian system obtained
> by Dr. Dee—the Trumps to the Aires, the Court Cards to the Gods,
> Seniors and Angels, and the numbers to the lesser angels.

What it all boils down to is that Parsons experimented on his own
with upper-degree OTO techniques usually characterized as "sex
magic," i.e., to affect or bring about events. In addition, he remains
the best example in support of the OTO's policy of keeping these techniques secret.

six

An Introduction to Enochian Magic

From Parsons' ritual references and other aspects of the occult world in which he so ardently participated, we can piece together the atmosphere surrounding his workings. For example, the Enochian system referred to by Parsons is a form of magic founded not by the prophet Enoch but by Dr. John Dee and Sir Edward Kelley in 16th-century England. Enochian magic is not necessarily sexual in nature; in fact, its Elizabethan originators deliberately refused injunctions towards sexual immorality.

John Dee was born July 13, 1527 in Mortlake, England, a small village on the Thames just outside of London. Dee was a bright boy, enrolling at the university at the age of 15. He began a large private library at his home and eventually became proficient in various sciences including mathematics, navigation (much of which he learned firsthand during his world travels), astronomy, optics, and cartography. He also studied the hermetic sciences and was appointed to be the Royal Astrologer to Elizabeth I.

Dee had been imprisoned by Queen Mary after drawing up an unfavorable horoscope for her (at her request). Elizabeth pardoned him, and in addition to his otherworldly duties he also acted as an agent of espionage, signing his secret communiqués to her "007." He seems to have developed some sense of esoteric duty to Elizabeth's person or position, as there is evidence he idolized her as the Egyptian goddess Isis. Indeed, his "esoteric duty" may even have included an application of the famous INRI formula, the "key word" used in Crowley's magic, in one of its many variations.

Dee married relatively late, in 1574, at the age of 47. History does not record the name of the wife, who died the following year. He remarried, this time to a Jane Fromond, one of the Queen's ladies-in-waiting. Dee's studies continued independently, and by 1581 he felt he had exhausted all known sources of worldly knowledge and that the only way to continue his quest for knowledge was to turn to the otherworldly.

A godly man, Dee was a good Christian and a member of the Church of England. He admired Enoch, the first man after the Fall said to have walked with God. According to tradition, Enoch was the author of several apocryphal books, in which he was said to have recorded what he learned during these walks. These lost books were in fact pseudepigraphical, i.e., not written by Enoch, but Dee longed to find them and proposed to do it with the help of angels.

Addressing God, he prayed, "I have read often in Thy books & records, how Enoch often injoyed Thy favour & conversation; with Moses thou was familiar; And also that to Abraham, Issack & Jocob, Joshua, Gideon, Esdras, Daniel, Tobias & sundry others Thy good angels were sent by Thy disposition, to Instruct them, informe them, helpe them, yea in worldly and domestick affaires, yea and sometymes to satisfie their desires, doubtes & questions of Thy Secrete."

In his quest, Dee acquired from various sources several magical "shewstones," with the intent of taking up crystal-gazing. Try as he might, however, he couldn't do it, as he was just too logical a thinker and his rational brain resisted all attempts to impose a trance state upon it. He decided he needed a helper and enlisted the services of Edward Kelley, who had changed his name from Talbott. Kelley had a reputation as an alchemist; it was said he had produced gold once. It also seems he was something of a rogue. John Weever recorded the following adventure of Kelley's in the 16th-century *Ancient Funerall Monuments*, the spelling of which appears to have been somewhat modernized:

> This diabolical questioning of the dead for the knowledge of future accidents was put into practice by the said Kelley, who, upon a certain night in the park of Walton-le-Dale in the County of Lancaster with one Paul Waring (his fellow companion in such deeds of darkness) invocated some of the Infernal Regiment, to know certain passages in the life, as also what might be known by the Devil's foresight of the manner and time of the death of a noble young gentleman, as then in wardship. The black ceremonies of the night being ended, Kelley demanded of one of the gentleman's servants what corse was the last buried in Law churchyard, a church thereunto adjoining, who told him of a poor man that was buried there but the same day. He and the said Waring entreated this foresaid servant to go with them to the grave of the man so lately interred, which he did; and withal did help them to dig up the carcase of the poor caitiff, whom by their incantations they made him (or rather some evil spirit through his organs) to speak, who delivered

strange predictions concerning the said gentleman. I was told this by the said serving-man, a secondary actor in that dismal abhorred business, and divers gentlemen and others are now living in Lancashire to whom he hath related this story. And the gentleman himself (whose memory I am bound to honor) told me a little before his death of this conjuration of Kelley, as he had it by relation from his said servant and tenant, only some circumstances except, which he thought not fit to come to his master's notice.

Kelley, called "the crop-eared wizard" because he had had his ears cropped as a punishment for earlier sorceries, moved with his family into a room in Dee's house, where they subsisted on a £50 per year salary paid by Dee.

On a cold evening in 1582, March 8, Dee and Kelley sat down and gazed into one of the shewstones. Impatient, Dee soon got up and moved toward the fire, but within 15 minutes Kelley was seeing angels. Dee came quickly but saw nothing and became content to assume the role of scribe, recording what Kelley relayed he was seeing.

According to Kelley, the angels showed him large tablets bearing unusual letters, which supposedly formed the oldest language of them all: the language of the angels. Kelley described the tablets to Dee, who wrote down what was said. The angel then proceeded to dictate the lost books of Enoch to Kelley, by spelling them out letter-by-letter. The angel would point to a letter, and Kelley would tell Dee which letter it was.

During these transmissions, Kelley was so afraid that the mere mention of these letters would be sufficient to invoke demons, that he only would call out the row and column of each letter as the angel pointed to it. Dee would then look up the corresponding letter and write it down. There were many more tablets, Kelley told Dee, which were not dictated.

The books completed, the angel next dictated the 30 "Aethyrs" (or "Aires") and their 19 Calls, which are for summoning angels to the caller, for the purpose of "scrying" or viewing what was in the Aethyr. The first five Calls were considered so powerful that the angel dictated them backwards to avoid conjuring up the guardians of the corresponding Aethyrs; the remainder were dictated in the usual way.

The Aethyrs are likened to the spheres of the ancients, the planetary orbits thought to surround the earth. According to ancient mythology and religion, souls ascending to heaven had to pass through each sphere in succession, aided by a series of holy names and passwords. Unsuccessful attempts led to reincarnation at best, or to hell. Tradition holds that many of the Aethyrs are guarded by harsh angels, even demons, who have no patience with men or magicians.

After the hazardous dictation process was completed, the angel provided Kelley with the English translations, which required that Dee had to go back over the entire collection of transcripts and substitute the English. Although each Enochian letter has its English counterpart, it is not a letter-for-letter substitution or a code. The letter correspondences were only provided as a pronunciation guide. An actual dictionary was dictated, and Dee had to translate accordingly. Enochian is thus a language unto itself, with its own grammar and syntax. It is very succinct and has an odd relationship to English that it does not have with other languages. One example of Enochian is the word "Babalon," meaning "harlot" in Enochian, as in the "Whore of Babylon." The Enochian system being complicated, the entire process of dictation and translation took seven years, from 1582 to 1589.

Amazingly enough, considering the language's complexity, the Enochian Calls translate into English remarkably well. Regardless of the fact that they were dictated backwards and forwards, and that the translations were only provided later, Enochian turned out to be a coherent language previously unknown to man.

The Calls, when translated, are quite evocative, and contain some very beautiful passages. Although it could easily be claimed Kelley was making the whole thing up, the Calls were nothing at all like his usual writing style, which was quite crude even when he wrote verse. It seems improbable for Kelley to have defrauded Dee in this regard, as the system is just too immense and well structured.

Along with the Calls were dictated instructions, such as when scrying or crystal-gazing the two were to arrange a special cedar table, around the perimeter of which was inscribed in Enochian, "This is the place of the outpouring of forgotten treasure in the form of ecstasy. Only fire is substantial here. This is the way of Babalon and of the Beast who is the first form. The eyes only need rest upon the name of any guardian and its representative will speedily be encountered." The whole thing is scrambled in the original, and the name "Babalon" is extremely so, in order to avoid summoning the Harlot.

In addition, a special ring and robes had to be worn. Some of these artifacts are preserved in the British Museum. The angels provided additional messages as well, some of which were cause for great concern on the part of Dee and Kelly. These communications parallel unorthodox messages received from 19th-century fairies and 20th-century occupants of UFOs. For example, at one point Dee and Kelley were told:

1. That Jesus was not God.
2. That no prayer ought to be made to Jesus.
3. That there is no sin.
4. That man's soul doth go from one body to another childes quickening [i.e., reincarnation].
5. That as many men and women as are now, have always been.
6. That the generation of mankind from Adam and Eve, is not historical but allegorical.

Such seemingly blasphemous messages made Kelley balk, and he grew more and more reticent to continue with their work. Dee had a devil of a time keeping him on, despite the £50 salary. The stress of the constant scrying once sent Kelley running into the street like a madman, at which point Dee had to catch him and calm him down.

However, being a pious man, Dee had occasional misgivings himself. At one point he burned his entire collection of "angelick" works, allegedly to find three of his books intact a few days later. Another time Kelley knocked over a lamp and accidentally burned several valuable manuscripts of Dee's.

Other messages were less onerous, such as one instance in which the angel supposedly began dictating in Greek. Kelley, however, did not know Greek and soon threatened to stop dictating if the angel persisted with this "Ghybbrish." Nevertheless, enough came through for Dee to recognize the message as a warning not to trust Kelley.

According to the story, the angel later told Dee and Kelley to swap wives, but the two were so shocked at this message that they and their wives all signed a pact (at Dee's prompting) never to reveal this message to anyone. As noted, the breaking of religious and sexual taboos, from the eating of meat and wine to incest and homosexuality, is considered a part of *tantra*. The shock is intended to decondition the initiate from his usual lifestyle. In the case of Dee and Kelley, living in prudish Elizabethan England, it was asking too much—at least for now. They did finally persuade their wives to agree to this seeming commandment from God: Dee recorded in his diary on May 3, 1587, "I, John Dee, Edward Kelley and our two wives, covenanted with God and subscribed the same, for indissoluble and inviolable unities, charity and friendship keeping between us four, and all things between us to be common, as God by sundry means willed us to do."

Dee and Kelley left Mortlake for a tour of Europe in 1583, continuing their work with the angels as they traveled. When they returned in 1587, they were horrified to see that a superstitious mob had sacked Dee's house and burned the contents, destroying most of his valuable library.

Undeterred by such a faith-destroying event, the two continued, their work with the Calls ending one day when Kelley was scrying alone in the 7th Aire, during which time he received the following proto-thelemic message:

I am the daughter of Fortitude and ravished every hour from my youth. For behold, I am Understanding, and science dwelleth in me; and the heavens oppress me. They cover and desire me with infinite appetite; for none that are earthly have embraced me, for I am shadowed with the Circle of the Stars, and covered with the morning clouds. My feet are swifter than the winds, and my hands are sweeter than the morning dew. My garments are from the beginning, and my dwelling place is in myself. The Lion knoweth not where I walk, neither do the beasts of the field understand me. I am deflowered, yet a virgin; I sanctify and am not sanctified. Happy is he that embraceth me: for in the night season I am sweet, and in the day full of pleasure. My company is a harmony of many symbols, and my lips sweeter than health itself. I am a harlot [BABALON] for such as ravish me, and a virgin with such as know me not. Purge your streets, O ye sons of men, and wash your houses clean; make yourselves holy, and put on righteousness. Cast out your old strumpets, and burn their clothes and then I will bring forth children unto you and they shall be the Sons of Comfort in the Age that is to come.

The entire passage is reminiscent of the gnostic text, "Thunder Perfect Mind," unearthed at Nag Hammadi in 1945 but written at least 1700 years earlier.

This message was the last straw for Kelley, and he finally snapped, robbing Dee of a large sum and leaving town with Dee's wife. The two did not return but ended up in Germany, where Kelley endeared himself to the Emperor. Focusing his attention increasingly on practical alchemy, Kelley was soon knighted but was later imprisoned (either for killing a man or simply to keep him close to the Emperor), and died during an attempt to escape. Dee was also imprisoned when James I, patron of the King James Bible, ascended to the English throne in 1603. Despite his own personal, extrabiblical peccadilloes, the pious King James was scared of magic and put a quick end to Dee's career as royal astrologer.

Dee was subsequently put on trial for witchcraft but was acquitted and spent his remaining years penniless. In 1608, he died, financially ruined but spiritually whole, apparently having used the Enochian system for little more than the satisfaction of his own curiosity. The papers he had hidden away near the end of his life were not found for 100 years, and his diary was not found for 200 years, but for at least one later student Dee's personal tragedy would eerily appear to repeat itself.

As is well known in the world of the esoteric and occult, crystal-gazing is not the only way one may scry in the Aethyrs, as tantric energy, or sex magick, may also be used to induce the same sort of ecstatic states that Kelley used so long ago. The provocative Parsons used this method, as did his libidinous mentor Crowley, who claimed to be the reincarnation of Kelley, although that role would in reality be played to Parsons' Dee by another man in his personal drama. In addition, Crowley further heightened his awareness through the use of psychoactive drugs (see his *Liber LXXXIV vel Chanokh*). Crowley's *The Diary of a Drug Fiend*, both well-received and vilified, was accused of encouraging drug abuse. During the course of his life, Crowley consumed massive amounts of alcohol, opium, cocaine, hashish, peyote and heroin, to which he was addicted at his death.

Like Dee and Kelley, Parsons eventually found himself in trouble, seemingly at the hands of the infamous Babalon, the Enochian Whore of Babylon, the traditional spirit of Rome who subjugated the children of Israel. Babalon, as the Harlot, is also a symbol of the material world in general, the root "mater" also meaning "mother," as in "Mother of Abominations." Adherents to the Jamaican religion of Rastafari use her this sensual way, as any listener of reggae music might know. A similar symbol for certain gnostic sects in the Middle East was the "Land of the Dead," i.e., Egypt. Like Egypt, Babylon was the land of corruption to the composers of the Bible, as in Revelation 17:3-6:

> He [the angel] carried my spirit away to the desert. I saw the Scarlet Woman sitting on the Beast with seven heads and ten

horns, covered with blasphemous names. The woman was clothed in purple and scarlet, and gilded with gold and precious stones and pearls, with a golden cup in her hand filled with abominations and the unclean things of her fornication. On her forehead a name had been written, a mystery: *Babylon the Great, the mother of harlots and of the abominations of the Earth.* I saw the woman was drunk from the blood of the Saints, and from the blood of the martyrs of Jesus. Seeing her, I wondered greatly.

According to Parsons, Babalon is the gnostic Sophia, slighted by John the Revelator, but justifiably so, as she is still in her fallen state. John fails to offer her redemption. She is also the Helen of Simon Magus mentioned by Parsons in his *Analysis By A Master of the Temple.* She is the *Chokmah* of the Kabbalah, the Holy Wisdom who cries out in the first and eighth Psalms, folded into the *Shekhinah* of the Hebrews.

The Greek name Babylon is derived from the Semitic *Bab-Il,* meaning "the gate of God." At one time or another every holy city believed it was at the center of the world, the mystical center where the gate between the upper and lower worlds is located. So it is with Jerusalem today for three of the world's major religions, with Benares for the Hindus, and with Mecca and Rome. Like so many other religious symbols, however, gates have a sexual symbolism as well.

The Hebrew for "gate of God" is *Bab-Al,* usually written *Bab-El* or simply *Babel.* The name (actually a title) of God usually translated *El* (if translated at all) is actually spelled with an "A" (or *aleph* in Hebrew).

Although he no doubt followed the Enochian spelling, Crowley claimed to have "corrected" "Babylon" to "Babalon" to give what was to him a meaningful *gematria,* a term used by medieval Jewish scholars to describe the ancient practice of substituting numbers for the letters in a word or name and adding them up to get a significant result. *Gematria* comes from a Greek word meaning "to measure (land)," and this practice dates at least to Babylon, when single letters were used to stand for numbers rather than spelling them out. In an age that has used Arabic numerals for centuries, the significance of this achievement may be hard to appreciate.

In this system of numeration, A = 1, B = 2, and so on. After the 10th letter ("I" in the Hebrew and Greek alphabets, sometimes written as "Y") there was no need for an 11 since "IA" stood for a 10 followed by a 1, which is the way we form numerals in our base 10 system. Eleven, in fact, is Crowley's "number of magick." The 11th letter is "K," which, according to gematria, equals 20, and so on. Thus BABYLON = 2 + 1 + 2 + 400 + 80 + 800 + 50 = 1335, which is not a meaningful result.

In the Book of Revelation the original Greek is BABYLON with an upsilon (Y), rather than an alpha, while the final vowel is not omicron but is the long "o," omega. Crowley's "corrected" spelling BABALON = 2 + 1 + 2 + 1 + 30 + 70 + 50 = 156, a number significant to John Dee as the product of 12 and 13, the dimensions of the table upon which he received the Enochian alphabet from the angel.

Crowley referred to the number 156 as that of the "City of the Pyramids," where initiates would spend the "Night of Pan." Babylon was known for its ziggurats, stepped pyramids built for the gods to descend and humans to ascend, serving as a model for the biblical Tower of Babel, also immortalized in the 16th card of the Tarot.

In the Enochian system, the City of the Pyramids lies in the 14th Aire, above which (i.e., 13th) is the Garden of Nemo, Nemo being Enochian for "Master of the Temple." The 12th Aire belongs to Babalon, and the 11th is called the Holy City. The 10th Aire will be discussed in a later chapter. While Dee and Kelley may have discovered the Enochian system and Babalon the Harlot, Parsons was to make the latter more infamous.[10]

---

10. The primary reference on Babalon remains Crowley's *Liber 418*, reproduced in *Magick* and elsewhere.

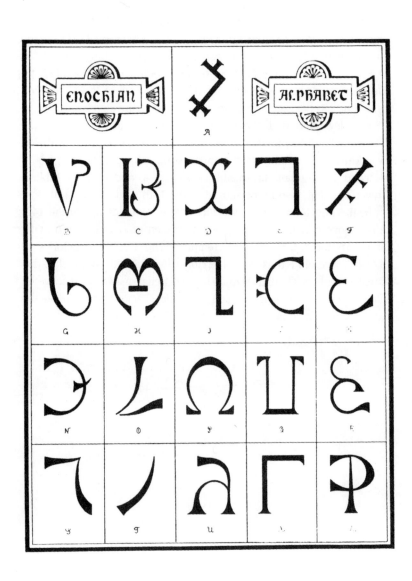

seven

The Babalon Working, Part 1: January–February 1946

Now that he had achieved extraordinary success in his physical jet propulsion, it seems Parsons was intent on creating high-flying adventures on the metaphysical plane. In early 1946, using the Angelic language of John Dee and Edward Kelley, Parsons planned his magickal operation, keeping diligent records per Crowley's constant advice. The surviving fragments of Parsons' Babalon Working have been circulated since the days of mimeograph machines, and are widely posted on the World Wide Web. They are not a part of *Freedom Is A Two-Edged Sword*, though the near future may see collected writings of John Parsons printed under one cover.

The working began January 4, 1946. At 9 p.m. Parsons wrote, "I followed this procedure for eleven days, from January 4 to 15," which is actually 12 days. Presumably, Parsons miscounted and carried on the working for one extra day, a simple mistake difficult to believe of a rocket scientist.

To begin the working, Parsons chose one of the squares from the Enochian "Air Tablet" (there are four 12-by-13 tablets, one for each element), also known as the "Great Watch-Tower of the East." He did not record which of the 156 possible squares he chose. After preparing the other magical weapons, at 9 p.m. he prepared and consecrated his "Air Dagger." An actual dagger purchased for this purpose, the weapon, he said, was the "special talisman of the operation."

Parsons then copied the symbols contained within the chosen square onto virgin parchment. These symbols consist of one of the seven planetary signs, one of the 12 zodiacal signs, a unique permutation of the four signs of the elements, and an Enochian letter in the center. Present as "Scribe" for the entire operation was none other than Hubbard, in what would eventually resemble the Dee-Kelley operation. The ritual was ready to begin.

Parsons first invoked the "Pentagram of Air," a five-pointed star traced in the air with the dagger. It starts at the upper right-hand point of the star, representing water, goes left towards air, then traces the remainder of the star through fire (lower right), spirit (top), earth (lower left), then back to water. As he proceeds in the ritual, the magician must visualize the outline of the pentagram in brilliant purple (different for each element invoked) as well as the symbol of air in the center. This ritual includes the oft-heard recitation invoking the four archangels as representatives of the four cardinal directions, and hence the four elements. "Before me, Raphael; Behind me, Gabriel," etc.

Parsons probably should have invoked with the hexagram next, which is the way the rite usually goes, but he does not record this being done. It may be that he assumed this step was understood, or that he deliberately left it out of his writing to deter prying eyes from repeating his operation. There are hexagrams invoked later in the operation, during the invocation of the "Six Seniors," and he may have felt these were sufficient.

Next Parsons recited from memory the "Invocation of the Bornless One," a short invocation translated by Crowley and appearing at the beginning of his and Mathers' translation of the Goetia, or *Lesser Key of Solomon*. It starts:

Thee I invoke, the Bornless One.
Thee, that didst create the Earth and the Heavens.
Thee, that didst create the Night and the Day.
Thee, that didst create the Darkness and the Light.
Thou art Osorronophris, whom no man hath seen at any time.
Thou art Jabas.
Thou art Japos.
Thou hast distinguished between the Just and the Unjust.
Thou didst make the Female and the Male.
Thou didst produce the Seed and the Fruit.
Thou didst form Men to love one another, and to hate one another.
I am Mosheh [Moses] Thy Prophet, unto whom Thou didst commit
    Thy Mysteries, the Ceremonies of Ishrael [sic].
Thou didst produce the moist and the dry, and that which nour-
    isheth all created Life.
Dear Thou Me, for I am the Angel of Paphro Osorronophris; this is
    Thy True Name, handed down to the Prophets of Ishrael . . ."

The original invocation is traditionally ascribed to Moses, but it bears an Egyptian flavor reflecting the mysteries of Egypt, into which the Bible says Moses was initiated. Later versions "corrected" some of the spellings to bring them in line with Crowley's work: "Osorronophris" became ASAR UN-NEFER (a form of Osiris), for example.

It would have been this corrected version that Parsons used. The complete text can be found in "Liber Samekh" in Crowley's *Magick*, and represents the lengthy rite Crowley used at Boleskine to attain to the Knowledge and Conversation of his Holy Guardian Angel and thus to the $6° = 5°$ of the A∴A∴, in the version quoted above. Although evidently undocumented, it is possible that success during this ritual would have allowed Parsons to claim the $6° = 5°$.

Parsons next recorded a "Conjuration of Air," a "Consecration of the Air Dagger" (apparently a redundancy), and the Key Call of the Third Aire, the latter of which is not to be confused with the element Air. The dagger is one of the four standard magical weapons used by the magician. The other three are the pentacle (or disk), the cup, and the wand.[11]

It seems that Parsons actually recited the "Third Key" (or Third Call), which is different from the Key Call of the Third Aire, as there is only one Key Call for all 30 Aires. However, the Third Call is appropriate to summon EXARP, the Angel of the Air Tablet, so it seems to have been a mistake in nomenclature only. In other words, Parsons used the correct call but called it by the wrong name in his notes. The Third Key, in English, is:

Behold! Saith your God! I am a circle on whose hands stand twelve Kingdoms. Six are the seats of living breath: the rest are sharp Sickles, or the Horns of Death. Wherein the creatures of earth are and are not, except in mine own hands; which sleep and shall rise!

In the first I made ye stewards, and placed ye in twelve seats of government: giving unto every one of you power successively over the 456 true ages of time: to the intent that from the highest vessels and the corners of your governments you might work my Power, pouring down the fires of life and increase continually on the earth. Thus you are become the skirts of Justice and Truth.

In the name of the same your God, lift up, I say, yourselves!

Behold! His Mercies flourish, and His Name is become mighty among us. In whom we say: Move! Descend! And apply yourselves unto us as unto the partakers of His Secret Wisdom in your Creation.

All this invocation should have been done from memory. Next was an Invocation of God and of the King associated with the Air Tablet.

---

11. See Crowley's *Liber A vel ARMORUM* in *Magick* for instructions for constructing each weapon as well as other magical accessories.

The Secret Name of God associated with the Air Tablet is ORO-IBAH-AOZPI, meaning "He who cries aloud in the place of desolation." The King associated with the Air Tablet is named BATAIVAH, which means "He whose voice seems to have wings." These odd names are all formed from the letters on the Enochian tablets taken in different order, much like a seek-and-find puzzle in the newspaper.

Parsons next invoked the Six Seniors of the Air Tablet, whose names are HABIORO, AAOZXAIF, HTNMORDA, AHAOZAPI, AVTOTAR, and HIPOTGA. They are equivalent to the "airy" parts of Mars, Jupiter, the Moon, Venus, Mercury, and Saturn, respectively—six of the seven "planets" visible to the naked eye, the seventh (the King) being the Sun, the same as the seven days of the week, albeit in a different order. The Kings and Seniors are each invoked with their own special hexagram, in this case a Hexagram of Air. Thus Parsons drew seven consecutive hexagrams in the air, visualizing the appropriate names and colors and pronouncing the names, then addressing each in turn, individually, with certain Enochian greetings. Again, from memory.

The next step is rather hazy in the record. Parsons says he invoked "blank by blank and blank to visible appearance." OTO scholars have filled in the first and last blanks, but the middle one remains a mystery. This first is written as RDZA, by which is surely meant ARDZA, Enochian for "He who protects," one of the "Calvary Cross" names, another long series that forms a certain pattern of letters traced out on the four elemental tablets.

ARDZA is the name that controls the force of the "Air of Air" (upper left) quadrant of the Air Tablet. This force, not recorded by Parsons, is named IDOIGO, "He who sits on the Holy Throne." Since the upper left is where the letters ARDZA (in Enochian) appear on the Air Tablet, the proximate name IDOIGO is probably what Parsons left unrecorded in the middle blank, as that is the only possible complement to ARDZA in this rite.

The last blank is filled in with the name EXARP, again the Angel of the Air Tablet, who controls all forces associated with the element of Air, the Kings and Seniors being invoked merely to preside over the rite. Parsons would have been facing the direction of the prevailing winds in Pasadena while invoking EXARP and, indeed, throughout the entire ceremony.[12]

The next statement is the simplest in Parsons' magical record, yet it is also the most important. Parsons merely writes, "Invocation of

12. Some versions read XARP—the final E is added to denote the element of Air.

wand with material basis on talisman," the "material basis" of which is the "Marrow of the Wand," the Wand, of course, representing the penis or phallus of the magician, while the Marrow is the semen. During the rite, the magician is to invoke the spirit and, while concentrating upon it, masturbate over the talisman. Parsons here was "energizing," even "fertilizing" the little parchment square bearing the chosen square from the Air Tablet, the form sympathetic magic takes: a symbolic fertilizing of Parsons' desire through a very literal application of the usual means of fertilization. Crude, perhaps, but traditional.

Parsons then wrote "Invocation with [Air] Dagger," presumably an invocation of the elemental he wished to attract, although he does not say. Lastly are the "License to Depart," a purification, and the banishings, which are a sign that the rite is over. The License to Depart is in the Goetia, or Lesser Key of Solomon, which Mathers and Crowley had translated years earlier. The first English-language edition appeared in 1903.

The License to Depart runs, "O thou Spirit N. [name of spirit, in this case EXARP], because thou has diligently answered unto my demands, and hast been very ready and willing to come at my call, I do here license thee to depart unto thy proper place; without causing harm or danger unto man or beast. Depart, then, I say, and be thou very ready to come at my call, being duly exorcised and conjured by the sacred rites of magic. I charge thee to withdraw peaceably and quietly, and the peace of God be ever continued between thee and me! Amen!" The invocation also occurs in Crowley's later *Magick*, as well as in other texts by various authors.

Banishings are as equally involved as the invocations, as they involve recreating (or, rather, "erasing") the various hexagrams and finally the pentagram in reverse of the original way they were traced. Needless to say, this is a very long ceremony, lasting at least an hour, and again, all from memory. All the Kings and Seniors have to be banished, one at a time. Interestingly, the procedure outlined here from the initial pentagram to the final banishing is slightly different from the textbook Enochian invocations. Parsons must have improvised somewhat.

In 1943, Parsons had published a brief poem in the *Oriflamme*, an OTO publication:

> I hight Don Quixote, I live on peyote,
> marijuana, morphine and cocaine,

I never know sadness, but only a madness
that burns at the heart and the brain.

I see each charwoman, ecstatic, inhuman,
angelic, demonic, divine.
Each wagon a dragon, each beer mug a flagon
that brims with ambrosial wine.

As documented by John Symonds and Robert Anton Wilson, narcotics and hallucinogens were a basic staple of Crowley's magical diet,
as they exist in esoteric ceremonies of several religions. Crowley
recorded using these drugs in his *Confessions*, as well as in the published portions of his Magical Record. Within the world of magick, it
is well known that it is easier to induce astral vision when one alter-
nately dulls and excites the senses by chemical means. Indeed, the
role of drugs in magick is common, and it is fairly certain they were a
part of the Babalon Working. In *The Book of Law*, (AL II:22), for example, Crowley wrote, "To worship me [Nuit] take wine and strange
drugs whereof I will tell my prophet, & be drunk thereof!" In addition,
Helen Parsons Smith told an interviewer that Parsons got into drugs
after their split in 1943, the same year he wrote his Don Quixote poem
and three years before the Babalon Working. Apparently she had been
his anchor to reality, and, once she was gone, he was wide open to
just about anything. She continued to follow the path of white magick, she said, while he turned down another, darker path.

Parsons' drug use also manifests itself in "Narcissus," one of his
poems from his later collection *Songs for the Witch Woman*, which is
dedicated to Cameron, the woman Parsons would claim to be the elemental he had purportedly invoked during the Babalon Working.
"Narcissus" reads:

Drug me with drugs
Slow acting, sensuous, sweet,
Co-mingle gin and musk,
Hashish and amber,
Let me drink and breathe
And hear slow, devious music
Until aroused
To subtle, languorous moods,
Until I see
Ochre and mazarine and purple

Emit lascivious sounds.
Then I shall go
Through dark and gothic ruins,
Gray and golden mists
Down to a forest, green
With an old dream.
I shall go naked
And magnolia and oleander
Datura and jasmine,
When blossoms will open and vaginally flower
In infinite time, for a relative hour,
Whose white, subliminal flowers
Will caress my breasts.
And I shall perform stately
Phallic arabesques
In the moonlight,
Pale and white.

The possibly drug-enhanced working continued the evening of January 5, when Parsons noted "a strong windstorm beginning suddenly about the middle of the first invocation," which was no surprise, as EXARP is the Angel of the *Air* Tablet. In writing, the "*first* invocation," Parsons was referring to the fact that he repeated the entire rite after finishing it the first time. The entire process took a full two hours, such that Parsons must have been reciting at breakneck speed to finish so soon.

On January 6, Parsons continued the invocation, which means he ran through the entire rite twice. The windstorm also continued. On January 7, he invoked twice more, and the wind subsided. At this point he began playing Sergei Prokofiev's *Violin Concerto No. 2* as background music; the actual recording of which is still available to the diligent searcher.[13]

The working continued, and on January 8 Parsons wrote, "Invoked twice, using blood" (presumably as a substitute for the

13. The concerto used by Parsons was Prokofiev's *Violin Concerto No. 2 in G Minor (Op. 63)*, which was the only recording available at the time. Recorded on December 20, 1937, it was performed by the Boston Symphony Orchestra, and conducted by Serge Koussevitzky, while Jascha Heifetz played violin. Prokofiev (1891–1953) was still alive at the time. Lasting just over 34 minutes, it is a haunting recording, though sentimental in places. It is unclear whether the Scribe restarted the record when it finished, or if the participants just allowed it to run until it stopped. The original was a 78-rpm phonograph record, and its CD is available on Biddulph from England. It is also available as item number 9167 in the Pearl-Koch catalog, entitled *Jacha* (sic) *Heifetz Concerto Recordings Vol. II-Brahms et al.*, a version released October 13, 1995 as part of a two-disc set.

"material basis" of January 4, or else applied to the Wand directly à la Crowley's *Mass of the Phoenix*).

On January 9, he wrote, "Invoked twice, replenishing material basis," which evidently means he did not apply the "material basis" (semen) to the talisman (the little parchment square) on the nights of the 5th through the 8th. In this sex magick, it seems he "invoked the wand" (gained an erection) but deliberately denied himself release so the secretions (sperm) created would be absorbed by the body, a practice found in tantra. This "magical masturbation" was evidently carried out in front of the Scribe, i.e., Hubbard.

On January 10, Parsons invoked twice and retired to bed around 11 p.m. He was awakened at midnight by nine loud, unexplainable knocks.[14] When Parsons got out of bed to investigate the knocks, he noticed a lamp lay smashed on the floor, which should have been taken as an omen, as it is not the desired result and represents a magical misdirection of energy. Parsons recognized as much in his record, but continued regardless. Considering Hubbard was the Scribe during this ritual, it is an interesting coincidence that HUBARD means "living lamps" in Enochian, as is the fact that a knocked-over lamp features in Dee and Kelley's enterprise as well.

On January 11, Parsons wrote, "Invoked twice, using blood," and on the 12th, "Invoked twice. A heavy windstorm." The invocations and the windstorm both continued on the 13th.

January 14 was the second-to-last day of the working—a very interesting day. As Parsons began invoking at 9 p.m., the electricity went out. Parsons records that "another magician who had been staying in the house and studying with me was carrying a candle across the kitchen when he was struck strongly on the right shoulder, and the candle knocked out of his hand." According to Cameron and others, this other magician was Hubbard, which is odd in that Hubbard was consistently referred to as "Scribe" throughout Parsons' record of the Babalon Working, rather than "magician," indicating the record may have been garbled here.

> He [the other "magician"] called us [the "us" apparently referring to Parsons and some unknown other] and we observed a brownish yellow light about seven feet high in the kitchen. I banished with a

---

14. This occurrence is curiously similar to the nine regular knocks that Whitley Strieber felt confirmed the existence of his otherworldly Visitors in his "non-fiction" book *Communion*. Strieber later said that these nine knocks signified his readiness to move to the next evolutionary level, just as three knocks signify a Master Mason is ready to enter the Lodge for initiation.

magical sword, and it disappeared. His [the other magician's] right arm was paralyzed for the rest of the night.

The final day was January 15, when Parsons wrote:

> At this time the Scribe [Hubbard] developed some sort of astral vision, describing in details an old enemy of mine of whom he had never heard [Captain Kynette, the car-bombing cop?], and later the guardian forms of Isis and the Archangel Michael. Later, in my room, I heard the [nine] raps again, and a buzzing, metallic voice crying "let me go free." I felt a great pressure and tension in the house that night, which was also noticed by the other occupants. There was no other phenomena, and I admit a feeling of disappointment.

Parsons sleepily performed the License to Depart, and the spirit was free to return to its home. In his record of the working Parsons wrote that the "tension and unease continued for four days" and that he didn't know what to do next.

Around this time, Jane Wolfe wrote to Crowley, "Last evening, when Jack brought me these various papers for me to post to you, I saw, for the first time, the small boy, or child. This is it that is bewildered, does not quite know when to take hold in this matter, or where, and is completely bowled over by the ruthlessness of Smith— Smith, who has a master hand when it comes to dealing with this boy."

Also around this time, Wilfred Smith described his own state to Crowley:

> Ill started, ill maintained, ill terminated. The shrine is desolate of the divine; has ever been; and I am completely empty; so much so, I do not know if I write accurately about myself. In fact I don't know anything at all. Have nothing; am nothing . . .
>
> The worst of it is, I have some years yet to go and the prospect of having to live with myself is—I assure you—not at all pleasant. For I can't see but that my brain will continually flog me till I go to sleep once and for all. I have ill understood your dealings with me these many years, and I am no better informed at this moment.

And Parsons wrote Crowley, "I have diligently followed the VIIIth Degree instructions as (a) creation of new orders of beings with consecrated talismanic images. Possible connective result: increase in writing output [a reference to *Freedom Is A Two-Edged Sword*?]; (b) Invocation of Mother Goddess, using Priest's call in [Gnostic] mass and silver cup as talisman [for the material basis?]; sometimes using suitable poetry such as Venus. Possible connective result: loss of Betty's affections as preliminary to (c) Invocation of Air Elemental Kerub [Cherub] . . . in Enochian Air Tablet." The "suitable poetry" is not recorded in his account of the working. The rite ended with Parsons commanding the elemental to appear in human form.

The "Kerub of the Air" of Air quadrant is called ERZLA. There are four Kerubs for each of the four Tablets, and 12 Lesser Kerubic Angels and 16 Lesser Angels for each as well, part of the complicated (but highly structured) system.

The Priest's Call in the Gnostic Mass is a short recitation in Greek that the Priest makes when the Priestess is behind the veil. It apparently was a preliminary to the lengthy rites of the Babalon Working (24 complete invocations in 12 days!) and is a call to the creative power of the Priest as represented by his "lance" (i.e., phallus). The call is:

IO IO IO IAO SABAO KYRIE ABRASAX KYRIE MEITHRAS KYRIE PHALLE. IO PAN, IO PAN PAN, IO ISCHYROCH, IO ATHANATON, IO ABROTON, IO IAO. CHAIRE PHALLE CHAIRE PANPHAGE CHAIRE PANGENETOR. AGIOS, AGIOS, AGIOS IAO, *which is* O, O, O, IAO, Sabao, Lord Abrasax, Lord Mithras, Lord Phallus. O Pan, O Pan Pan, O Strong One, O Immortal One, O Divine One, O IAO. Hail Phallus, Hail All-Devourer, Hail All-Begetter. Holy, Holy, Holy IAO.

Iao, Sabao, and Abrasax are Greek deities with long histories: They are solar in nature, and the rising sun is the Phallus invoked in the call.

Following the working, Parsons was at first despondent: "Nothing seems to have happened. The windstorm is very interesting, but that is not what I asked for," he wrote Crowley. On January 18, Parsons and Hubbard went into the Mojave Desert to relax. At sunset the feeling of tension suddenly left Parsons, and he turned to Hubbard "in absolute certainty that the operation was accomplished" and said simply, "It is done," echoing Jesus' "It is finished" spoken on the cross.

At this time, Grady McMurtry, whom Parsons met at a science fiction meeting, returned from England and moved to San Francisco with the intent of starting a lodge there. He spent the week of January 14th to the 20th at 1003 S. Orange Grove, interviewing the various members of the lodge to determine what was going on and what could be done about it. Crowley had sent him in to see if there was any way to fix the mess he had been hearing about. McMurtry's report is dated January 25 and includes signed statements from Parsons and several others. Parsons was surprised to see McMurtry, who had left as an inferior in the Order, return as his superior.

McMurtry told Crowley that Parsons was ". . . a man of integrity and aspiration, all he lacks is an experienced instructor. He is easily the outstanding personality of the whole group." He also mentioned a new female interest of Parsons' named Helen Parker, but apparently nothing of note developed between the two.

McMurtry's report found the lodge in a mess, as many of the members were bickering about almost everything, yet he saw hope for the future. Parsons, he said, was "shaking the debris of Agape from his shoulders and preparing to make a clean start with a more ambitious program than ever. A lesser man would have washed his hands of the whole affair."

McMurtry further outlined a program of advertising, initiation, training, and performance of the Gnostic Mass as the immediate needs of the lodge. Parsons wanted to incorporate the OTO, which McMurtry endorsed. Parsons would stay in Pasadena with the Agape Lodge, while McMurtry would return to San Francisco and open the Thelema Lodge. This plan did not materialize until 1977, long after Parsons' death.

Parsons wanted to pursue the advertising campaign as a "Synagogue of Satan"; McMurtry thought this angle was fine for some but not all-inclusive. He wanted to pursue a less sensationalistic campaign in San Francisco, modeled after the Abbey of Thelema in Cefalu, Sicily.

McMurtry closes by referring to Agape Lodge as "Hodge Podge Lodge," which he says the residents of 1003 S. Orange Grove call "Ghastly Gables." Neither title is flattering. Parsons' attached statement says that he sold the big home to finance an explosives manufacturing plant, such that he evidently didn't own the house very long. Another member, Max Schneider, with whom Parsons seems to have been bickering the most, said Parsons was trying to "combine a Lodge, a profess house, and a rooming house for thrill seekers all under one roof." The other statements speak well of Parsons, but say that the influence of Smith was still too strong.

One interesting remark was made by Roy Leffingwell, who told McMurtry that Parsons was "impregnating statuettes with a vital force by invocation, and then selling the statuettes." He further said that Parsons reminded him "of the young Crowley—he is so set on overturning the present system that he will stop at nothing." No mention is made of the Babalon Working in any of McMurtry's reports.

Parsons' disappointment at the results of the working had been alleviated by the next month, when, on February 23, 1946, he triumphantly wrote to Crowley, "I have my elemental! She turned up one night after the conclusion of the Operation, and has been with me since, although she goes back to New York next week. She has red hair and slant green eyes as specified. She is an artist, strong-minded and determined, with strong masculine characteristics and a fanatical independence. If she returns she will be dedicated as I am dedicated!"

The elemental was Marjorie Elizabeth Cameron, sprung from Parsons' head like Sophia from the Godhead or Pallas Athena from Zeus. She actually arrived at the lodge before Parsons left for the desert with Hubbard. McMurtry had just left, and the Babalon Working was still in progress (but was not known to Cameron). Cameron came back two weeks later after some friends of Parsons tracked her down at the employment office. This time she came to stay.

Parsons described Cameron as an "air of fire type with bronze red hair, fiery and subtle, determined and obstinate, sincere and perverse, with extraordinary personality, talent, and intelligence." She remained in the dark about the Babalon Working until long after it was finished—even though she was to participate in its next phase. Parsons made her a protective talisman, which she wore around her neck for years until police took it away because it had a potent poison sealed inside.

Parsons exultantly wrote in his notes that Cameron answered all the requirements of the elemental he had invoked. She adopted the magical name "Candida" (the Latin root of "candid"), calling herself "Candy" for short. He wrote that she "demonstrated the nature of woman to you [referring to himself] in such unequivocal terms that you [Parsons] should have no further room for illusion on the subject." Parsons and Cameron would marry in October of that year, just eight months later. Shortly after they met, the ever-romantic Parsons composed a poem for her, "Witch Woman," which opens his poetry collection *Songs for the Witch Woman*:

I hear your voice low in the dusk
Like the notes of the harp player
That carve the still air
Into a sensuous and subtle imagery of sound.

And my senses are drowned
By the scent of the oleander and the musk
Of the datura dimly shining in the dark,
While your voice troubles the still air,
And I recall
An ancient garden and a secret call
And your slant eyes and your red hair
Engender dreams of days beyond despair.

And under your sorcery I fare forth
To fabulous lands and meadows green with Spring
And caught on the gossamer web of evening
I behold incredible things no poet ever told.

Marjorie Cameron was born on April 23, 1922 in Belle Plain, Iowa,
which is located in Benton County in east central Iowa. Her parents
were Hill Lislie Cameron, originally from Illinois, and Carrie V.
Ridenour, a native of Iowa. Cameron actually grew up in northern
Wisconsin, "a country of ferocious grandeur." When she met
Parsons, she was 5'5", 126 pounds, fair-complected with freckles, red
hair and blue (not green) eyes. An "air of fire type," as Parsons called
her, is typically a Leo in the Enochian system (on the Fire Tablet
rather than the Air Tablet), and is associated with the Prince of
Wands in the Tarot.

Cameron had served in the WAVES during WWII, at which time she
had been stationed in Washington, D.C. She had also served as an
aide to the Joint Chiefs of Staff there, after entering the Navy as an
Apprentice Seaman on December 9, 1942 at Chicago, Illinois. She
was honorably discharged from Washington, D.C. as a photographer
on November 16, 1945, after which she moved to Los Angeles, where
one of her Navy friends took her to the Agape Lodge. Interestingly,
Cameron, Hubbard and Heinlein were all in the Navy. A Freedom of
Information Act request revealed that the FBI had no file on her.

From January 19 (the very day Cameron arrived!) to February 27,
Parsons daily recorded that he "invoked the Goddess BABALON with
the aid of my magical partner, as was proper to one of my grade."

The magical partner was, of course, Cameron, though some writers have tried to make it Hubbard, who was in actuality not present. The grade Parsons referred to is the IX° of the OTO, a rite involving sexual intercourse in much the way that the VIII° involves masturbation. However, Parsons evidently never held this grade, nor was this a IX° working, based on the way Crowley ran the higher grades in the 1940s. At that time, Agape Lodge was the only operating lodge of the OTO. Members there could request the grade, as it were, and Crowley would confirm their right to work it despite the fact that they had not attained the intermediate grades. However, just because a few members were working with the IX° material does not mean they could demonstrate attainment, as there were no other legitimate IX° members present to guide them and confirm their results. The Babalon Working in particular was far too unorthodox to have been a part of this degree; it was specially designed by Parsons for this one purpose.

According to Cameron, the rite consisted of her and Parsons spending two weeks in bed. Unfortunately, Parsons did not record the details of his daily invocations, or if he did they have not survived. Cameron said the two talked incessantly: "He educated me . . . that's what he was supposed to do." She also related that he made her aware she "had a mission in the world." Of course, she was ignorant of the entire Babalon Working, of which she was supposed to be the elemental invoked, until well past its completion.

On February 27, Cameron went back to New York to visit her boyfriend, a photographer named Napoleon, spending two weeks there, during which time she dumped him. She later said she returned to Pasadena when she discovered she was pregnant by Parsons. The day after she left for New York, Parsons returned to the Mojave Desert without Hubbard, who had gone away for awhile, perhaps to the VA hospital in San Francisco. Parsons invoked Babalon in the desert, presumably through a solo sexual rite of some sort, though he does not say. What resulted was phenomenal: "The presence of the Goddess came upon me," he wrote, "and I was commanded to write the following communication."

The communication Parsons was commanded to write was *Liber 49*, often mistakenly referred to as *The Book of Babalon*, of which it is only a part. *Liber 49* is too long to reproduce here, but it has been reproduced widely in print and on the internet in unauthorized versions. The communication falls well outside the orthodoxy of the OTO's system, their test of its genuineness and spiritual coherence being its claim to be the fourth chapter of *Liber AL*—which is described internally as "threefold."[15]

Parsons took *Liber 49* to be an affirmation of the need to produce a "magical child." *Liber 49* has 77 verses: The seven-pointed star is sacred to Babalon (which has seven letters), and $7 \times 7 = 49$, a number also sacred to Babalon. Besides being two sevens side-by-side, 77 is 7×11, and 11, as we have already seen, is the number of Crowley's magick.

Parsons came to see *Liber 49* as the fourth chapter of *The Book of the Law*. Parsons saw the four chapters as corresponding to the four letters of the ineffable name of God: YHWH, the Hebrew *Yod Hé Vau Hé*. He assigned one chapter to each letter and to what each letter represented: Father, Mother, Son, Daughter, or God, Holy Ghost, Christ, and the gnostic Sophia, the *Puer, Vir, Puella, Mulier* of *Liber 36*.

Of the 77 original verses of *Liber 49*, 73 survive. *Liber 49* begins:

1. Yea, it is I, BABALON.
2. And this is my book, that is the fourth chapter of the *Book of the Law*, Hé completing the Name, for I am out of NUIT by HORUS, the incestuous sister of RA-HOOR-KHUIT.

Five of the surviving verses mention fire, flame or burning, which seems appropriate for a man working with rockets and explosives. Three mention the "Black Pilgrimage," which we will also discuss later. Two mention the number 11, albeit one incorrectly: Verse 65 calls it the number of a witches' coven, but that number is 13. References to Crowley's work, especially *The Book of the Law*, abound, and those familiar with that work will find this one easy enough to interpret.

Verses 28 and 29 refer to Crowley's *Liber Astarte*, with the statement that the working is of "nine moons." *Liber Astarte vel Berylli sub figura CLXXV* is "The Book of Uniting Himself to a Particular Deity by Devotion" and is reproduced in Crowley's Magick, but not in *Magick in Theory and Practice*. The deity in Parsons' case was Babalon. There is no timeframe specified in the book, but Babalon's purported message to Parsons regarding a nine-month working seems excessive, and there is certainly no surviving record to bear this out.

---

15. UFO researcher Jacques Vallee says Parsons claimed to have met a Venusian in the Mojave desert during the course of 1946. The Venusian apparently was the implied source of *Liber 49*.

Parsons may have interpreted this nine-month figure to mean that the working in this case involved a magical birth rather than a literal one.

Verse 48 reads, "Now is the hour of birth at hand. Now shall my adept be crucified in the Basilisk abode," a reference to Crowley's Magus initiation from 1916. One of the entries in Crowley's magical record for the period reads, "He hath crucified a toad in his basilisk abode," reflecting the time Crowley christened a frog "Jesus," crucified it, then ate its legs and burned the rest. This incident was a ritual affirmation of the supersession of what Crowley called "the slave-gods."

The "basilisk abode" refers to the womb, as tradition held that the basilisk, or "legendary reptile with fatal breath and glance," was born of menstrual blood. In Greek, *basileos* means "king," and the frog is a symbol of transition, living as it does in two worlds (water and dry land).

Two chapters survive of Parsons' original *The Book of Babalon*. One, "The Star of Babalon," is in *Freedom Is A Two-Edged Sword*. It consists of directions from Babalon to the expected Magical Child, and is not to be confused with Parsons' record of the Babalon Working. The other chapter consists of quotes from a secret OTO document of the VIII°.

eight

The Babalon Working, Part 2: March 1946

In March 1946, the red-haired elemental Cameron returned from New York and moved in with Parsons. She was to be an integral part of the Babalon Working, though did not know it at the time. She did feel like she was in the middle of something, so much so that she felt as if she were "spying." Parsons wrote that he knew not in whom Babalon was incarnate, but Cameron said he had been warned in the desert not to tell her it was she. To prove herself to him, Cameron would provide a sign, which she claimed was her sighting of a silver, cigar-shaped UFO. This incident was the only time the two ever discussed UFOs, she said. She actually derided his magick at the time, but later proved to herself that it worked.

On March 1, Parsons again prepared the altar and the various magical weapons, this time "in accordance with the instructions in *Liber 49*." What changed? In verses 18 through 22, Babalon specifies sandalwood incense, a green and gold cloth to cover the altar, her book *(Liber 49)* and the other magical implements, including a three-inch copper disk with the sevenfold Star of Babalon painted in gold on a blue background, which was to be the new talisman, replacing the parchment talisman of the original Enochian rite. The talisman was to be anointed in much the same way, although this time with the sexual secretions of both partners—Parsons and Cameron.

The operation began as directed on March 2, when Hubbard, who had been away since the 27th or 28th of February, returned with a description of "a vision he had that evening of a savage and beautiful woman riding naked on a great cat-like beast," Parsons wrote. "He [Hubbard] was impressed with the urgent necessity of giving me [Parsons] some message or communication. We prepared magically for this communication, constructing a temple at the altar with the analysis of the key word [INRI]. He was robed in white, carrying the lamp, and I in black, hooded, with the cup and dagger [two of the magical weapons]. At his suggestion we played Rachmaninoff's 'Isle of the Dead' as background music, and set an automatic recorder to transcribe any audible occurrences. At approximately 8 p.m. he began to dictate, I transcribing directly as I received."[16]

After Parsons' initial contact with the astral plane during this second working, Hubbard began acting as seer, although Parsons continued to call him "Scribe" in his notes, and it was actually he who was "scrying in the Aethyr" while Parsons took notes. In regard to Hubbard's vision of the catlike beast and naked woman, it should be recalled that Crowley repeatedly referred to the Beast and his Scarlet Woman in the Book of Revelation, which Crowley identified as himself and his current consort, corresponding also to the Gnostic-Christian heresiarch Simon Magus and his Helen. The woman was Sophia incarnate, and Hubbard's vision was once again seen as the cover picture for the first edition of Williamson's *Darker Than You Think* (from 1948).

It is uncertain whether or not the tape recording of the March 1946 session still exists, but the incredible transcript has survived, however, quoted here verbatim, since a summary would not do it justice. The words are Hubbard's, or rather, Babalon speaking through Hubbard as recorded by Parsons:

The Angel of TARO[17]. A three-day retirement to greet her [Babalon]. Purify thyself. The symbol is seven by three.[18] It is BABALON. Keep secret. The communications are sacred.

These are the preparations. Green gold cloth, food for the Beast [Crowley], upon a hidden platter, back of the altar. Disrobe only when the doors are bolted.

Transgression is death.

Back of main altar. Prepare instantly. Light the first flame at 10 p.m., March 2, 1946.

The year of BABALON is 4063.[19]

Beware of the use of profaned rituals.

She is flame of life, power of darkness, she destroys with a glance, she may take thy soul. She feeds upon the death of men.

Beautiful—Horrible.

The first ritual. Tomorrow the second ritual. Concentrate all

---

16. The definitive version of "Isle of the Dead" (Op. 29) is conducated by Sergei Rachmaninov himself. Recorded April 20, 1929 with the Philadelphia Orchestra and released on 78, it lasts 18 minutes, which means Parsons let it run out during the invocation, or else the Scribe had to restart it several times. The recording is available on the Magic Talent label as CD48038, as well as on a CD entitled *Rachmaninoff Conducts Rachmaninoff.*
17. The Golden Dawn's spelling of "tarot"; as with INRI it has multiple meanings.
18. Possibly a reference to the seventh and third Enochian Calls.
19. 4063 dates the Year 1 to 2017 BC, the meaning of which is uncertain.

force and being in Our Lady BABALON. Light a single light on Her altar, saying: Flame is Our Lady, flame is Her hair. I am flame.

A plate of food, unsalted. An altar cloth hitherto undefiled.

Make a box of blackness at ten o'clock. Smear the vessel which contains flame [Cameron?] with thine own blood. Destroy at the altar a thing of value.[20] Remain in perfect silence, and heed the voice of Our Lady. Speak not of this ritual or of Her coming to any person. If asked, answer in a manner that avoids suspicion. Nor speculate at any time as to Her future mortal identity. To receive flattering communications to thy damnation. Press not to receive teachings beyond those given.

Questions you may ask but three. Spend one half hour in composing these at 11:30 p.m. The answers must be written at midnight.

Thou shalt take the alkahest[21] in thine own mouth, and in the box of darkness carefully store this matter.

Display thyself to Our Lady; dedicate thy [sex] organs to Her, dedicate thy heart to Her, dedicate thy mind to Her, dedicate thy soul to Her, for She shall absorb thee, and thou shalt become living flame before She incarnates. For it shall be through you alone, and no one else can help in this endeavor.

It is lonely, it is awful.

Retire from human contact until noon tomorrow. Clear all profane documents on the morrow, before receiving further instructions. Consult no book but thine own mind. Thou art a god. Behave at this altar as one god before another. And so be prosperity.

Thou art the guardian and thou art the guide, thou art the worker and the mechanic. So conduct thyself. Discuss nothing of this matter until thou art certain that thine understanding embraces all.

Upon the completion of Babalon's message, Parsons immediately set about following the instructions dictated by her, as well as those received the night before (March 1), although he did not record what those instructions were.

As a part of this March 2 ceremony, he recited passages from several key works of Crowley's and elsewhere, passages that are vital to understanding the rite:

1. The Lesser Ritual of the Hexagram.

---

20. A statue of Pan was destroyed.
21. The "universal solvent" sought by the alchemists, an obvious reference to sexual fluids.

2. Excerpt from the Gnostic Mass.
3. Excerpt from Crowley's *The Vision and the Voice*.
4. A short verse dedicated to Babalon.
5. The Key Call of the Seventh Aire.
6. Excerpt from Crowley's *Tannhäuser*.

Parsons opened with an esoteric analysis of what he called "the key word," INRI, which is a part of the "Lesser Ritual of the Hexagram" he actually performed, though he did not record the fact by name and only wrote "analysis of the key word." He probably also performed the other rituals of the Hexagram and Pentagram, but he does not say.

Parsons recorded the analysis of the key word as follows: "The temple is opened with the analysis of the key word: INRI. *Yod Nun Resh Yod.* Virgo Isis Mighty Mother. Scorpio Apophis Destroyer. Sol, Osiris slain and risen. IAO. The sign of Osiris slain (given). The sign of the mourning of Isis (given). The sign of Apophis and Typhon (given). L.V.X., Lux, the Light of the Cross."

During the ritual, the magician must adopt at each stage of the analysis certain postures. Crossed arms, for example, represent Osiris slain, as the posture a corpse takes during burial. The entire ritual is recorded by Crowley in *Magick* and elsewhere. The gods invoked are Egyptian gods.

INRI is not a word but an acronym, representing the initials of the message Pontius Pilate had nailed upon the cross in the gospel story: *Iesus Nazaraeus Rex Iudaeorum*, Latin for "Jesus of Nazareth, King of the Jews." The acronym is often seen depicted in paintings of the crucifixion, possibly arising as a painter's expedient. Medieval clerics manipulated the letters to find different phrases that described Jesus while conforming to the same acronym.

Mystics and alchemists found other, less orthodox interpretations as well. In *Morals and Dogma*, Albert Pike gives a few possible meanings of INRI, withholding the one which he says Masons learn when they attain the 18th degree of Scottish Rite Freemasonry, known as Knight Rose Croix (Rose Cross). The meanings Pikes does give are: *Igne Natura Renovatur Integra* (All of Nature is Renewed by Fire); *Igne Nitrum Roris Invenitur* (The Cleanser of Fire Comes Like Dew); and the Jesuits' alleged *Iustum Necare Reges Impius* (To Judge not but the Impiety of Royalty).[22]

---

22. May scholars of Latin forgive my crude translations.

In the Golden Dawn the analysis of INRI was part of the 5°= 6° material. Crowley records a few of the interpretations in his *Sepher Sephiroth* ("Book of Books"): *Igni Natura Renovata Regnum* (Birth by Fire Renews the Kingdom), *Intra Nobis Regnum deI* (Within the Noble is the Kingdom of God), and even *Isis Naturae Regina Ineffabilis* (Isis, the Ineffable Queen of Nature). This last interpretation may be the one Pike chose to withhold; it also hearkens back to John Dee and Queen Elizabeth.

In the gospel tale, the original message was posted in three languages: Latin, Aramaic (Hebrew), and *koine* Greek. *Yod Nun Resh Yod* are the Hebrew names for the letters INRI. They are also words in the Hebrew tongue: hand-fish-head-hand, respectively. Each of these has further esoteric meanings that could be expanded indefinitely. The hand, for instance, represents the creative force, as it is with our hands that we build tools, heal the sick, express our love. *Yod* is also Hebrew slang for "penis," another sort of creative power. *Nun*, the fish, is Scorpio, hence death. *Resh* is the back of the head, and looks like a large *yod*; for this reason Crowley associated it with the *kundalini*, the mysterious energy source in yoga that runs along the spine and out the top of the head. A whole treatise could be written on the analysis of INRI; the same could be said of TARO, which Babalon mentioned on March 2.

The analysis complete, the invoking hexagrams are drawn in the air in the four cardinal directions (representing the four elements), and the name ARARITA "vibrated" in each quarter. When one "vibrates" a name, it is not merely spoken but visualized as written, originating within the magician and going outward until it fills the entire universe. ARARITA is also mentioned in the Star-Sapphire ritual from *The Book of Lies* and is a Hebrew acronym for one of the names of God.

The second part of Parsons' invocation is from the Gnostic Mass, recited as the Priest steps onto the first step leading to the altar, and as the Priestess disrobes behind the veil. Parsons recited the part of the Priest, and Cameron (representing Babalon) recited the part of the Priestess:

THE PRIEST: "O circle of Stars [the Milky Way] whereof our Father [the sun] is but the younger brother, marvel beyond imagination, soul of infinite space, before whom Time is ashamed, the mind bewildered, and the understanding dark, not unto Thee may we attain, unless Thine image be Love. Therefore by seed and root

and stem and bud and leaf and flower and fruit do we invoke thee."
[Parsons deleted the second part of this invocation, which is a quote of AL I:27].

THE PRIESTESS [here Parsons actually wrote "BABALON"]: "But to love me is better than all things; if under the night-stars in the desert thou presently burnest mine incense before me, invoking me with a pure heart and the Serpent flame [kundalini] therein, thou shalt come a little to lie in my bosom. For one kiss wilt thou then be willing to give all. But whoso gives one particle of dust shall lose all in that hour. Ye shall gather goods and store of women and spices; ye shall wear rich jewels; ye shall exceed the nations of earth in splendour and pride; but always in the love of me, and so shall ye come to my joy. I charge you earnestly to come before me in a single robe, and covered with a rich head dress. I love you! I yearn to you! Pale or purple, veiled or voluptuous, I who am all pleasure and purple, and drunkenness of the innermost sense, desire you. Put on the wings, and arouse the coiled splendour [kundalini] within you: come unto me! To me! To me! Sing the rapturous love-song unto me! Burn to me perfume! Drink to me, for I love you! I love you! I am the blue-lidded daughter of Sunset, I am the naked brilliance of the voluptuous night sky. To me! To me!"

This priestess's recitation is an expansion of AL I:61.

The third part of the invocation comes from Crowley's *The Vision and the Voice* and was part of his working of the 12th Aire in 1909, spoken to Crowley by a celestial "charioteer":

Glory unto the Scarlet Woman, BABALON[23] the Mother of Abominations, that rideth upon the Beast, for She hath spilt their blood in every corner of the earth, and lo! She hath mingled it in the cup of Her whoredom.

With the breath of Her kisses hath she fermented it, and it hath become the wine of the Sacrament; the wine of the Sabbath; and in the Holy Assembly hath She poured it out for Her worshippers; and they have become drunken thereon, so that face to face they beheld my Father. Thus are they made worthy to partake of the Mystery of this holy vessel, for the blood is the life.

sex and rockets

---

23. Crowley's original reads "Babylon."

Beautiful art thou O BABALON, and desirable, for thou hast given Thyself to everything that liveth, and thy weakness hath subdued their strength. For in that union Thou didst *understand.* Therefore art Thou called Understanding, O BABALON, Lady of the Night!

O my God, in one last rapture let me attain to the union with the many. For She is Love, and Her Love is one, and She has divided the one love into infinite loves, and each love is one, and equal with the One, and therefore is She passed from the Assembly and the Law and the enlightenment into the anarchy of solitude and darkness. For ever thus must She veil the brilliance of Herself.

Parsons actually abbreviated this passage, as he did with the excerpt from the Gnostic Mass, and did not recite it verbatim. It is longer in the original.

The fourth invocation was, "O BABALON, BABALON beloved, come now, partake of the sacrament, possess this shrine. Take me now! Let me be drunken on the wine of your fornications; let your kisses wanton me to death. Accept thou this sacrifice willingly given!" This passage seems to have been an original verse by Parsons, not found anywhere in the works of Crowley.

The fifth invocation was written as the Key Call of the Seventh Aire, but the text Parsons recorded is actually the Seventh Call, evidently the same type of shift Parsons made when he wrote that he used the "Key Call of the Third Aire" but actually utilized the Third Call. The Seventh Call in English is:

The East is a house of Virgins singing praises among the flames of first glory [the rising sun] wherein the Lord hath opened his mouth; and they are become 28 living dwellings [the phases of the moon, hence days] in whom the strength of man rejoiceth; and they are apparelled with ornaments of brightness, such as work wonders on all creatures. Whose kingdoms and continuance are as the Third and Fourth [Aires], strong towers and places of comfort, the Seats of Mercy and Continuance. O ye Servants of Mercy, Move! Appear! Sing praises unto the Creator; and be mighty amongst us. For that to this remembrance is given power, and our strength waxeth strong in our Comforter!

The following is the original Enochian, in Roman letters. Although the words are the same, Parsons' spellings vary considerably from those recorded by Crowley.

Ra-asa isalamanu para-di-zoda oe-cari-mi aao iala-pire-gahe Qui-inu. Enai butamonu od inoasa ni pa-ra-diala. Casaremeji ujeare cahire-Ianu, od zodonace lucifatianu, caresa ta vavale-zodirenu tol-hami. Soba lonudohe od nuame cahisa ta Da o Desa vo-ma-dea od pi-beliare itahila rita od miame ca-ni-quola rita! Zodocare! Zodameranu! lecarimi Quo-a-dahe od l-mica-ol-zododa aaiome. Bajirele papenore idalugama elonusahi—od umapelifa vau-ge-ji Bijil—IAD!"

The original ends with "IAD," which means "God" (Crowley translated it "comforter," which usually refers to the Holy Spirit). In Parsons' notes he has replaced "IAD" with "BABALON."

The sixth invocation was from Crowley's play *Tannhäuser*, alternating verses originating with the worshiper and his goddess. A Wagnerian opera, *Tannhäuser* was based on a 13th-century German epic poem. The main character, Tannhäuser, was a mortal who spent some time as the goddess Venus' lover but eventually left her to return to earth and the sweetheart of his youth. Tannhäuser inadvertently reveals his tryst with Venus, a disclosure that means certain death. His mortal love, Elisabeth, pleads for his life, and he is spared but banished as punishment for his deed. Alone, he longs for Venus. She hears him, and is about to return him to her when Elisabeth intervenes once again. Tannhäuser is redeemed, and is escorted by angels to paradise.

Here again, Parsons and Cameron probably took turns reciting their respective lines. Parsons played the part of Tannhäuser, while Cameron was Venus. Parsons began the romantic interlude:

Isis art thou, and from thy life are fed
All showers and suns, all moons that wax and wane,
All stars and streams, the living and the dead,
The mystery of pleasure and of pain
Thou art the mother, thou the speaking sea
Thou art the earth, and its fertility,
Life, death, love, hatred, light, darkness return to thee
To Thee!

Hathoor am I, and to my beauty drawn
All glories of the Universe bow down,
The blossom and the mountain and the dawn
Fruits blush, and women, our creations crown

I am the priest[ess], the sacrifice, the shrine
I the love and life of the divine
Life, death, love, hatred, light, darkness are surely mine, Are Mine!

Venus art thou, the love and light of earth,
The wealth of kisses, the delight of tears
The barren pleasures never came to birth,
The endless infinite delight of years.
Thou art the shrine at which my long desire
Devoured me with intolerable fire.
Thou wert song, music, passion, death upon my lyre—
My lyre.

I am the Grail and I the glory now;
I am the flame and fuel of thy breast
I am the star of God upon thy brow;
I am the queen, enraptured and possessed,
Hide thee sweet river, welcome to thee, sea
Ocean of love that shall encompass thee
Life, death, love, hatred, light, darkness return to me—
To me!

After the completed invocation, which was more like a bard's love poem, Parsons burned the Enochian Air Tablet he had used in the January stage of this working. He then smashed a small statue of Pan, which had been a favorite possession. He recorded that at the same instant the roof on his guest house caught fire and was damaged, apparently attributing this destruction to supernatural forces, although the burning parchment may have had something to do with it as well.

Regarding such sacrifices as the smashed statue, Crowley's *Liber Astarte*, verse 37, reads:

Having made by thine Ingenium a talisman or pantacle to represent the particular Deity, and consecrated it with infinite love and care, do thou burn it ceremonially before the shrine, as if thereby giving up the shadow for the substance. But it is useless to do this unless thou do really in thine heart value the talisman beyond all else that thou hast.

Crowley noted in his *Confessions*, "I have noticed that every time

I receive an important initiation, some cherished article mysteriously disappears. It may be a pipe, a pen or what not: but it is always an object which is impregnated with my personality by constant use or special veneration. I cannot remember a single occasion when this has not happened. The theory is that the elementals or familiar spirits in attendance on the Magician exact, so to speak, a tip on all important occasions of rejoicing." In such magical workings, evidently, if you don't offer something to the spirits, they will take it anyway.

At 11:30 p.m. that same night, Parsons prepared three questions as directed, and at midnight he asked them of Babalon (and was answered through Hubbard).

> How can I communicate directly with BABALON, hear her, see her, feel her, be sure that I am working aright?
>
> *At the altar in meditation, as you know how. Also, invoke me carnally with all your passion. Thus will you feel my desire and increase my substance.*
>
> How can I serve best?
>
> *Follow instructions exactly and in detail. Avoid loose interruptions. Be diligent. Do not hesitate or question, act. All depends on your time.*
>
> How can I be certain of the vehicle [of incarnation]?
>
> *Do not trouble yourself with this. It does not concern you. I will provide the vehicle, I will show you a sign, and signs. It is the now which concerns us. Keep your faith, think not overmuch.*

While meditating the following morning, Parsons was interrupted by one of his tenants, whom he then cursed "in the Anglo-Saxon fashion." The man became ill, and Parsons realized he had erred. He apologized to him, but the day continued badly. That night Babalon purportedly continued her message, but the speaker, curiously, seems to be another (all parenthetical remarks are copied from the original):

> In the presence of our Lord PAN, at the feet of Our Lady BABALON, at the feet of Her (servants?) (changing?) we declare unto thee this message (consecrated, dedicated, never to be defiled?) (the Scribe was uncertain here) containing the rituals of the second and third days, of the welcome and preparation in the Name of Our Lady of the Night most gracious, to pure lewd and whoresome Lady BABALON. Oh thou who art mortal tremble; given it is unto thee a

feat never before performed in the annals of your histories, never before accomplished successfully. Many have dared, none succeeded.

Our Lady BABALON must descend to triumph.

Mortality. We have not asked this of another, nor shall we ever. Even now we doubt thy faith. Is this accepted, are you willing to proceed. Answer aloud.

I am willing.

Then know thou art already faulty in thy delivery. These are extraneous things. The elemental was not properly released (this was corrected), thou wert guilty of human rage, the current of force has been disturbed. Beware, shouldst thou falter again, we will sure slay thee.

But insofar as thy working was consecrated it has succeeded. Rectify thy mortal fault and error. Consecrate all. Now receive the second and third rituals.

Consecrate thyself as instructor of Our Lady Incarnate.

Take the black box, concentrate upon its emptiness for one hour, gaze into it, and thou wilt see, imprinted upon it, a shape, a sign, a sacred design, which shall be the sign delivered by Our Lady Babalon Incarnate. When thou hast finished, when thou hast recognized this pattern, construct it in wood.[24]

This is the sigil.

Ten be the hour appointed. Invoke long, to music indicated.[25]

When thou canst feel Our Lady incarnate in thy being, take the black box and perform the consecrated rite. Wear thou scarlet, symbolic of birth. Be sashed in black. It matters not the quality of goods. Take then the box, make then the sign.

Paint upon it a second sign which thou knowest. If thou hast forgotten, gaze into thy crystal.

Meditate while gazing on the qualities of an instructor. Thou inscribe in Her book, for Her guidance.

Thou art forbidden to leave thy room.

The end of the second ritual.

At this point, Hubbard rested a while, then they continued.

---

24. The "black box" is evidently the same as the scrying device used by Dee and Kelley. Karl Germer thought the sign "imprinted upon it" to be a small circle inside of which was inscribed an inverted triangle—the sign for water, but inside a circle. Cameron remembered otherwise.
25. Following this instruction, Parsons deliberately omitted recording one line of the message.

Begin four hours prior to dawn.

A period of eradication of all inimical influences. Complete perfection. Wear black. Cut from thy breast the red star. Renew the blood. Lay out a white sheet. Place upon it blood of birth[26], since She is born of thy flesh, and by thy mortal power upon earth.

Thou shalt recognize by the sign. BABALON is born! It is new birth, all things are changed, the signs, the symbols, the everything!

Thou shalt compose with the aid of the muse suitable invocation of the birth of BABALON, and this thou shalt deliver to the flames which now burn too.

This last instruction certainly refers to Parsons' poem, "The Birth of Babalon," which, fortunately for us, survived the flames. The mystical yet racy message continued:

Now thou shalt flame the third, chanting the invocation. She is born in the third flame.

In verse, seven verses of seven lines, seven magick words. Stand and chant seven times. Envision thyself as a cloaked radiance desirable to the Goddess, beloved. Envision Her approaching thee. Embrace Her, cover Her with kisses. Think upon the lewd lascivious things thou couldst do. All is good to BABALON. ALL.

Then rest, meditating on this:

Thou as a man and as a god hast strewn about the earth and in the heavens many loves; these recall, concentrate, consecrate each woman thou hast raped. Remember her, think upon her, move her into BABALON, bring her into BABALON, each, one by one until the flame of lust is high.

Then compose a verse of undetermined lines on this, to BABALON. This verse shall be used in worship when she appears.[27]

Then meditate upon thy desire, think upon Her, and, touching naught, chant these verses. Recall each lascivious moment, each lustful day, all set them into the astral body, touching naught.

The part about "consecrating each woman thou hast raped" is likely not meant literally, and the instruction to "touch naught" evidently refers to a tantric practice, as does the entire instruction, essentially. It resumes:

---

26. i.e., menstrual blood.
27. This verse is now lost.

Preserve the material basis.[28]

In the box?

Yes.

The lust is hers, the passion yours. Consider thou the Beast raping.

Leave thy casual loves—all belongs to BABALON, thy lust is BABALON's. She is with thee three days. The sign is hers, secret, and no man knows its correspondence. Guard!

The instruction was followed by "a prophecy" of unknown length, which Parsons deliberately omitted recording.

Directly following the message, Parsons records instead a poem entitled "The Birth of Babalon" that he wrote as a means by which to invoke Babalon. It is unclear at which point in these proceedings he used it, but it may have been the seventh part of the invocation, as a six-fold invocation makes little sense here. Parsons also seems to have ignored the instructions to burn it, already noted.

A longish, well-composed poem, "The Birth of Babalon" begins:

What is the tumult among the stars that have shone so still till now?
What are the furrows of pain and wrath upon the immortal brow?
Why is the face of God turned grey and his angels all grown white?
What is the terrible ruby star that burns down the crimson night?
What is the beauty that flames so bright athwart the awful dawn?
She has taken flesh, she is come to judge the thrones ye rule upon.
Quail ye kings for an end is come in the birth of BABALON.

Afterwards, Parsons expressed his confidence in the working, but wrote, "Now I can do no more than pray and wait." On the sixth of March, Parsons recorded in a letter to Crowley:

I hardly know how to tell.

I am under the command of extreme secrecy.

I have had the most important and devastating experience of my life between February 2nd and March 4th.

I believe it was the result of the 9th [degree] working with the girl [Cameron] who answered my elemental summons. (She is now in New York.)

I have been in direct touch with One, who is most Holy and

---

28. i.e., the "elixir," or sexual secretions.

Beautiful, mentioned in *The Book of the Law*.

I cannot write the name at present.

First instructions were received direct, further through Ron acting as seer.

I have followed them to the letter.

There was a desire for incarnation.

I was the agency chosen to assist the birth, which is now accomplished.

I do not yet know the vehicle, but it will come to me, bringing a secret sign I know.

Forgetfulness was the price.

I am to act as instructor, guardian, guide, for nine months.

Then it will be loosed in the world.

That is all I can say, now.

There must be extreme secrecy.

I cannot tell you the depth of reality, the poignancy, terror and beauty I have known. Now I am back in the world, weak with reaction.

But the knowledge remains. I have found my will. It is to serve, and serve I shall. All I am or will be is pledged.

I must put the Lodge in Roy's [Leffingwell] hands, prepare a suitable place, and carry on my business to provide the suitable material basis . . .

It is not a question of keeping anything from you, it is a question of not dwelling or even thinking unduly on the matter until the time is right. Premature discussion or revelation would cause an abortion.

A manuscript is prepared, which will be released to the proper persons at the right time . . .

All the tests are right, all the signs are right. There is no danger, save in weakness or pride.

Although he claimed there was no danger, in his metaphysical life, the fearless Parsons thus showed the same methodology he used in his rocket propulsion work, a tenaciousness in testing and a thrill-seeker's lack of caution concerning what he may "conjure." Secretly Parsons did write the name of the "One, who is most Holy and Beautiful": he called her *Babalon*. He further directed Crowley to contact no one save himself or Hubbard regarding this matter. Unfortunately, he does not seem to have tested this spirit with the rigorousness of his rocket-testing or thoroughness that Crowley used when he was contacted by entities such as Abuldiz, Amalantrah, Aiwass, and Lam. Crowley always required proofs during such contacts, proofs established by the *gematria* of certain key words, i.e., the entity's name, location, or some other word or phrase. If Parsons subjected "Babalon" to such a test, no record survives.

Again Parsons wrote, "For the last three days I have performed an operation of birth, using the air tablet, the cup, and a female figure [Cameron?], properly invoked by the wand [penis], then sealed up in the altar. Last night I performed an operation of symbolic birth and delivery." This operation is not part of the instructions contained in *Liber Astarte*, which *Liber 49* told him to enact, but it seems to have satisfied Parsons.

On March 15, Crowley sent Parsons an admonishment about Cameron: "I am particularly interested in what you have written me about the elemental [Cameron], because for some little time past I have been endeavouring to intervene personally on your behalf. I would however have you recall [Eliphas] Levi's advice that 'the love of the Magus for such things [elementals] is insensate and may destroy him.'" "Eliphas Lévi" was the pseudonym of Alphonse-Louise Constant, a "magic theoretician" who wrote two books, *Dogma and Ritual of High Magic* and *History of Magic*, published in 1854 and 1856, respectively. Although he died in 1875 in relative obscurity, his works gained popularity with French intellectuals such as Victor Hugo. Lévi's popularity stems from his ability to be romantic yet rational at the same time. Crowley was so impressed that he considered himself the reincarnation of Lévi. Crowley's claim to have intervened personally on Parsons' behalf is interesting, as it certainly took place by use of the OTO's "key," i.e., magically.

Crowley cautioned Parsons yet again about his own worst traits, in the letter of March 15, 1946:

> It seems to me that there is a danger of your sensitiveness upsetting your balance. Any experience that comes your way you have a tendency to over-estimate. The first fine careless rapture wears off in month or so, and some other experience comes along and carries you off on its back. Meanwhile you have neglected and bewildered those who are dependent on you, either from above or from below.
>
> I will ask you to bear in mind that you have one fulcrum for all your levers, and that is your original oath to devote yourself to raising mankind. All experiences, all efforts, must be referred to this;

as long as it remains unshaken you cannot go far wrong, for by its own stability it will bring you back from any tendency to excess.

At the same time, you being as sensitive as you are, it behoves [sic] you to be more on your guard than would be the case with the majority of people.

As it had so many times before, the warning fell on deaf ears.

The same day, Parsons wrote Crowley a letter, in which he formally turned the operation of Agape Lodge over to Roy Leffingwell, so he could focus on his project. Parsons wrote that the "IXths"—meaning Leffingwell, Jane Wolfe, and himself—would hold council monthly to discuss lodge policy. Whatever had happened to Parsons in the desert must have been quite amazing for him to react so. He finally had direction, something he had lost when he sold out of Aerojet—something he never really had spiritually, except perhaps when he first encountered Crowley and the OTO. A letter dated one day later was sent to all Agape Lodge members, declaring Leffingwell "executive head" of the lodge.

Crowley was now a dying man with a heroin problem brought on by his physician's treatment of his respiratory problems. As further letters arrived from the States, he became increasingly unhappy about Parsons' claims, no doubt concerned about the future of his life's work.

On April 19, Crowley wrote Parsons, "You have got me completely puzzled by your remarks about the elemental—the danger of discussing or copying anything. I thought I had a most morbid imagination, as good as any man's, but it seems I have not. I cannot form the slightest idea what you can possibly mean."

And to Karl Germer, Crowley wrote, "Apparently he, or Hubbard, or somebody, is producing a Moonchild. I get fairly frantic when I contemplate the idiocy of these goats."[29]

The purpose of Parsons' Babalon Working seems to have been the birth of a child—the Moonchild—into whom Babalon would incarnate. It had said in *The Book of the Law* four decades earlier that this child would be "mightier than all the kings of the Earth" (AL III:45). Aleister Crowley had once thought Frater Achad was this magical child, the birth of which occurs on the astral plane rather than the physical and represents a possession of sorts. Jane Wolfe wrote that Jack Parsons might be this child, but Parsons himself thought differently.

---

29. The last word is often misquoted in secondary sources as "louts."

The fact that Cameron later claimed to have been impregnated by Parsons during their first two weeks together casts doubt upon the literal application of the term Moonchild. She said she had an (illegal) abortion with Parsons' consent (and another abortion later on), then just a few days later they were performing another working. If a literal child were what he was seeking (remember, she didn't know the purpose of the working), the purported pregnancy probably would have gone another way. This abortion story actually serves as good evidence that Parsons was looking for an adult female to arrive, perhaps in a manner similar to Cameron's arrival.

In any case, the "magical child" is an ages-old concept found in the mythologies of certain cultures. The magical child concept Parsons was pursuing was given definition by Crowley, of course. In *De Arte Magica* Aleister Crowley wrote, "It is said by certain initiates that to obtain Spiritual gifts, and to aid Nature, the Sacrament should be as it were a Nuptial of the Folk of the Earth; but that Magick is of the Daemon, and that by a certain perversion of the Office, may be created Elementals fit to perform the will of the Magician." The "perversion," no doubt, refers to unorthodox acts of sex by which may be created elementals or "magical" children.

Also called a "homunculus" ("little man"), the Moonchild's creation is described in Crowley's novel by the same name, *Moonchild* (originally titled *The Butterfly Net*):

> But other magicians sought to make this Homunculus in a way closer to nature. In all these cases they had held that environment could be modified at will by the application of telesmata or sympathetic figures. For example, a nine-pointed star would attract the influence which they called Luna—not meaning the actual moon, but an idea similar to the poets' idea of her. By surrounding an object with such stars, with similarly-disposed herbs, perfumes, metals, talismans, and so on, and by carefully keeping off all other influences by parallel methods, they hoped to invest the original object so treated with the Lunar qualities, and no others. (I am giving the briefest outline of an immense subject.) Now then they proceeded to try to make the Homunculus on very curious lines.
>
> Man, said they, is merely a fertilized ovum properly incubated. Heredity is there even at first, of course, but in a feeble degree. Anyhow, they could arrange any desired environment from the beginning, if they could only manage to nourish the embryo in some artificial way—incubate it, in fact, as is done with chickens

to-day. Furthermore, and this is the crucial point, they thought that by performing this experiment in a specially prepared place, a place protected magically against all incompatible forces, and by invoking into that place some one force which they desired, some tremendously powerful being, angel or archangel—and they had conjurations which they thought capable of doing this—that they would be able to cause the incarnation of beings of infinite knowledge and power, who would be able to bring the whole world into Light and Truth.

I may conclude this little sketch by saying that the idea has been almost universal in one form or another; the wish has always been for a Messiah or Superman, and the method some attempt to produce man by artificial or at least abnormal means.

Crowley speaks of a (female) magical child who would be the product of her environment rather than her heredity, a development that distinguishes magical children from the regular type. One relatively recent attempt at producing a messianic child occurred with the occult society of Theosophy, whose leaders at the time tried to raise the young Indian boy, Jiddhu Krishnamurti, as their own World Savior. The plan failed, as Krishnamurti eventually abandoned the Theosophists and started his own movement, for which he became world-renowned. In Parsons' case, however, he (and Crowley) seem to have been using the phrases "magical child" and "Moonchild" interchangeably—and not as literally as Crowley's description would suggest.

Although like Jones before him Parsons himself was viewed as the magical child, he evidently felt otherwise, such that he was determined himself to produce it—or, rather, *her*—as Parsons wrote of a *female* messiah. Indeed, the purpose of Parsons' operation has been underemphasized, as the Babalon Working itself was a preparation for what was to come: a *thelemic* messiah. This messiah would mature in a magically influenced environment. She would then assume a leadership role. In addition, the word "child" was symbolic, intended not for an infant but for one woman in particular (or perhaps even all women in general).

It seems clear that Parsons was seeking not an idea but a living being, who evidently was not Cameron. "There was a desire to incarnate," he wrote. He considered Cameron his elemental, though he did occasionally (and paradoxically) refer to her Babalon—as she later did herself. But the Babalon Working was clearly aimed at bringing Babalon down to earth from somewhere else. This plan backfired.

It was not nine months but nine years later that Cameron would claim to be Babalon herself and to have given birth to a magical child on the astral plane. In the meantime, Parsons started to look elsewhere for this "child"—to a physical incarnation embodied in some unknown person. He wrote, "The invocation of Babalon served to exteriorize the Oedipus complex; at the same time, because of the forces involved it produced extraordinary magical effects. However, this operation is accomplished and closed—you [referring to himself] should have nothing more to do with it—nor even think of it, until Her manifestation is revealed, and proved beyond the shadow of a doubt."

With the Babalon Working, it may also be that Parsons was trying to compete against Smith for Crowley's attention, even though Smith had been forced into exile. Indeed, the Babalon Working has parallels with Crowley's *Liber 132*, in which he exalted Smith in order to send him on a "retreat."

The Alphabet of Daggers:

nine

Parsons' Final Years: 1946–1952

On February 20, 1946, in between the two parts of the Babalon Working, Parsons, Hubbard and Betty formed a company called "Allied Enterprises." To Hubbard's $1,183.91, Parsons put up $20,970.80, which was his "laundromat money," while young Betty contributed nothing. In this enterprise, they were to buy boats on the East Coast and sail them back to California for resale (or tow them by trailer, if cheaper). They also stated an interest in investments of a "varied and eclectic nature," from which it may be inferred that they went beyond boats—perhaps into explosives. Some of the money, Parsons said, as did Rypinski, was used to buy the house at 1003 S. Orange Grove Ave. as well, which Parsons leased first.

In April 1946, after the second part of the Babalon Working, Ron left with Betty and $10,000 of the company's money. Later that month Parsons started to think that they had cheated him. He threatened to chase them, but a call to Hubbard soon calmed him down. Astrologer and initiate Louis Culling overheard the call and couldn't believe the formerly angry Parsons could be so easily swayed. Parsons ended the call with, "I hope we shall always be partners, Ron," a comment that made Culling cringe.

Culling wrote to Karl Germer on May 12, "As you may know by this time, Brother Jack signed a partnership agreement with this Ron and Betty whereby all money earned by the three for life is equally divided between the three. As far as I can ascertain, Brother Jack has put in all of his money . . . meanwhile, Ron and Betty have bought a boat for themselves in Miami for about $10,000 and are living the life of Riley, while Brother Jack is living at rock bottom, and I mean rock bottom. It appears that originally they never secretly intended to bring this boat around to the California coast to sell at a profit, as they told Jack, but rather to have a good time on it on the east coast." Indeed, Hubbard had written the Chief of Naval Personnel before he headed east, asking permission to sail to South America and China.

On May 22 Crowley wired to Germer, "Suspect Ron playing confidence trick—John Parsons weak fool—obvious victim—prowling swindlers." Crowley again, in a follow-up to Germer dated May 31:

> Thanks for yours of May 23rd enclosing one from Frater Achad [Charles Stansfeld Jones]. It is very good that he should come crawling back to the penitent's form after thirty years, but I do not quite see how it is going to make up for the time he has wasted on his insane vanity, and you might let him know this view.
>
> I am glad that his submission should have taken place at this moment, however, because his case serves as very useful to quote in discussing the business of Jack Parsons . . .
>
> The question of Frater 210 [Parsons] seems to me very typical. He reminds me up to a point—though he is on a much lower plane than they—of two men who joined the Order shortly after I took it over [Jones and Victor Neuburg]: both cases seem to me to have certain significance if applied to the present position of Frater 210.
>
> It seems to me on the information of our Brethren in California (if we may assume them to be accurate) Frater 210 has committed both these errors [i.e., those of Jones and Neuburg].
>
> Both cases were alike in this—that after a very short period of training both had more than fulfilled their early promise; they could claim not only attainment, but achievement—and that in no small degree. I am sorry that there is no possibility of making any similar claim on behalf of Frater 210 . . .
>
> He has got a miraculous illumination which rimes [sic] with nothing, and he has apparently lost all his personal independence. From our brother's [Louis Culling] account he has given away both his girl and his money—apparently it is the ordinary confidence trick.
>
> Of course, I must suspend judgement until I have heard his side of the story, but he promised me quite a long while ago to write me a full explanation, and to date I have received nothing from him . . .

By June, a sadder but wiser Parsons could wait no longer and went to Florida after Hubbard and Betty, discovering they had purchased three boats. He found two of the boats, but not Ron and Betty. One, the *Harpoon*, was anchored at Howard Bond's Yacht Harbor. Another, *Blue Water II*, was at the American Ship Building Company. Parsons then rented a room and waited. Two days later, someone from Bond's called Parsons to say that the *Harpoon* had just sailed. He was too late to catch them, so he returned to his room and consecrated a circle. Parsons wrote Crowley on July 5:

Here I am in Miami, pursuing the children of my folly . . . Hubbard attempted to escape me by sailing at 5 PM, and I performed a full invocation to Bartzabel [a form of Mars] within the Circle at 8 PM. At the same time, so far as I can check, his ship was struck by a sudden squall off the coast, which ripped off his sails and forced him back to port, where I took the boat in custody . . . I have them well tied up. They can not move without going to jail. However, I am afraid that most of the money has already been dissipated. I will be lucky to salvage three to five thousand dollars. In the interim I have been flat broke.

Bartzabel had a little help from the U.S. Coast Guard, who rescued and detained the pair. Betty later described her and Hubbard's situation during the storm as "desperate," relating that the two were very scared that they would not make it back to shore.

On July 1, 1946, Parsons sued Allied Enterprises in Dade County, Florida Circuit Court, case number 101634. In an instance of remarkably swift justice, the court approved a settlement on July 10, and on July 11 the three partners signed an agreement dissolving the company. Parsons recovered two boats: *Blue Water II* (a schooner) and *Diane* (a yacht). Hubbard was allowed to retain possession of the *Harpoon*, a two-masted schooner, and use it as collateral against a promissory note in the amount of $2900. Hubbard was also ordered to pay Parsons' legal fees. Parsons returned to Pasadena and never heard from either party again. Hubbard and Betty eventually married and had a daughter. Hubbard's career with Scientology is well-documented, in various versions, elsewhere.

The incident affected not just Parsons, as his bad luck now forced him to stop sending money to his ex-wife, Helen, and Wilfred Smith, who had married. The fact that he was sending money to them in the first place reveals how much he thought of Smith, as well as his generosity. Parsons' regular contributions to Crowley, however, would continue until the latter's death the next year. At the time of the financial disaster, Smith wrote to Crowley:

It all seems to be folding up together. [Jack] can't send any more money. Grimaud's [Helen] is running out. These, and the fierce stab of Regina's [Kahl] death occurred all within a day or two. But above all I feel I have shot my bolt, such as it was, and missed the mark.

From the utterly desolate state in which I started out, which held for months, I am glad to say very recently the joy in some of the masterpieces has returned to me. I expected never to write to you again; hardly know why I do. But there is a feeling one owes a gentleman a letter when one fails to turn up at a dinner engagement. Besides, I don't think I could get Grimaud to write you this; she refuses steadily to accept my negative view of this Grand Magical Retirement. You must be so inured to disciples' failures that just one more won't surprise you.

On August 20, Parsons sent a formal letter of resignation from the OTO to Crowley. Instead of the usual "Thrice Illuminated, Thrice Illustrious, and Very Dear Brother" salutation, he began it "Dear Aleister." He gave no explanation but merely said the resignation was his will, although it certainly may have been a reflection of his disillusionment in the face of such misfortunes. He expressed his continued sympathy to the Crowley's "Rights of Man" *(Liber OZ)*, quoted below, but finished by saying, "I do not believe that the OTO, as an autocratic organization, constitutes a true and proper medium for the expression and attainment of these principles [the Rights of Man]." Many resigning members have made similar remarks.

Regarding Parsons' source of extra income, Louis Culling remarked that Parsons was "bootlegging nitroglycerine," presumably meaning he was selling it illegally. But to whom? Cameron apparently was bold enough to help him in this enterprise, whatever it was. She and Parsons were married in San Juan Capistrano on October 19, 1946 by a Justice of the Peace named Marco F. Forster, with Ed Forman and his wife Jeanne witnessing the event. Recorded in the Orange County Recorder's Office, the marriage took place just before Parsons' JPL partner Frank Malina was invited by Julian Huxley to go to France and work for UNESCO. Rypinski opined that Malina left the country to distance himself from the scandal revolving around Parsons, as there apparently was an investigation into the house and possibly some newspaper exposure. But Malina himself says he was just looking for something different to do, which rings closer to the truth.

In late 1946, Parsons and Cameron left 1003 S. Orange Grove Ave., and the lodge, which met at several different places after this. The big house was later torn down to make way for apartments. Parsons also left his job with the Vulcan Powder Company, having been offered employment with the North American Aviation Corporation in nearby Inglewood, California, where he worked until 1948, when Hughes Aircraft in Culver City hired him.

In addition, Parsons engaged in consulting work. As such, he was often called on by the Los Angeles District Attorney's Office, the Los Angeles Police Department, the Los Angeles Superior Court, Northrup Aircraft Company, General Chemical Company, the National Defense Research Council, and the Office of Scientific Research and Development. Parsons was also a member of several technical societies, including the American Chemical Society, the Institute of Aeronautical Sciences, the American Institute for the Advancement of Science, the Society of Sigma Xi, and the Army Ordnance Association. His obituary said he had refused several honorary degrees, but there is no further evidence to support this claim. A membership in Sigma Xi seems unlikely due to his lack of a degree but is reported by two different sources, such that it is possible his reputation was enough to gain him entrance.

Disillusioned by the incident with Hubbard and Betty, Parsons drifted away from magick and focused his will on his technical career, although the two aspects of his life could never be completely separated. Unfortunately, his misfortune continued, and he had little success, nothing to equal the glory of his World War II efforts. On May 17, 1948, his two worlds collided, as he lost his government security clearance "because of his membership in a religious cult . . . believed to advocate sexual perversion . . . organized at subject's home . . . which had been reported subversive." Elsewhere the FBI describes it as a "mythic love cult," despite Parsons' insistence it was "dedicated to the freedom and liberty of the individual." The same old plagues were still haunting him.

In a letter to Karl Germer dated June 19, 1949, Parsons said he lost the clearance for membership in the OTO and for publicly circulating *Liber OZ*, a statement of "the rights of man." Known also as *Liber LXXVII*, certain elements of the statement are understandably disturbing to different factions of society and, although Parsons may have viewed himself a teacher destined to affect the powers that be, the latter, according him, evidently perceived him and his ideas as a security risk. *Liber OZ* reads in full as follows:

The law of the strong: this is our law and the joy of the world.

—AL II:2

Do what thou wilt shall be the whole of the Law.

—AL I:40

Thou hast no right but to do thy will. Do that, and no other shall say nay.

—AL I:42-3

Every man and every woman is a star. —AL I:3

There is no god but man.

1. Man has the right to live by his own law—
   to live in the way that he wills to do:
   to work as he will:
   to play as he will:
   to rest as he will:
   to die when and how he will.

2. Man has the right to eat what he will:
   to drink what he will:
   to dwell where he will:
   to move as he will upon the face of the earth.

3. Man has the right to think what he will:
   to speak what he will:
   to write what he will:
   to draw, paint, carve, etch, mould, build as he will:
   to dress as he will.

4. Man has the right to love as he will: —
   Take your fill and will of love as ye will,
   when, where, and with whom ye will.—AL I:51

5. Man has the right to kill those who would thwart these rights.

   The slaves shall serve.—AL II:58
   Love is the law, love under will.—AL I:57

According to Parsons' FBI file, however, the investigation was actually caused by his association with known Communists, a problem shared by his JPL/GALCIT comrades Frank Malina, Hsue-shen Tsien and Martin Summerfield. As early as 1938, the self-described anti-war, anti-capitalist Parsons had subscribed to the *Daily People's World*, a Communist paper, and had attended a few meetings of different groups during the subsequent years, joining the "subversive" American Civil Liberties Union in 1946. One of the early victims of what would become the McCarthy witchhunts, Parsons later testified in closed court that his interest was merely an intellectual one. He told them that *thelema*, the "will" aspect of Crowley's work, was definitely anti-communist and anti-fascist, which it is, and his clearance was finally reinstated on March 7, 1949. Nonetheless, Cameron left him soon after.

Humorously, Parsons' FBI file is full of references to the "Church of *Thelma*." There is also an unclear reference to Parsons doing something on September 21, 1948 to bring the attention of government officials upon him once more, but apparently nothing came of it. Parsons then spent two years on the staff of the University of Southern California's Pharmacology Department starting in 1948.

Despite his occupational troubles based in part on his occult activities —or possibly because of them—Parsons was unable to avoid the exotic lure. On Halloween of 1948, Babalon called on Parsons in some unspecified manner and urged him to resume his magick. Like so many who suffer the ills of the physical world, Parsons would turn once more to religion in his time of need, beginning a 17-day "working of the wand" (17 is a masculine number because of its association with Mars), the climax of which was Babalon's manifestation in a dream. He had Smith christen him "Belarion Armiluss Al Dajjal, AntiChrist" as he took the Oath of the Abyss. Oddly enough, considering the friction between them, Parsons remained close to Smith, the man who had married Parsons' wife and who was also his superior in the A∴A∴. Their relationship was probably more formal than personal by this time.

At the conclusion of his 17-day working, Babalon instructed Parsons on an "astral working," i.e., an out-of-body experience. Parsons had, by his own accounts, a "well-developed body of light," so apparently this travel was an easy task for him. Indeed, he claimed success with a vision wherein he "went into the sunset with Her sign and into the night past accursed and desolate places and cyclopean ruins, and so came at last to the City of Chorazin. And there a great tower of Black Basalt was raised, that was part of a castle whose further battlements ruled over the gulf of stars."

Chorazin was a small town on the Sea of Galilee that, according to the gospel story, Jesus cursed when the citizens would not repent (Mt. 11:21; Lk. 10:13). Later legends claimed that the Antichrist would be born in Chorazin, whose modern name is Kerazeh. The black basalt ruins of the city's old synagogue to which Parsons refers are still standing.

Regarding the title with which Parsons had himself christened by Smith, *Belarion* is an alternate spelling (presumably from the Greek) of "Belial," a demon named in the Bible, the Dead Sea Scrolls and the Jewish apocrypha (hidden texts of dubious authenticity) whose name means "Without God," as "Bel" or "Ba'al" means "God" or "Lord." Belarion is often identified by Christian writers with the Beast in Revelation, with whom Aleister Crowley in turn identified himself. Rather than emulating his mentor, however, Parsons may have acquired the moniker from a fantasy novel which featured a character by that name.

The term *Armiluss* is the Jewish equivalent of the Antichrist. As the end approaches, Jewish eschatology states, the Messiah ben Ephraim ("born of Ephraim" or Israel, the northern kingdom) will come first, following by Armiluss who will lead the armies of Gog and Magog against the armies of the Messiah at the battle of Armageddon, murdering him. Ben Ephraim's corpse will be left for the scavengers, but the Messiah ben David (whom the Christians believe was Jesus) will appear and resurrect him.

The next word in Parsons' title, *Al-Dajjal*, is the Islamic version of the Antichrist, whose name is Arabic for "the deceiver." He does not appear in the Koran but rather in the *hadith*, which are the sayings of Mohammed as recorded by his disciples. Al-Dajjal is blind in one eye but is able to perform miracles, the greatest of which will be bringing order to a world in chaos. On Judgment Day he will be defeated by the Mahdi, whom most Muslims believe is the return of Mohammed.

The beastly-named Parsons then took the Oath of the Abyss. "Crossing the Abyss" involves the total denial of the world and detachment from the ego. The oath has survived along with some of Parsons' other papers from this period and begins as follows:

> I, who am called John Whiteside Parsons in the outer, and Fra. 210 in the inner, do hereby in the presence of Fra. 132 [Wilfred Smith], take this oath of a Magister Templi [Master of the Temple], which for me is the Oath of Antichrist. And I swear that my name is BELARION ARMILUSS AL DAJJAL, ANTICHRIST who am come to fulfil the law of the Beast 666 [Crowley].
>
> And I hereby accept all things needful for the fulfillment of my will, and do swear to persevere in this my chosen work unto the end.

Parsons' personalization was followed by the Oath of the Abyss or "Great Obligation" that Aleister Crowley took and that is contained in his 1908 diary "John St. John" in *The Equinox* vol. I, number 2 special supplement:

Then did I take upon myself the Great Obligation as follows:

I. I, O.M. & c., a member of the Body of God, hereby bind myself on behalf of the whole Universe, even as we are now physically bound unto the cross of suffering:

II. that I will lead a pure life, as a devoted servant of the Order:

III. that I will understand all things:

IV. that I will love all things:

V. that I will perform all things and endure all things:

VI. that I will continue in the Knowledge and Conversation of My Holy Guardian Angel:

VII. that I will work without attachment:

VIII. that I will work in truth:

IX. that I will rely only upon myself:

X. that I will interpret every phenomenon as a particular dealing of God with my soul.

As a part of this venture, Parsons prepared two important papers: *Analysis By A Master of the Temple*, which is autobiographical in nature, and *The Book of AntiChrist. Analysis* seems to have been prepared prior to Parsons' attempt to cross the Abyss, as "Frater Belarion" speaks to Parsons in the third person, saying "I await you in the City of the Pyramids."

Subsequently writing *as* Belarion, Parsons refers to the OTO as "an excellent training school for adepts, but hardly an appropriate Order for the manifestation of Thelema," a statement tantamount to heresy. Obviously, he was frustrated by attempts to discipline him, and his notion of Thelema was almost fundamentalist, based on little more than *Liber OZ*. Trying to make lemonade out of lemons, he writes in the third person, "The experience with the OTO and Aerojet were needed to dispel your romanticism, self deception, and reliance on others. Betty was one link in the process designed to tear you away from the now unneeded Oedipus complex, the overvaluation of women and romantic love."

Evidently on account of such failures, Parsons listed seven things to begin working on immediately:

Works of the Wand—of the Will alone avail in this state. No other weapons should be used, no other ritual save the hymn to the Unnamed One in the Anthem of the [Gnostic] Mass.

You should be meticulous in all observations pertaining to the Will, even the most petty. Fulfill all obligations and promises, undertake nothing which you cannot fulfill, be prompt in the discharge of each responsibility.

Be neat in personal and domestic habits; indicate your self respect to yourself.

Do not become unduly involved with any person, and practice all your hard-earned wisdom in your relations with women.

Set up your personal affairs in business order. Keep your accounts current and your papers neatly filed.

Finish your poetry for publication. Finish the synthesis of the Tarot and start work on the preparation of the lessons of class instruction from your book.

Pay no attention to any phenomena whatsoever, and continue in a sober and responsible way of life under all circumstances.

Originally in Crowley's play *The Ship*, which he wrote shortly after learning the Key of the OTO, "The Hymn to the Unnamed One" is recited during the Gnostic Mass, where it is referred to as the "Anthem." Written to portray the essence of that Key in dramatic form, the hymn invokes the "centre and secret of the Sun/And that most holy mystery/Of which vehicle am I." [30]

After taking the oath, which he and Smith both signed, Parsons endured an unspecified 40-day ordeal—longer than the entire Babalon Working—that probably involved a retreat of some sort and fasting. He emerged to claim the grade of a Master of the Temple. Parsons was 33 when he took the Oath of the Abyss; Crowley was 34 when he attempted the same. Little survives of Parsons' account; all we have is his statement in *The Book of AntiChrist*. Parsons should have kept detailed records of his attempt at crossing the Abyss, but if such records existed they must have been lost or destroyed. It is doubtful he succeeded in his attempt.

In order to try to reconstruct what Parsons might have done to cross the Abyss, we need to review what Crowley himself did in this regard. It may not be the same procedure as that attempted by Parsons, but it was in print at that time as *The Vision and the Voice*,

---

30. *The Ship* was published by Crowley in *The Equinox*.

and Parsons did in fact idolize Crowley, such that he probably stuck to the original, at least to some degree. It is important to note that crossing the Abyss is a part of the A∴A∴'s doctrine, and has nothing to do with the OTO. In fact, by this time Parsons had resigned from the latter.

Crowley carried out his Abyss-crossing process during 1908 and 1909. A key part of this working was a 30-day walk across the Algerian desert, upon which he took along *Frater Omnia Vincam*, known in the "world of men" as Victor Neuburg, the acolyte who was in love with him and received Crowley's abuse. Although this endeavor was a full three years before Crowley would learn the sexual secret of the OTO, on one occasion he used Neuburg in an act of sex magic, taking the submissive role to Neuburg's dominance. Neuburg took notes as Crowley described what he saw.

The crossing of the Abyss is part of the old Enochian system, which posits a universe of 30 concentric Aires (or Aethyrs) with the earth at the center, much as the ancients did with the seven planetary spheres, although there are other arrangements. The 30th Aire is the lowest; hence, it is the closest to the earth. The First Aire is thus the highest, but there are said to be unknown, unnumbered Aires above it.

Each Aire, as seen in the discussion of the Babalon Working, has its angels, kings, Seniors, cherubs, etc. associated with it. Working with each Aire requires invoking these entities, just as Parsons invoked EXARP in January 1946. The full ritual is full of consecrations, hexagrams and pentagrams, and takes at least an hour to perform for each Aire. The ritual must be recited from memory, and "vibrated" in the original Enochian language.

The Aires are transversed in reverse order, as the highest numbered Aire is closest to the earth. Crowley worked with the 30th Aire first, then the 29th, and so on. On the 21st day, the day of his working with the 10th Aire, Crowley had his Abyss-crossing experience. The 10th Aire is guarded by the demon Choronzon, who dwells in the Abyss.

For Crowley, Aires 30 through 11 involved astral vision ("skrying in the Aethyrs"). The working of the 10th Aire involved a full-blown possession experience in which Crowley's psyche was overtaken by Choronzon for a time. Neuburg was extremely frightened by this intense change in his usually amicable master, and was glad that Crowley was bound inside a consecrated circle. Unlike the invocations of the previous nights, there was no physical contact between the two men. The possession lasted until the energy produced by the blood of three sacrificed pigeons ran out, and then it ended.

Crowley emerged with his sanity intact, having survived a face-to-face encounter with the blind forces of the Abyss. He had tasted madness and survived. He had crossed the Abyss by giving up his ego. He was now a *Magister Templi* (Master of the Temple) in the A∴A∴.

Crowley scryed the remaining Aires during the course of the next nine days, then finished the rite (and his desert walk). A detailed account of these endeavors and his ordeal can be found in Crowley's *The Vision and the Voice*, as well as in his *Confessions*.

As noted, it is unclear to what extent Parsons emulated his master in his Abyss working, for which he may very well have retired to the Mojave desert, as Crowley had to that of Algeria. This period was a low point in Parsons' life: his former glory lost, he was employed at a gas station. The working lasted 40 days, whatever form it took— longer than the entire Babalon Working, and longer than Crowley's own Algerian working with Neuburg. Unfortunately, most of the records documenting the endeavor are now gone, if they even existed.

Whatever form it did take, this operation was Parsons' Black Pilgrimage, foretold by Babalon three years earlier in *Liber 49*, vs. 33, 58, and 61. After the end of the 40 days, Parsons wrote a two-page document called *The Book of AntiChrist*. In it he predicted the manifestation of Babalon upon the earth within seven years, which he would not have done had he considered Cameron to be Babalon. He also predicted that an entire nation would embrace *Thelema*. Babalon told him these things would come to pass only if he survived the next seven years. He did not, and it is odd that Babalon, or Parsons' own psyche, or whatever it was, would even suggest that the young man might not, as if it or he knew his sad fate.

In "The Black Pilgrimage," which was the first part of *The Book of AntiChrist*, Parsons compared himself to several infamous but obscure figures from the past. He referred to them as past lives of his, though probably just as a literary device. The first, Simon Magus, was the legendary first-century Samaritan magician who made a living selling miracles to the populace. According to the Bible, after his baptism by Philip (Acts 8:9 ff), Simon continued to peddle his wares under a Christian guise, giving rise to our word "Simony." Simon preached a gnostic message in which his consort Helen, found in a brothel, was the fallen Sophia (i.e., wisdom) whom he had redeemed.

The second past life was Gilles de Retz (usually spelled "Rais" or "Raiz"), a child torturer and killer also known as Bluebeard the pirate. Parsons mentioned an incident apparently not documented elsewhere, in which de Rais (ca. 1404–1430) allegedly tried to make Joan of Arc (ca. 1412–1431) the "Queen of the Witchcraft."

The third figure was "Francis Hepburne, Earl Bothwell," but Parsons must have been referring to Francis *Stewart*, the fifth Earl of Bothwell. The fourth Earl had been named Hepburn. The fifth Earl was the "Arch-Dianist" of Scotland, meaning the spiritual leader of the Diana-worshipping witches, who saw in Stewart the incarnation of the "horned god." He also had a claim to the throne, toward which he directed his supernatural efforts. In fact, Stewart was the first cousin of King James VI of Scotland, the same murderous King James I of England whose translation of the Bible remains a standard, and who had John Dee arrested. As noted, the King feared witchcraft greatly, and he saw in his cousin the very devil whom he knew the witches worshiped. When Stewart busted into the King's house on July 24, 1593, the King asked whether Stewart came for his life or for his soul. Had James died heirless, Stewart could have claimed the throne. Some of Stewart's anti-Christian writings are even used in our age. Parsons mentioned him specifically in regard to a Gille Duncan, about whom there seems to be no information.

The fourth life was Count Cagliostro, the famous 18th-century alchemist who studied under St. Germain, the supposedly immortal miracle worker, and Seraphina (AKA Lorenza Feliciana), Cagliostro's wife. During the witchhunts, Seraphina testified against her husband—admittedly under the threat of torture—and he was sentenced to death. His sentence was commuted to life in prison, and Seraphina was allowed to retire to a monastery of nuns.[31]

The common thread in all of these past lives is the poor relationship with women: Parsons was still beating himself up for having trusted Betty. In addition to pummeling himself, Parsons also trounced Christianity and "the lying priests, conniving judges, [and] blackmailing police," ending the second part of *The Book of AntiChrist*, called "The Manifesto of the AntiChrist," with the following:

> I, BELARION, ANTICHRIST, in the year 1949 of the rule of the Black Brotherhood called Christianity, do make my Manifesto to all men.
> And I, THE ANTICHRIST, come among you, saying:

---

31. Crowley claimed to have been Cagliostro as well. Presumably at least one of them is wrong.

An end to the pretense, and lying hypocrisy of Christianity.

An end to the servile virtues, and superstitious restrictions.

An end to the slave morality.

An end to prudery and shame, to guilt and sin, for these are of the only evil under the Sun, that is fear.

An end to all authority that is not based on courage and manhood, to the authority of lying priests, conniving judges, blackmailing police, and

An end to the servile flattery and cajolery of mobs, the coronations of mediocrities, the ascension of dolts.

An end to restriction and inhibition, for I, THE ANTICHRIST, am come among you preaching the Word of the BEAST 666, which is, "There is no law beyond Do what thou wilt."

And I, BELARION, ANTICHRIST, do lift up my voice and prophesy, and I say: I shall bring all men to the law of the BEAST 666, and in His law I shall conquer the world.

And within seven years of this time, BABALON, THE SCARLET WOMAN HILARION will manifest among ye, and bring this my work to its fruition.

An end to conscription, compulsion, regimentation, and the tyranny of false laws.

And within nine years a nation shall accept the Law of the BEAST 666 in my name, and that nation will be the first nation of earth.

And all who accept me the ANTICHRIST and the law of the BEAST 666, shall be accursed and their joy shall be a thousandfold greater than the false joys of the false saints.

And in my name BELARION shall they work miracles, and confound our enemies, and none shall stand before us.

Therefore I, THE ANTICHRIST call upon all the Chosen and elect and upon all men, come forth now in the name of Liberty, that we may end for ever the tyranny of the Black Brotherhood.

Witness my hand and seal on this [deleted] day of [month deleted], 1949, that is the year of BABALON 4066.

"Hilarion" was the magical motto of the Scarlet Woman Jeanne Foster, an American member of the A∴A∴, whom Crowley called "the Cat." Foster had completed a working with Crowley in 1915 that he later believed produced a Magical Child in the form of Charles Stansfeld Jones (Frater Achad). The name "Hilarion" comes from one of the "Mahatmas," or Ascended Masters, of Theosophy: Hilarion Smerdis, who was said to have been the angel who dictated the book of Revelation to St. John of Patmos. It is unknown why Parsons referred to Babalon by this name, which was later one of Cameron's magical names as well. She may have chosen it because of this document.

On May 8, 1949, some months after the Abyss working—and possibly because of it, in Parsons' mind—he was hired by the Hughes Aircraft Company. At that time, he wrote Crowley, "It has now been almost a year since I last wrote—at that time I was near mental and financial collapse. Since that time I have laboriously gained some sort of mental equilibrium and gradually regained something of a position in my old field in a large aircraft company. My one aim is to rebuild myself."

Also in 1949, Cameron returned from Mexico and made Parsons a green box with the Hebrew letter *shin* painted in red on the lid. He kept his Babalon Working documents in it.

In January of 1951, Parsons made a striking discovery and wrote Germer:

> I have the text of Dee's skrying in the Seventh Aire, which as he said ". . . so terrified him that, beseeching God to have mercy upon me, I finally answered that I will from this day forward meddle no more herein." The Voice, speaking from Kelley, resulted in a sinister dissociation of Kelley's personality. The parallel with my own Working with Ron is appalling. After this Kelley robbed Dee, absconded with his wife, and developed ["continued" would be more appropriate] a criminal confidence career . . . In view of the fact that this mss [manuscript] was unknown to Hubbard and I [sic], the parallelism is really extraordinary. I have another prophecy in *Khaled Khan*,[32] which I shall send later.

This realization of history repeating itself may have hit Parsons too late to do anything about it, but he was not defeated. Parsons worked in the Propellants Section at Hughes, and by March 1950 he was listing his title as "Group Leader in Charge of Propellants, Propulsion and Launching Group of the Research and Development Laboratories." Circumstances had gone well from the date of his hiring May 8, 1949 until June 1950, at which time the Israelis, with whom he had been negotiating since October 1948 via the American

---

32. The reference is to Crowley's *Heart of the Master*, which was written under the pseudonym Khaled Khan.

Technion Society, requested a detailed proposal for "the construction of Explosive Plants and the development of rockets and other armaments," which Parsons would design, build and operate. In order to accomplish this goal, he planned to relocate to the newly formed Israel. According to Parsons' FBI file he negotiated with no less than the head of the American Technion Society, a man named Rosenfeldt.

Parsons worked on the proposal in July and August. In September, Hughes had him working on a proposal for a "Rocket Propellant Loading Plant." The pricing data in this proposal was what Parsons needed to finish his proposal to the Israelis. He took 17 of his own documents from Hughes, many of which were still designated as "Confidential" or "Restricted," and passed them on via Cameron to a friend for typing. His FBI file says this (female) friend was a part of the typing pool at Hughes. This incident occurred, in Parsons' own words, "about the 16th of September," at the recommendation of von Kármán, who was also interviewed by the FBI with regard to the Chinese Tsien's espionage case. Von Kármán's participation was later found to be incidental in both cases.

These 17 documents were said to be rough drafts of the proposal he was writing for Hughes, but they were mostly old JATO documents Parsons was using to pad his résumé. His "friend," whom he said he had known for five years, turned him in, and on September 25 the FBI confiscated the documents. On September 26 at noon, they interviewed Parsons. His signed statement denies any wrongdoing, relating his claim that he was merely using excerpts from those documents, specifically the pricing data, to help complete his proposal to the Israelis, who had not seen any of the documents, or even the excerpts. In fact, the only person who had seen them was his "friend" the typist. Parsons said he knew that she and her husband both had confidential clearances, so he didn't see where any violation of security had occurred. This incident transpired before the more recent and restrictive "Need to Know" rules were in effect.

Parsons did admit that removing Hughes Aircraft property without permission was a "serious error of judgement," but he had a property pass that he showed to the guard when he removed the papers, a common practice, Parsons told them. Displaying his characteristic trust and generosity of spirit, in his statement Parsons nobly absolved his "friend" of any complicity. He further said that he intended to check with the State Department when his proposal was complete, before sending it to Israel, where he only planned to work on projects that the U.S. had approved, and that the Technion Society had been set up to regulate such things.

Copies of Parsons' statement were forwarded to the Air Force, the OSI, and the CIA. The Air Force replied that the incident was an Army matter. Subsequent statements were taken, and many acquaintances of Parsons and Cameron were interviewed. One referred to the couple as "characters and screwballs." Another called Parsons a "crackpot." References to earlier investigations of his "cult" at 1003 S. Orange Grove occupy much of the FBI file. One witness claimed to have gone to the house for a "weekend party" that turned into a rite wherein everybody removed their street clothes, put on ceremonial robes, and were subsequently drugged.

Another witness' statement bears quoting in its entirety:

> [T]he Parsons are an odd and unusual pair in that they do not live by the commonly accepted code of married life, and are both very fascinated by anything unusual or morbid such as voodooism, cults, homosexuality, and religious practices that are 'different.' Subject seems very much in love with his wife but she is not at all affectionate and does not appear to return his affection. [Two lines deleted.] She is the dominating personality of the two and controls the activities and thinking of subject to a very considerable degree. It is the opinion [deleted] if subject were to have been in any way willfully involved in any activities of an intentional espionage nature, it would probably have been on the instigation of his wife.

An FBI memorandum of January 27, 1951 shows Parsons was at that date still under investigation for "espionage," stating that Parsons intended to turn the documents over to an individual who had offered him the promise of a position in Israel. It also describes him as a "former employee" of Hughes, meaning that he had been fired by then. Apparently he was fired immediately in September, when the breach of security was discovered. In the file is also a routing slip signed by J. Edgar Hoover.

In March 1951, Parsons moved from the house at 424 Arroyo Terrace in Pasadena to 1200 Esplanade in Redondo Beach, California, the address given by Jim Brandon but which does not appear in Parsons' FBI file. Other addresses provided for Parsons and Cameron are 3416 Manhattan Avenue and 3212 Highland Avenue, both in Manhattan Beach, California.

On October 25, 1951, the Assistant United States Attorney decided not to prosecute the case, even though on December 15, 1950 seven additional classified papers were found to be in Parsons' possession during the course of the investigation. These additional papers had highly technical titles such as "Ignition Studies of Restricted Burning Solid Propellant Jet Motors." Curiously, the titles of the original 17 documents Parsons took (13 finished papers and four drafts) are still censored from the FBI file as of this writing. Although it is unverified, it has also been said that Parsons inadvertently employed jargon used by the Manhattan Project, the U.S. nuclear weapons program established in 1942 by Enrico Fermi.

On January 17, 1952, after one year and four months of investigation, the Board informed Parsons this they were pulling his clearance, which was never reinstated. The lack of reinstatement is curious, as officials at Wright-Patterson Field informed the investigators that the entire project had been declassified right after the war, even though some of the individual papers were still classified. Indeed, they recommended declassification of the papers in Parsons' possession, as most of them were rather old. Regardless, his superiors just didn't trust him anymore. The combined effects of several investigations into the magical and sexual activities at the house on South Orange Grove Avenue, alleged communistic activities, previous loss of clearance, and two separate cases of taking classified documents all added up to mistrust. This tragedy hastened Parsons' decline.

The investigation stressed Parsons, and sometime in late 1950 he turned to his chosen form of spirituality for relief, despite its troublesome implications. Expressing his discontent, Parsons wrote a short text addressed to the Moonchild who was yet to come. The text was to be a part of the *Book of Babalon* and read mournfully:

My daughter, it is now four years since I entered the infernal chapel, and partook of the sacrament of your incarnation. Since then, much that was prophesied at that time has come to pass. I have been stripped of wealth, of honor, and of love; and have participated not once but twice in my own betrayal, as it was foretold. But how else would I come to the understanding needful to make this your Book?

For thereby I have taken the Oath of the Abyss, and entered my rightful city of Chorazin, and seen therein the past lives whereby I came to this, the grossest of all my Workings. Now it would seem that the further matters of the prophecy are at work; events press on tumultuously, and 'Time Is' is write large across the sky [see *Liber 49*, vs. 3].

And against the time when 'Time Has Been' looms up in blood and fire to complete this labor, for your instruction and for the instruction and help of all men and women who shall survive that day.

God knows, there is much unsaid and badly said; obscurity, peevishness, haste and bad workmanship mar these pages, until sometimes I wonder if I do not do disservice to our cause. There is so much needful, so little available. Yet, since I have been chosen, I do my best.

Although I have had indications, they are not certain. I do not know who you are, nor where you are at this writing; nor have I ever sought to know. This I do know—that you are incarnate, that you will manifest at the appointed time, to carry on the work that is from the beginning: that shall be until we have all entered the City of the Pyramids. The links are certain—the Beast 666 [Crowley], the Pole Star 132 [Wilfred Smith], the dark passionate star Regina [Kahl], the bright deceitful star Cassup [Betty Northrup], the disastrous star of the White Scribe [Hubbard], and the wandering star, now nameless, in whom you were incarnated.

It is through them that this work is possible. To them, you are BABALON, and through you to all men it is dedicated.

Parsons didn't abandon demonic spirituality, or his love for women. He and Cameron reunited after a short separation, moving into the coach house of the F.G. Cruikshank mansion at 1071 S. Orange Grove Ave. Cruikshank still lived in the house, while Parsons and Cameron and several others rented rooms above the garage at 1071½ S. Orange Grove, just three doors down from the Parsonage. At this location, Parsons spent his nights painstakingly creating an exact duplicate of Dee's Enochian tablets, which have not survived.

Prior to the FBI investigation, Parsons had been planning to quit his job at Hughes Aircraft and finance a trip to Israel to pursue the proposal he had been trying to sell them for several years. Parsons and Cameron were now heading to Mexico to test an explosive "more powerful than anything yet invented," to quote filmmaker Renate Druks, who was an acquaintance of Cameron. Parsons was also still working on what he called "The Gnosis" and "The Witchcraft," and reportedly had employment possibilities in Spain.

During this period, in one of his last letters to Karl Germer (Frater Saturnus), Parsons wrote:

No doubt you will be delighted to hear from an adept who has undertaken the operation of his H.G.A. [Holy Guardian Angel] in accord with our traditions.

The operation began auspiciously with a chromatic display of psychosomatic symptoms, and progressed rapidly to acute psychosis. The operator has alternated satisfactorily between manic hysteria and depressing melancholy stupor on approximately 40 cycles, and satisfactory progress has been maintained in social ostracism, economic collapses and mental disassociation.

These statements are mentioned not in any vainglorious spirit of conceit, but rather that they may serve as comfort and inspiration to other aspirants on the Path.

Now I'm off to the wilds of Mexico for a period, also in pursuit of the elusive H.G.A. before winding up in the guard finally via the booby hotels, the graveyard, or—? If the final, you can tell all the little Practicuses [3° = 8° in the A∴A∴] that I wouldn't have missed it for anything.

[Signed] No one. Once called 210.

Although he had intimately expressed to Germer some of the strain he was under, Parsons hated the German man he wrote, who succeeded Crowley as head of the OTO, and the letter was actually intended to sneer at Germer, as Parsons was leaving behind another job at a filling station for much greater things.

Expressing the glory of his life, Parsons wrote a poem, one of his last surviving, called "Star," which closes the volume *Songs for the Witch Woman*:

I remember
When I was a star
In the night
A moving, burning ember
Amid the bright
Clouds of star fire
Going deathward
To the womb.

Oh moon
Red moon of my desire
My sisters' and my brothers' fire
Down the great hall of heroes
I the star seed
Wooed the incredible flower.

I alone
My need, my power
attained the dark house
and my bride.

I remember
When I was a god
In my hour
and like a god I died
By the deep waters,
Crucified.

And I dreamed
and the great powers
moved over me
And a voice cried

Go free, star, go free
Seek the dark home
On the wild sky
Good bye, star, good bye.

LATE NEWS

Los Angeles Times

9 A.M. FINAL

VOL. LXXI | IN FOUR PARTS | WEDNESDAY MORNING, JUNE 18, 1952 | 64 PAGES | DAILY, 10c

ROCKET SCIENTIST KILLED IN PASADENA EXPLOSION

Tragedy Drives His Mother to Suicide

JOHN W. PARSONS
Killed in Explosion

MYSTERIOUS NOTES FOUND IN WRECKAGE

Police Pressing Investigation of Explosion

ten

Death and Beyond

By 1952, Parsons' various appeals and endeavors seemed to have been working, as good fortune appeared to be shining upon him again at last. In fact, he was working for several different concerns, including one with JPL employee Charles Bartley, who had a pyrotechnics license and let Parsons store explosives at his Pacoima facility, at which the two worked as consultants doing special effects explosions for films. Parsons also was working at least part-time for the Bermite Powder Company in Saugus, California, where Cameron helped him mix explosives. And he had the job at the service station.

This seeming upturn was short-lived, however, as the ultimate catastrophe lay just around the corner. Six years earlier, on March 2, 1946, Hubbard had channeled an eerily prophetic message, after which, Parsons wrote, the ex-Navy man was "pale and sweaty": "She [Babalon] is the flame of life, power of darkness, she destroys with a glance, she may take thy soul. She feeds upon the death of men. Beautiful—horrible . . . She shall absorb thee, and thou shalt become living flame before She incarnates."

In addition, utilizing one of the two abilities Cameron claimed Parsons had taught her, i.e., to use her epileptic seizures to enter the astral plane (the other one being the tarot), Cameron claimed to have discovered a bottle of mercury beneath the floorboards in his laboratory, which, if Parsons had planted it there, was extremely careless for someone so experienced with dangerous chemicals. However, Parsons was indeed somewhat reckless with chemicals, which in the end may have been his doom.

On Tuesday, June 17, 1952 at 5:08 p.m. an explosion erupted in the lower level of 1071½ S. Orange Grove Ave. that was heard as far as a mile away. Tragically and horribly, Parsons was at the center of it. A second explosion occurred almost immediately, as if set off by the first. Flame consumed Parsons, as Babalon had predicted, and his right forearm was blown off so completely that only a few small pieces of it were found. The blast broke his other arm and both legs, left a "gaping hole" in his jaw, and shredded his shoes. Parsons was conscious when upstairs neighbors dragged him out from under an old-fashioned washtub, which can be seen in a photo reproduced in the *Los Angeles Times* on June 18.

The lower level of the coach house had been a stable, and the upper level had been servants' quarters, which had been turned into apartments that Parsons, his mother, and Cameron occupied until June 1. At the time of the blast, Parsons' mother, Ruth, had taken a summer position as caretaker for one Mrs. Carpenter, who was out of town with her husband, residing at 21 W. Glenarm St. with her friend Helen Rowan who was confined to a wheelchair.

The explosion blew the stable doors from their hinges, knocked over two walls, and tore a hole in the ceiling as well as a hole in the floor. Smaller doors and windows were blown from their frames, and two greenhouses 25 feet away were shattered. A grand piano upstairs shifted enough for one of its legs to break, and a chandelier fell. Windows were broken on the home next door. Artist Salvatore Ganci, one of the upstairs residents, was on the phone when the explosion occurred. "I was lifted off the couch by a violent blast," he told the *Pasadena Star-News* reporter. The apartment was shared by 21-year-old Jo Ann Price, an actress and model, as well as actor Martin Foshaug, 31, and his mother Alta. No one upstairs was hurt.

Ganci and Mrs. Foshaug rushed downstairs and pulled Parsons from the wreckage, propping him up against a wall until paramedics could get there. Parsons was coherent enough to give them instructions as he was loaded into the ambulance and taken to Huntington Memorial Hospital at 100 Congress St. in Pasadena. The remarkable man died there at 5:45 p.m., some 37 minutes after the explosion. In March 1946, Parson had cryptically written, "And in that day [the manifestation of Babalon] my work will be accomplished, and I shall be blown away upon the breath of the father." As Parsons lay dying, according to John Bluth, his last words are said to have been, "I wasn't done." According to Jane Wolfe, Cameron related them as, "Who will take care of me now?" But it was not he who needed looking after, as he had passed on into the other side that he had so fervently tried to bring into this world.

From his birth, both Parsons and his mother shared a strong bond. After the sickening tragedy, Ruth Parsons and Helen Rowan went to a friend's home at 424 Arroyo Terrace, where her son and Cameron had been staying since June 1, which was described in a newspaper as a "two-story mansion." Another friend, Mrs. Nedia Kibort, age 59, of 320 Waverly Drive, was in the house with them, where presumably they sought a little comfort after the dreadful news. Ruth was drinking heavily, and took two Nembutals from a prescription she received after the explosion. When she learned of her son's death she shouted, "I can't stand to live without him. I adored him." She also said that she had a gun upstairs and then gulped the remainder of the sleeping pills—23 or 43, depending on the account—while Mrs. Rowan looked on helplessly. Another friend, a nurse named Nellie Smith, arrived soon after and found Ruth slumped over in a living room chair. She phoned Dr. J.R. Huntsman of 65 N. Madison Ave., who pronounced Mrs. Parsons dead at 9:06 p.m. Her death was investigated by Lt. John C. Elliott, who had been at the scene of her son's death, and by Sgt. Woody Pollard.

Cameron was buying supplies for the Mexico trip at the corner grocery when the explosion occurred. The *Pasadena Independent* reported Cameron as being "stoic in the face of her double loss." She told reporters and police that she and her husband were headed to Mexico for a vacation. Their luggage was sitting in the hallway at 424 Arroyo Terrace when Ruth committed suicide. Others told a different story.

Cameron's brother Robert, age 28, of 125 N. Rampart Blvd., stated that Parsons was headed to Mexico on business, "the nature of which was very secretive." Presumably Robert would know, as he and Cameron's other brother, sister and father all worked at JPL. Someone else told the *Independent* that Parsons was going to set up his own business in Mexico, but Cameron insisted it was merely an extended trip. The amount of baggage, however, indicated a long-term stay. In fact, the couple were headed next to Israel, where they intended to raise a family.

Motorcycle officer Ernie Hovard was the first policeman on the scene of the explosion and was later joined by Donald M. Harding, a Pasadena police force criminologist. Harding found numerous containers of explosives, many of which had already been placed outside by Parsons, in preparation for the trip, which was obviously not for sightseeing. The legality of the explosives was questioned, and the 58th Army Ordnance Disposal Unit was called in from Fort MacArthur to help determine the cause of the explosion, as well as to inspect the immediate area and the house at 424 Arroyo Terrace for further explosives. As photographers took flash photos, Harding shielded certain of the remaining bottles, afraid that the light would set them off as well. The Disposal Unit removed the rest of the explosives from the premises, and the investigators and others began to speculate as to what caused the blast—nitroglycerin? Rocket fuels? Or the more exotic-sounding trinitrobenzene or PETN?[33]

In addition to the explosion, Harding found numerous scientific notes in the debris, most of which contained chemical formulas. One interesting document contained Parsons' notes concerning industrial explosions: "Texas City Disaster Report: 433 dead, 128 missing. [The explosive] cannot be detonated with rifle bullets, blasting caps or dynamite." Parsons also had notes about a Los Angeles electroplating company explosion in 1947 that killed 15, and another explosion at Aerojet that killed eight. He had been a member of the coroner's jury on the 1947 incident.

A more curious fragment was obviously not a part of his professional work. The note read, "Let me know thy misery totally. And spare not and be not spared. Sacrament and Crucifixion. Oh my passion and shame . . . Mothers . . . Sisters . . ." Unfortunately, he got his morbid wish, as did his devoted mother.

Harding eventually determined that the blast occurred just behind Parsons, and to his right, just above floor level. Had the building not been of heavy timber construction, it probably would have been leveled. As it was, the entire half of the lower level containing his lab was gutted. Firemen reported that they noticed a "funny odor" when they arrived on the scene. Interestingly, considering she had purportedly found mercury there, Cameron said that the explosion occurred *beneath* the floorboards, *lifting them up*.

Martin Foshaug said that Parsons "had been experimenting in an effort to produce a 'Super' fog effect for motion pictures," but this work certainly had nothing to do with the blast that killed him, since Parsons had left his special effects job with the Bermite Powder Company on the previous Friday, June 13.

On June 19, the newspapers reported that the cause of the explosion had been determined to be "fulminate of mercury," a very sensitive and powerful detonator that Army Ordnance had stopped using because of the number of deaths it had caused. However, the size of the explosion seems excessive for fulminate of mercury. Harding, who had just joined the Pasadena police force, was assigned to his first investigation with the Parsons blast. He could have both been inexperienced and had based his conclusions on hearsay, rather than science, about mercury. Harding was told by a neighbor that Parsons was manufacturing the mercury explosive (illegally) in the garage

---

33. PETN is still used for demolition and special effects today.

laboratory. It was to be his last batch, Parsons had told the neighbor. Obviously, he was right. Harding searched for other storage places Parsons might have maintained, and stated that enough explosives remained in the lab to "blow up half the block."

Harding's determination of the bomb device's origin was based on his discovery in the rubble of ingredients needed to make fulminate of mercury. Shrapnel from a coffee can was found in the wooden floor and in the walls, radiating out from the hole at ground zero, which led Harding to surmise that Parsons must have reached for the can when it dropped but wasn't quick enough. This development, Harding inferred, was why the explosion occurred low to the floor and why Parsons' right arm was missing, since it was closest to the blast. Harding believed Parsons was mixing the chemical in the can when it dropped. Fulminate of mercury, he reasoned, "is made wet and gets more sensitive as it dries. A little friction, percussion, heat or agitation is enough to set it off."

Based on Harding's findings, Detective Lieutenant Cecil H. Burlingame was told by the coroner's office that no inquest would be held. After an autopsy performed the next day by Deputy Coroner I.G. Mcfarland, the death was ruled accidental and attributed to "multiple injuries of entire body." Burlingame told reporters that police had received reports in 1942 that Parsons was illegally storing explosives at 1003 S. Orange Grove Ave. Nevertheless, a search conducted in conjunction with the FBI had turned up nothing.

The *Pasadena Independent* talked to J.H. Arnold of the Bermite Powder Company, who told them that Parsons had stayed long enough with his company to finish a special effects project. Parsons had, in fact, been working on a "rocket propellant detonation and pyrotechnic short-interval delay" project, which was a confidential program at the company. Contrary to Cameron's testimony, his co-workers related that he had told them he was heading to Mexico to continue his research with explosives and miniature special effects. Arnold had asked him to stay long enough to see the tests of the confidential project, but Parsons was eager to get to Mexico. "He had been working hard," Arnold told the investigators, also stating that Parsons was extremely safety-conscious. Said Arnold, "He worked carefully, had a thorough knowledge of his job and was scrupulously neat." But Harding called him "criminally negligent" in the way he handled the explosives at his home lab. Arnold was surprised to hear that Parsons had so many explosives at home, which police learned had been there at least six months. Arnold added that Parsons at one time had his own powder magazine near Rialto, which was a legal storage place. His home, however, was in obvious violation of the Pasadena fire marshal's code. In addition, Arnold noted, six or eight months earlier Parsons talked about going into the dynamite business. Other comments came from T.E. Beehan, Secretary-Treasurer of Aerojet, who described Parsons as a "loner" and said, "He liked to wander, but he was one of the top men in the field."

In their reportage about his life and death, the *Pasadena Independent* dug up some of the older stories about Parsons when he was at 1003 S. Orange Grove and recalled that in 1942 a letter had been sent from San Antonio, Texas by "A Real Soldier," who wrote that a "black magic" cult was operating in the house. The same Detective Lt. Burlingame had investigated the letter incident and was told by Parsons that the "cult" was merely a "non-sectarian and non-political fraternity" which "held open forums on Sunday afternoons, and discussed philosophy, religion, personal freedom, and fortune telling."

However, in 1944 police investigated a small fire at the house, during which investigation Detective O.A. Nelson found "considerable paraphernalia . . . which indicated that spiritual seances may have been held in the house." Said Nelson, "It appears to be the home of some type of secret society." Nevertheless, the matter was dropped.

Smelling a good story, the sensationalistic *Independent* announced in its obituary that on July 19 "secret rites" were held for John Parsons at Turner & Stevens Mortuary, Marengo Ave. and Holly St. However, the funeral home referred to the ceremony as a "private prayer service." The obituary used his birth name, Marvel, and reported that Cameron was the only survivor. It also stated that cremation took place earlier that day at the Live Oak Crematory and that his body was embalmed by W.T. Stahlman. The Social Security number given on his death certificate, presumably provided by Cameron, is incorrect and belongs to a Virginia Wilson, also of California, who had been born the same year as Parsons and who lived until 1980.

On July 20, a private service was held for Ruth Parsons, also by Turner & Stevens, and her body was cremated as well. She was survived by a Mrs. Emma Aldrich of Santa Monica, California, apparently no relation to lodge member Meeka Aldrich.

On June 22, both the *Los Angeles Times* and the *Pasadena Independent* addressed a new development: George W. Santmyer (or Santmyers), a Los Angeles chemical engineer working with Parsons in a Naval Ordnance Department research project since January 1, suggested to the papers that something was amiss with the investigation. Police had found 500 grams of cordite (an ammunition component) and six filter papers containing fulminate of mercury residue in Parsons' trash can, which was either at the back of the lab or just outside it, depending on the account. "For Parsons to have disposed of such materials in that manner," said Santmyer, "would be the same as for a highly trained surgeon to operate with dirty hands. It's completely out of character for him." Criminologist Harding, when asked, admitted that Parsons' supposed sloppiness seemed "incongruous." Harding also said that enough cordite and fulminate of mercury were found in the trash to blow up the garbage truck and drivers who would have picked up the can.

In his statement to the papers, Santmyer argued that someone else must have put it there, that Parsons would not have disposed of highly dangerous explosives at the last minute, nor would he have prepared them for transportation on a long drive into Mexico, as everything he needed to produce fulminate of mercury could be easily purchased once he arrived there. Santmyer also stated that Parsons was "on the trail" of a completely new explosive that "was to be far superior to any existing commercial blasting material" and much safer to handle. According to Burlingame, however, Santmyer's questions weren't "sufficient to warrant us reopening the case." Nevertheless, Santmyer was not the only person who smelled something fishy in the untimely death of John Parsons.

Something else was allegedly found after the death of Parsons that didn't make the 1952 *Los Angeles Times*. Amateur rocket advocate Harold Chambers, who worked at a technical bookstore in downtown Los Angeles for 40 years, was told on separate occasions by both Harding and Santmyer that an "odd, bizarre, fairly big box, decorated with snakes and dragons" was found in a trailer at Parsons' residence. The odd box was found to contain home movies of Parsons and mother having sex, not only with each other, but also with Ruth's "big dog." According to reports from Pasadena police, passed down to their friend Harold Chambers, we now have circumstantial evidence that John Parsons indeed fulfilled his goal to "exteriorize [his] Oedipus complex."

Ruth Parsons' "big dog" also made it difficult for police to attend to her suicide scene. After being attacked by Ruth's agitated beast, Pasadena police officers shot the dog in the head.

Chambers also reports that Don Harding, having discovered a syringe among the blast debris, partially filled with a morphine-like substance, believes that Parsons' drug use contributed to his mishandling of explosives.

The high-reaching pioneer Parsons was gone but not forgotten. In 1969, *Darker Than You Think* author Jack Williamson wrote, "In Pasadena not long ago, walking across the grounds of the Jet Propulsion Laboratory, I was jolted to see Parsons' name on a memorial tablet set up to honor the first martyrs to space. He had written me once about testing multicellular solid-fuel rockets designed after those in my story 'The Crucible of Power.' When I first heard about his death I wondered if my own rockets had killed him, but [L.] Sprague de Camp tells me that he dropped a bottle of picric acid." It wasn't picric acid, but he had the right idea.

Rather than any "martyrs to space," the JPL plaque actually honors the first successful series of JATO tests, which began on Halloween 1936. The monument was unveiled on Halloween 1968, the 32nd anniversary of the original date. "The Crucible of Power," contained in the anthology *The Best of Jack Williamson*, describes the multi-cellular, solid-fuel rockets as follows: "[I]t was a four-step rocket, each step containing thousands of cellules, each of which was a complete rocket motor with its own load of alumilloid fuel, to be fired once and then detached." No doubt Parsons would have also been interested in the solar religion of the story's Martians, whose high priest was called the "Lance of the Sun."

While the police were content to let the tragedy stand as an accident ostensibly caused by his professional endeavors, others felt it had to do with the occult. In *The Occult Explosion* (published 1972), Nat Freedland interviewed filmmaker Renate Druks, who said, "Cameroun [sic] stayed with me at my Malibu Beach house for six months, pulling herself together after Jack died. I have every reason to believe that Jack Parsons was working on some very strange experiments, trying to create what the old alchemists called a homunculus, a tiny artificial man with magic powers. I think that's what he was working on when the accident happened." Druks evidently was the source of Michael Hoffman's statement in *Apocalypse Culture* that "In 1952 Parsons was blown up in what is officially described as an accident but which others have said was a homunculus experiment that went bananas." Before moving in with Druks, Cameron stayed briefly with Wilfred and Helen Parsons Smith. She also spent time alone in the desert.

Parsons' friends did not believe he killed himself, at least intentionally. Indeed, he had too many plans, as reflected by his dying words: "I wasn't done." It is somewhat ironic that these were the dying words of the man who claimed to be the Antichrist, while, according to the gospel tale, the dying words of Christ were the opposite: "It is finished."

Druks, who later worked with avant garde filmmaker Kenneth Anger and who also studied magic under Jane Wolfe, related that Parsons was going to Mexico "to experiment with his new formula for an explosive 'more powerful than anything yet invented.'" According to JPL employee Charles Bartley, Parsons told him he was going there to start a fireworks company, yet von Kármán stated that Parsons told him it was an explosives factory—which is admittedly not much different—that the Mexican government had hired him to set up. Von Kármán also said that Parsons told him the government was furnishing a 17th-century castle for him to stay in while he was there. Since there are few if any castles in old Mexico, perhaps Parsons or von Kármán confused *palacio* for *castillo*. Cameron related a similar account but stated it was in Baja California, rather than Mexico proper. These experiments were to be a step toward their eventual plans for working with the Israelis.

Decades later Cameron spoke of the explosion as coming from under the floorboards, implying murder rather than an accident or suicide. In the OTO newsletter *The Magical Link*, she stated that a good suspect was the explosives expert against whom Parsons had testified and who had been paroled immediately prior to the fatal explosion, a reference to Captain Kynette of the Los Angeles "spy squad," found guilty of murdering another police officer in 1938. The weapon Kynette used was a car bomb, and Parsons' testimony had been crucial in his conviction.

In recent years, one researcher was informed by the City of Los Angeles' Hall of Records that Parsons' will was still sealed and that he would have to get permission from the executor to obtain a copy. The executor was Ed Forman, who is dead. When I visited the Hall of Records, the clerk was unable to find any listing for Parsons' will in the probate records for Los Angeles county. The will, in fact, was never probated.

On August 13, 1952, just a month after his tragic death, *People Today* published a half-page piece on Parsons in its "People in Crime" section, which included a delightfully sinister photo of Parsons. The article was entitled "L.A.'s Lust Cult" and is worth quoting in full, to demonstrate the general attitude toward Parsons at the time. The bold print appears in the original.

Rich, rock-ribbed Pasadena, famed for its roses, the California Institute of Technology, and as a retirement haven for Eastern millionaires, looks like the last place a black magic cult dedicated to sex would thrive. Nevertheless, the Church of Thelema (the name means "will"), **a cult practicing sexual perversion, has been making converts of all ages, sexes, there since 1940. Among the believers: many prominent residents of the Pasadena-Los Angeles area; at least one member of Hollywood's movie colony.**

The existence of the cult, reported to police in an anonymous letter mailed from San Antonio, Texas, in September '42 by "A Real Soldier" and in an October '44 letter, was only proven this June with the "accidental" death of high priest John W. Parsons.

Parsons, bushy-haired, 37-year-old scientist who was one of the inventors of JATO (jet-assisted take-off), was killed when an explosion rocked his lab in the carriage house of the old F.G. Cruickshank [sic] estate along Pasadena's "Millionaire's Row," where he lived with his artist-wife and mother. **Within hours of her son's death, the elder Mrs. Parsons had committed suicide by swallowing 50 sleeping pills. The estate, investigators soon learned, had been the 'Temple' where Thelemites ran their strange sexual orgies.**

Parsons had served as high priest since the death, in '44, of local prophet Wilfred Smith, a disciple of Aleister Crowley, called "the sinister man" by French authorities. Crowley's chief commandment: **"Take your fill of love . . . with whom ye will."**

Says an ex-member: "The inner circle followed this rule, especially at the fertility rites at the spring and fall equinoxes." **Torch-carrying hooded cultists, chanting prayers to "Thou burning rapture of girls, that disport in the sunset of passion," concentrated on "begetting a royal race before dawn." Other rituals: a Black Mass,** patterned on a religious ceremony, in which High Priestess disrobed to tune of uninhibited chanting; **"purifying" fire torture.** Members are accepted in the cult—which also existed in Chicago and New York—on a probationary basis, must pass through 10 degrees before qualifying for participation in sex rites.

With the bizarre death of Parsons and the suicide of his mother, Thelemites have gone further underground. But, still active, they conducted a secret funeral for their dead high priest.

A sidebar to the article reads:

Thelemites follow code set down by founder Aleister Crowley, Englishman who died 25 years ago after a stormy life. Expelled from France and Italy, exiled from England, Crowley published his teachings under the title: *Equinox*. Its gist: Do anything you please.

Both the article and the sidebar contain a number of errors, including the date of Crowley's death, which was in reality in 1947, and of Smith's, which was in 1957.

In addition, at the time of the explosion Parsons was not the "high priest," since, as early as January 1946, Crowley wrote a letter naming a successor to Parsons. Indeed, by October of the year Crowley had become disillusioned with Parsons and wrote to Culling, "About J.W. P. [Parsons]—all that I can say is that I am sorry—I feel sure that he had fine ideas, but he was led astray firstly by Smith, then he was robbed of his last penny by a confidence man named Hubbard." And in December he wrote, "I have no further interest in Jack and his adventures; he is just a weak-minded fool, and must go to the devil in his own way. *Requiescat in pace.*"

Although Crowley may have found Parsons naïve and ineffectual, there are many who realize his key role in the aerospace/military industries, and not a few who believe he accomplished amazing things esoterically, leaving behind an extraordinary legacy that included "flying saucers," which would not be surprising considering his fervent interest in space and his attempts both chemically and alchemically to "shoot for the stars."

Death and Beyond

In fact, Kenneth Grant writes, "The [Babalon] Working began . . . just prior to the wave of unexplained aerial phenomena now recalled as the 'Great Flying Saucer Flap.' Parsons opened a door and something flew in." Indeed, this notion has entered certain fringe areas of pop culture.

Crowley sensationalizer Francis King mentions that Parsons felt flying saucers "would play a part in converting the world to Crowleyanity." When Cameron later became obsessed with flying saucers she never whispered a word about Parsons' interest. She believed saucers were not high-tech, but rather a "restoration of the elemental powers."

An unconfirmed statement attributed to conspiriologist John Judge claimed that Parsons may have flown with the pilot Kenneth Arnold, who in 1947 saw several silver disks over Mt. Rainier in Washington State and coined the term "flying saucer" to describe them.

Another Aerojet employee, Daniel Fry, saw a saucer in 1950 and went on to become an active figure in 1950s contacteeism. Some wonderful footage of him in his final years is recorded in the film *Farewell, Good Brothers*. Still another occult-oriented employee in the aerospace engineering industry, the Californian Orfeo Angelucci, claimed to have been a contactee in the 1950s.

Other momentous events were attributed to Parsons. Referring to the date of Parsons' death, Arthur Lyons said, "It was 13 years later, the period of human maturation, that twins were born in San Francisco—the counterculture and the Church of Satan." Gerald Suster, in his biography of Israel Regardie, credits Parsons with helping birth the sixties.

After his death, Cameron continued Parsons' work—not the Babalon Working, but that involving personal growth and exploration. She moved to the desert, living in an American artists' colony in northern Mexico (San Miguel de Allende), next door to David Siquieros and Max Ernst's wife Lenora Carrington. Cameron and Soror Estai (Jane Wolfe) struck up a voluminous correspondence. Here's hoping that this potentially fascinating communication will be made public by the OTO or whomever has it.

On December 15, 1952, Cameron wrote to Jane Wolfe, "Seven years ago, Jack began an operation which he referred to as the Babalon Work—and this set into motion the second part of a great force which was divided into three. Aleister Crowley began the first, three years before I was born [a possible reference to Frater Achad]. I never knew the man, yet his desire gave me birth. His paternity sings in my veins." Cameron is saying that she is the third and final part of that "force"; she referred to her life as one of the "strangest and wildest voyages into the unknown that has ever been told."

Cameron declared that Babalon actually came to exist as her own self. This large claim comes despite the known fact that Parsons believed Cameron was an elemental who he hoped would later give "birth" to Babalon. He would not have predicted Babalon's physical manifestation to occur within seven years, as he did in 1949 in *The Manifesto of the AntiChrist*, if she were already on earth. After the three-day working of March 1946, Parsons proclaimed, "Babalon is incarnate upon the earth today, awaiting the proper hour of Her manifestation." In 1949 Parsons revised this statement, perhaps anticipating Cameron's return. The year 1949 must have been significant to Parsons—the book that purportedly came from Babalon is titled *Liber 49*.

Parsons' *Songs for the Witch Woman* is dedicated to Cameron, "in whom She is incarnate." But in "The Star of Babalon" Parsons says that Her spirit is within all women who proclaim their equality to men. If this is indeed the case, a billion women on planet Earth are now wearing Babalon's tiara.

In 1953, Cameron wrote:

For some months now I have been aware of the heightening intensity of what I call a third beam of hearing. I can describe it as the sound of a radio beam that one picks up on shortwave. It is independent of my normal hearing—if I close my eyes it is not affected in any way. There are moments when it is so intense that I can actually tune it in—by turning my body. It seems to be heightened in power by the presence of some other humans . . . I have the feeling that there is someone on the other end, or let me say that I have the feeling that the beam transcends time and space and that I am hearing the sound of my transmitter echoed in incredible places.

While her auditory experiences were being inhumanly heightened, Cameron saw a flying saucer. In a letter to Jane Wolfe dated January 22, 1953, Cameron speculated the UFO was the "war-engine" mentioned in *The Book of the Law* III: 7-8 ("I will give you a war-engine. With it ye shall smite the peoples; and none shall stand before you.") Eight years earlier Crowley wondered if the atomic bomb constituted this engine.

In another letter Cameron wrote about:

[Mars], which I believe, is somehow my home. Earth will explode in a collision with the two Star Islands which are reported now moving towards each other in the heavens [reference uncertain]. And resulting therefrom, my star, the great Seven-pointed Star of Babalon, shall be born in the heavens. [Marginalia scribed by Gerald Yorke in 1969 on a copy of *Liber 49* states Cameron is "nutty as can be."]

In order to contact her "Holy Guardian Angel," Cameron began to illustrate *Songs of the Witch Woman* with her "desire." We don't have any record of Cameron contacting her Guardian Angel, but soon we will have Cameron's illustrations of Parsons' poem in print, or so it is said by their current owner, Carl Abrahamsson.

The fateful year of 1953 also saw the death of Mark M. Mills, Parsons' former associate, in a helicopter crash at an Eniwetok atomic bomb test site. Mills holds some of the solid fuel patents with Parsons and also co-authored some once-classified papers on solid fuel.

Next year Cameron played both the Scarlet Woman and Kali, the Hindu goddess of destruction, in Kenneth Anger's short film, *Inauguration of the Pleasure Dome.* Notorious for his underground films and authorship of the *Hollywood Babylon* books, Anger is also known for rescuing Crowley's paintings and ephemera in the Sicilian "Abbey of Thelema," from which Crowley and company were tossed by Benito Mussolini in 1932. In a letter to Wolfe, Cameron said that rituals acted out in Anger's film helped bring down Babalon.

The widowed Cameron married a man named Sharif Kimmel. With some bikers on Catalina Island in 1955, she destroyed the black box from the Babalon Working. Cameron had a daughter, Crystal, as well as grandchildren and great-grandchildren. Wilfred Smith, with whom she had lost contact, died in 1957. Jane Wolfe died a few months later, in 1958.

In 1957, a drawing by Cameron in Wallace Berman's *Semina* magazine prompted a raid on the Ferus Gallery by the police and an obscenity trial, after which Berman served a few days in jail. Dean Stockwell paid his bail. The picture showed a sun-headed man penetrating a woman from the rear. A photo of Cameron was on the cover. Cameron the painter was also involved in the L.A. art scene of the 1960s, with George Herms, Bruce Connor and Wallace Berman, and continued showing her work well into the 1980s.

The American actors Dennis Hopper and Dean Stockwell are said to have been Cameron's roommates. In fact, Cameron appeared with Hopper in the 1961 Curtis Harrington horror film *Night Tide*, playing a Lovecraftian "Deep One"—her few lines spoken in "R'lyehian." Harrington appeared in *Inauguration of the Pleasure Dome* as well; his film *Wormwood Star* is an impressionistic profile of Cameron.

Ithell Colquhoun's *The Sword of Wisdom*, written in 1975, mentions an "OTO Lunar Lodge" with which Cameron was supposedly working around 1960, somewhere in California. However, it does not seem to have been chartered, and those who knew Cameron say there was no lodge at all.

On Halloween 1968, JPL honored the 32nd anniversary of its nativity by dedicating a plaque behind its visitors' center. During the dedication, JPL held a large celebration, even going so far as to invite wives and ex-girlfriends who had been present during the tests. But they did not invite Ed Forman or Rudolph Schott, both of whom were still alive and living in the area. Nonetheless, Forman donated an old rocket and papers he had saved from the original tests, all of which have since been lost.

In 1969, the *London Sunday Times* ran an article on L. Ron Hubbard's early involvement with magick. The Church of Scientology protested, and in return the paper printed verbatim the Church's statement concerning Hubbard's involvement with Parsons.

Hubbard broke up black magic in America: Dr. Jack Parsons of Pasadena, California, was America's Number One solid fuel rocket expert. He was involved with the infamous English black magician Aleister Crowley who called himself 'The Beast 666.' Crowley ran an organization called the Order of Templars Orientalis over the world which had savage and bestial rites. Dr. Parsons was head of the American branch located at 100 Orange Grove Avenue, Pasadena, California. This was a huge old house which had paying guests who were the U.A.S. nuclear physicists working at Cal. tech. Certain agencies objected to nuclear physicists being housed under the same roof.

L. Ron Hubbard was still an officer of the U.S. Navy [and] because he was well known as a writer and philosopher and had friends among the physicists, he was sent in to handle the situation. He went to live at the house and investigated the black magic rites and the general situation and found them very bad.

Parsons wrote to Crowley in England about Hubbard. Crowley

"the Beast 666" evidently detected an enemy and warned Parsons. This was all proven by the correspondence unearthed by the [London] Sunday Times. Hubbard's mission was successful far beyond anyone's expectations. The house was torn down. Hubbard rescued a girl they were using. The black magic group was dispersed and never recovered. The physicists included many of the sixty-four top U.S. scientists who were later declared insecure and dismissed from government service with so much publicity.[34]

Despite the vilification and brouhaha, in 1972 the International Astronomical Union in France honored Parsons by naming a crater on the moon after him. "Parsons Crater" is at 37° N latitude, 171° W longitude, and, appropriately enough, on the *dark* side of the moon. Due to the Ranger survey, the first to photograph the dark side and reveal hundreds of new craters in need of names, NASA turned to its own past to provide them. Parsons was the only GALCIT scientist to earn this honor, in which Frank Malina, now living in France, may have had a hand.

Parsons' buddy, Ed Forman, died in 1973 of heart trouble while employed by Lockheed in El Segundo. Despite his lifelong closeness with Parsons, Forman never joined the OTO. (Parsons' mother, Ruth, also worked at Lockheed during the war.)

It is evident that Parsons was considered an important if dangerous figure by the authorities. His FBI file, which was requested prior to the Freedom of Information Act as part of a JPL history project, is heavily censored. Although FOIA rules have since changed, when one requests the file one normally gets a photocopy of the file that has already been processed. There have been no updates, simply because the FBI hasn't noticed or doesn't want to bother with it.

Among the many reasons Parsons was investigated was not only the "black magic" but also his association with communist sympathizers. Fellow GALCIT group member, Frank Malina, whose efforts served the U.S. quite effectively, was also a victim of the Communist witchhunts. After the war, Malina had become head of the scientific

---

34. [Publisher's Note: After hearing that Feral House was issuing a biography of John Parsons, The Church of Scientology became interested in seeing how L. Ron Hubbard would be depicted within. After contacting Scientology's Office of Special Affairs in Los Angeles for information they were said to have concerning Hubbard's involvement with Naval Intelligence, Feral House was sent, in June 1999, a copy of a certificate given Hubbard for attending and completing "the prescribed course in training for military government" at the Naval School of Military Government, Princeton University. Scientology's package also contained a 19-page document by L. Fletcher Prouty, a former Colonel in the U.S. Air Force, author of *The Secret Team: The CIA and its Allies in Control of the United States and the World*, and perhaps best known as being the mysterious character played by Donald Sutherland in Oliver Stone's *J.F.K.*. Prouty's affidavit discusses the probability that Hubbard's Naval Records have been altered and "sheep-dipped."]

research division of UNESCO in France, a post he held until his political beliefs and longstanding membership in the Communist Party were discovered. He resigned and turned to a successful career in "kinetic art." Several of his pieces are still on display in England, and the art/science journal he founded, *Leonardo*, is still published by MIT. Malina died in France in 1981.

It may have been Malina who first introduced the late John Parsons to the UFO-researcher and debunker, Jacques Vallee, who was the role model for the French scientist in *Close Encounters of the Third Kind*. Vallee suggests that JPL would deny Parsons ever existed; but, as evidenced by a memorial plaque on JPL grounds (and numerous conversations with the staff of JPL) the opposite is actually the case.

After the war, group leader and rocket scientist von Kármán was invited to Germany to inspect various Nazi research installations like the one at Peenemünde. This visit occurred at the invitation of Hap Arnold and his other old friends in Washington. Von Kármán's autobiography, *The Wind and Beyond*, contains pictures from his trip to Germany, including one shot of him interrogating a German scientist. As previously noted, von Kármán worked in Germany during the decade following World War I. After World War II, he was instrumental in recruiting Nazi scientists to the United States. Declassified documents refer to this effort as "Operation Paperclip." Some of Parsons' letters to Cameron are from Alabama, where Paperclip rocket scientist Wernher von Braun was a prisoner of war, and it is possible the two had met. Von Kármán spent the next two decades engaged in various aeronautics research projects and died in 1963, a giant among men.

GALCIT member and alleged spy Hsue-shen Tsien had an interesting if troubled life after the war ended. Evidently he was accused of being a Communist simply because he was Chinese, as, years later, Malina's widow told an interviewer, "We never saw him at any of the cell meetings." This incident embarrassed Tsien so much he decided to return to China—something he thought he'd never do. However, immigration stopped him at the docks and detained him for five years, by which time, the authorities figured, anything he knew would be obsolete. Then they deported him, and subsequently he singlehandedly built the Chinese missile program from scratch using what he had learned at GALCIT. Tsien's fascinating life is recounted in Iris Chang's biography, *Thread of the Silk Worm*.

In 1989, a collection of Parsons' unpublished essays, *Freedom Is A Two-Edged Sword*, appeared and renewed interest in the man, which has surged with the advent of the World Wide Web. The book includes Parsons' commentary on the "Red Scare." Much of the other material reproduced in *Freedom Is A Two-Edged Sword* deals with two of Parsons' post-OTO projects: The Gnosis and The Witchcraft. The former was an attempt to set up a regular form of worship for Parsons and for whomever would follow.

Parsons christianized his Gnosis by having Sophia, the incarnation of wisdom, play the role of the daughter of God, equating her with the Holy Ghost. In Parsons' version, Sophia's union with Christ was equal to God. In "traditional" Gnosticism, Sophia was usually the mother of God, and Christ the savior of both. Only in Parsons' work do we find the alternative formula, to which end Parsons wrote "On Magick," "The Gnostic Creed," and "The Gnostic Doctrine."

Parsons' other project was The Witchcraft, a course on magick for the layman. Surviving documents include "Basic Magick: Fundamental Theory and Practice," "Manifesto of The Witchcraft," and a few chapters of a book called *The Cup, the Sword and the Crux Ansata*. Parsons wrote the manifesto June 15, 1950, but he still thought enough of Babalon to note this as the year 4000. However, the date is inconsistent with previous Babalon-influenced dates. In 1946, Hubbard proclaimed the year Babalon 4063, and in 1949 Parsons dated *The Book of AntiChrist 4066*. The year 4000 may indicate a change of his numbering system; it is not a misprint.

Parsons' purpose in creating these texts was clear: To Cameron he wrote, "Simplicity has been the key to victory in all the idea wars and, at present, Magick does not have it. There is the skeleton in the Rights of Man [Crowley's *Liber OZ*], and the coverings in the main literature. But the true body has never been shown forth."

In addition, short outlines on "General Field Theory" that Parsons left unfinished could almost be taken as precursors of the late Rupert Sheldrake's "morphogenetic field theory." Notes on Wagner's *The Ring* take us to the final chapter of *Freedom*: it is "The Star of Babalon," already mentioned. Part of Parsons' *The Book of Babalon*, this chapter consists of instructions received from Babalon herself for the Magical Child. Much like the magical letter in the beautiful gnostic "Hymn of the Pearl," these instructions would serve to effect an *anamnesis* (awakening) on the child's part, to further her mission on Earth. This text serves as further evidence that it was not Cameron who was to become Babalon, but someone as yet unknown.

As noted, Cameron occasionally showed her art, but she never sold it. In fact, much of her early work she destroyed. The rest remains in private collections, although several showings have been held, such as at the Los Angeles Municipal Art Gallery and at the Los Angeles County Museum of Art in 1989. Cameron was included posthumously in the "Beat Generation" show at the Whitney Museum in New York in late 1995. Near the end of her life she requested permission from JPL to give her grandson Silver a tour, wanting him to see where his "grandfather" had worked, a request that was granted. Cameron died of cancer on July 24, 1995, aged 73.

Having reviewed the life of John Parsons in more depth than most writers, I have come to the conclusion that he has been misunderstood—even misrepresented. Historians of rocketry and the space program seem to have underestimated his contributions to the field, while writers on the occult have romanticized him as some sort of great sorcerer. Without his contributions to both solid and liquid fuels, the American space program would not be where it is today. In less than five years, Parsons accomplished what Robert Goddard could not do in a lifetime. The list concerning the top leaders in the world of rocketry contained in von Kármán's 1958 letter, written the same year as the solid-fueled *Explorer I*, was self-aggrandizing, as von Kármán himself admitted. To wit, Malina had written to von Kármán concerning opinion on who were the top 10 Americans who had contributed to the program. "Starting, of course, with ourselves, the list is of the following," von Kármán replied. Parsons name was at the top.

While one cannot take von Kármán's name off the top of that list, there is justification for placing Parsons' name above Malina's, as Parsons is the individual who persevered in the face of repeated failures, and Parsons and the others funded their own research until someone (Hap Arnold) finally took notice. Furthermore, Parsons was the one in the field blowing up rocket after rocket until he found just the right combination that worked. Von Kármán encouraged him, but Parsons did the difficult and extremely hazardous work. Everything today in the field of solid fuel rockets is essentially Parsons' work, if slightly modified. Obviously, it cannot be said that Parsons single-handedly won the war, but his JATOs were deployed in several areas for its last three years. In addition, the global company Aerojet was founded upon Parsons' innovations with solid fuels, and nothing else.

It is likely that Parsons' underestimation had little to do with his occult activities, which seem to have been tolerated as one of many eccentricities associated with his brand of genius. Amo Smith had his pith helmet, Malina was a communist, and von Kármán talked about the golem—this was the normal state of affairs at Caltech. In reality,

Parsons is forgotten because he was not a part of Caltech proper, not a "scientist" in the stuffy sense of the word. He did not hold a degree from an accredited university.

One of the biggest questions remaining is why Parsons and Forman abandoned rockets altogether at the end of the war. Their early work was diverted into other directions as the war demanded new technologies, yet it was not they but Malina who took up pure rocketry after the war ended. Was Parsons' work with the OTO more important now than his profession? Did Aerojet make him sign a non-competition agreement? Was he resting on his laurels when he should have been pursuing other fields of research? Or was there simply no funding for such things anymore? Hopefully, and likely, considering Parsons' mentality, his original interest was more than a matter of mere profit, but what had started as a passion got lost in the distraction of war and personal upheavals.

Today, Parsons' inspired ingredient for rocket fuel, ammonium perchlorate, is causing its own problems. According to Jonathan Parfrey, president of Physicians for Social Responsibility, toxicological studies by the EPA show that perchlorate is an endocrine disruptor which also harms fetal development. Perchlorate has also been linked to conditions like aplastic anemia and hypothyroidism. After having leached into groundwater at Aerojet's Sacramento, San Gabriel and Chino Hills facilities, multimillion-dollar perchlorate cleanups are currently underway.

In contradistinction to the underestimation in the field of rocket science and the aerospace industry, Parsons' accomplishments in the arcane sciences have been highly overrated and grossly exaggerated. As a magician he was essentially a failure. As a Thelemite he learned the hard way what was required. He loved Crowley's "Law" but couldn't adhere to it—though he tried harder than most. He violated the rules, undertook unauthorized and unorthodox magical operations, and claimed the grade of *Magister Templi* without first completing all the grades below it. He couldn't handle working under authority—his ego was too big. His record of failure is valuable in that regard. He was a great promulgator of thelemic ideals in his essays, but as an idealist his elitism ruined his work. Indeed, some would say he was guilty of *hubris*, which the gods always punish.

In his (short) personal and business lives Parsons also scored poorly. His romantic naiveté led him to trust those whom he should not have trusted. He chose some very good friends but also some very bad associates. He wisely joined in on the founding of Aerojet, only foolishly to sell out a few short years later, which, admittedly, even the great man von Kármán did. However, there is little excuse but naiveté for what Parsons did with the money he received from that sale. In addition, his mix-up with the Israelis was perhaps a simple mistake in judgement, but one that he could have avoided quite easily. He admired them but misjudged U.S. policy.

The whole matter of his death has also been greatly overemphasized. Suicide is simply not tenable, and the only clear possible murder suspect is Kynette, the crooked cop, although there may be others. A U.S. scientist who attempted to pass government "secrets" onto the Israelis, and who was loading explosive chemicals on a truck bound for Mexico and then Israel, may have won himself a few anonymous enemies.

Despite these suspicions and the fact that Parsons was an experienced handler of explosives, his death may truly have been accidental. As noted, Parsons sweated profusely, as two separate acquaintances have testified, one of them also pointing out how hot it was that June day in 1952. Even a safety-conscious expert could let a tin can slip out of a sweaty hand. The hole in the floor, the shrapnel stuck in low places, the loss of the right arm, all point to a dropped container. And it is questionable just how "safety-conscious" was a man who stored all sorts of dangerous explosives in his kitchen, on the back porch, in unlicensed labs in residential areas.

The only evidence not easily explained is the detective's original comment that the explosion occurred *behind* Parsons, and the fact that the trash can was full of explosive substances which should not have been there. Murder cannot be ruled out, but a sad accident seems more likely. Had the notorious Los Angeles police investigated the scene, we could consider a coverup. But it was the *Pasadena* police, assisted by Army Ordnance. If someone had wanted him dead, a car bomb would have been easy enough to rig. But fulminate of mercury is not stable enough for a murder scheme that had to be clever enough to fool an expert. Had it been mixed ahead of time and planted in his lab, Parsons would have noticed it right away. It's true that fulminate of mercury becomes more dangerous as it dries, but as soon as Parsons had seen a can of dried fulminate of mercury, he would've known someone had planted it there. Of course, unless it was beneath the floorboard, as Cameron claimed to have discovered, and cordite with a fulminate of mercury fuse may be a possibility.

Based on the evidence—admittedly obscured by 40 years of time—it seems that John Parsons' death was accidental. Of course, there

197

Death and Beyond

remain the accusatory remarks of Cameron—not the best witness for later events, but she was the closest person to Parsons at the time of his death. Furthermore, the discovery of additional evidence might lead one to believe that it was murder.

As a boy, I read an odd little science fiction story, one that Parsons never could have seen, as it was published in 1955, three years after his death. The title was "End as a World," and the author was F.L. Wallace. I found the story in an anthology edited by H.L. Gold entitled *The Third Galaxy Reader,* for which I paid a dime at a garage sale. "End as a World" wasn't the best story in the book, but it wasn't the worst, either. It was a different kind of story. Its surprise ending stuck in my memory for a long time.

The story started with newspaper and radio accounts of the end of the world. Day-to-day activity stopped as people look up and wait for the end. Suddenly a loud noise was heard, and a bright flash of light was seen overhead. It was not what was expected, i.e., the explosion of the planet: It was the first rocket ship. It was indeed the end of the world, the story concluded, but the beginning of the universe.

John Parsons, self-professed Antichrist, may not have brought about the end of the world, but through his contributions to science he played a part in bringing about the beginning of the universe.

STATE OF CALIFORNIA
CERTIFICATION OF VITAL RECORD

STATE OF CALIFORNIA
DEPARTMENT OF HEALTH SERVICES

P625

52-045285 CERTIFICATE OF DEATH

STATE OF CALIFORNIA — DEPARTMENT OF PUBLIC HEALTH

REGISTRATION 1904 REGISTRAR'S NUMBER 753

1a. NAME OF DECEASED—FIRST NAME	1b. MIDDLE NAME	1c. LAST NAME	2a. DATE OF DEATH
Marvel aka Jack	John Whiteside	Whiteside Parsons	June 17, 1952

5:45 P.

3 SEX	4 COLOR OR RACE	5	6 DATE OF BIRTH	7 AGE
Male	White	Married	October 2, 1914	37 YEARS

8a. USUAL OCCUPATION — Chemist

8b. KIND OF BUSINESS OR INDUSTRY — Powder Co.

9 BIRTHPLACE — California

10 CITIZEN OF WHAT COUNTRY — U. S. A.

11 NAME AND BIRTHPLACE OF FATHER — Marvel H. Parsons - Mass.

12 MAIDEN NAME AND BIRTHPLACE OF MOTHER — Ruth Whiteside - Unk.

13 NAME OF PRESENT SPOUSE — Marjorie Cameron Parsons

14 WAS DECEASED EVER IN U.S. ARMED FORCES?

15 SOCIAL SECURITY NUMBER — 559-10-7396

16 INFORMANT — Mrs. Marjorie Cameron Parsons (Wife)

5016

PLACE OF DEATH

17a. COUNTY — Los Angeles

17b. CITY OR TOWN — Pasadena

17c. LENGTH OF STAY IN THIS CITY OR TOWN — 37 years

17d. FULL NAME OF HOSPITAL OR INSTITUTION — Huntington Memorial Hospital

18 ADDRESS — 100 Congress Street

LAST USUAL RESIDENCE

18a. STATE — California

18b. COUNTY — Los Angeles

18c. CITY OR TOWN — Pasadena

18d. STREET OR RURAL ADDRESS — 424 Arroyo Terrace

PHYSICIAN'S OR CORONER'S CERTIFICATION

19a. CORONER — Autopsy

19b. SIGNATURE

19c. ADDRESS — HALL OF JUSTICE, LOS ANGELES

19d. DATE SIGNED — 6/18/52

FUNERAL DIRECTOR AND REGISTRAR

20a. Cremation

20b. DATE — 6-19-52

20c. CEMETERY OR CREMATORY — Live Oak Crematory

21 SIGNATURE OF EMBALMER — 311

22 FUNERAL DIRECTOR — Turner and Stevens — Pasadena, California

23 DATE RECEIVED BY LOCAL REGISTRAR — JUN 19 1952

24 LOCAL REGISTRAR

MEDICAL AND HEALTH DATA

916.0

CAUSE OF DEATH

25 DISEASE OR CONDITION DIRECTLY LEADING TO DEATH — Multiple Injuries of entire body

ANTECEDENT CAUSES — DUE TO (a) / DUE TO (b)

APPROXIMATE INTERVAL BETWEEN ONSET AND DEATH

26 OTHER SIGNIFICANT CONDITIONS

27a. SPECIFY OPERATION

27b. MAJOR FINDINGS OF OPERATION

28 AUTOPSY — YES

DEATH DUE TO EXTERNAL VIOLENCE

29a. SPECIFY ACCIDENT, SUICIDE OR HOMICIDE — Accident

29b. PLACE OF INJURY — Home

29c. LOCATION CITY OR TOWN — Pasadena COUNTY L.A. STATE Calif.

29d. TIME — 6 17 52 5:45 P.

29e. INJURY OCCURRED — NOT AT WORK

29f. HOW DID INJURY OCCUR? — Explosion in home due to chemicals

601885

This is to certify that this document is a true copy of the official record filed with the Office of Vital Records.

S. Kimberly Belshé, Director and State Registrar of Vital Records
by:

MICHAEL L. RODRIAN, CHIEF
STATE REGISTRAR

DATE ISSUED

This copy not valid unless prepared on engraved border displaying seal and signature of Registrar.

ANY ALTERATION OR ERASURE VOIDS THIS CERTIFICATE

Afterword

Helen Parsons Smith died July 27, 2003 at Tahoe Forest Hospital, close to her longtime home in King's Beach, CA. She was survived by her son Kwen Smith and his wife, along with their two children and their two grandchildren. Helen was the oldest OTO initiate at the time of her death, the numerologically significant age of 93. Her obituary says that for a long period in her life "she may well have been the only regularly active priestess in the world who carried forth the celebration of the mass of *Ecclesia Gnostica Catholica*." Per her wishes there was no funeral; she enjoyed her privacy to the end.

One other notable event took place since this book was first published four years ago. I was able to uncover the inspiration for Parsons' Black Pilgrimage, which I discussed in chapter 10. The source was M.R. James' short story "Count Magnus," published in 1904. It has been reprinted in several places; my copy is in *Collected Ghost Stories*, published by Wordsworth Editions, Ltd. in 1992. I believe the story may also be found online.

The fictional Count Magnus De la Gardie was a late 16th-century/early 17th-century mage residing in a huge manor in Vestergothland, Sweden. He seems to have been named for a real Count Magnus who lived in the same area from 1622 to 1686, but the two have nothing else in common. The center of the story is the mysterious Black Pilgrimage he was said to have undertaken, what form it actually took, and what he brought back from it. The nature of the pilgrimage itself is never discovered, though the thing he brought back is hinted at. It seems to have been some sort of supernatural beast, a demon or familiar spirit that protected Magnus even in death.

James does specify the destination of the Black Pilgrimage. It was Chorazin in Palestine (now in Israel), the city which Jesus cursed, the city which later legends said would birth the Antichrist, the city which Parsons also named as the destination of his pilgrimage. Its unique black ruins still stand; they are black because they are made of the local basalt. Of all of Chorazin's ruins, the best-known is the unfinished synagogue. James has Magnus write of his *Liber nigrae peregrinationis*, "If any man desires to obtain a long life, if he would

sex and rockets

200

obtain a faithful messenger and see the blood of his enemies, it is necessary that he should first go into the city of Chorazin, and there salute the prince [of the air]." The story doesn't specify how long Magnus lived, but based on internal evidence one may deduce it was around 120 years. The story does make clear that Magnus obtained his faithful messenger, and did have occasion to see the blood of his enemies.

On February 28, 1946 Parsons wrote *Liber 49*, a book from Babalon whose 58th verse says, "Thou shalt make the Black Pilgrimage." No further details were given until Parsons wrote *The Book of AntiChrist* a few years later. In *The Book of AntiChrist*, the first section of which is entitled "The Black Pilgrimage," Parsons wrote that he began his pilgrimage in November of 1949, in response to a dream he says came from Babalon. He describes the pilgrimage as an astral working conducted in his temple.

Parsons wrote, "And I went into the sunset with Her sign, and into the night past accursed and desolate places and cyclopean ruins, and so came at last to the City of Chorazin. And there a great tower of Black Basalt was raised, that was part of a castle whose further battlements reeled over the gulf of the stars. And upon the tower was this sign [a circle inscribed with an inverted triangle]. And one heavily robed and veiled showed me the sign, and told me to look, and behold, I saw flash below me four past lives wherein I had failed in my object." Parsons goes on to name these past lives; I have described each of them in detail in chapter 10. After this he writes, "And thereafter I was taken within and saluted the Prince of that place . . .," echoing Magnus' instructions to go into the city and salute the Prince of the Air. Judging from hints in Parsons' letters to Karl Germer in 1949 and later, his purpose was not long life, a faithful messenger, nor to see the blood of his enemies; it was always the furtherance of Thelema. (But if the furtherance of Thelema necessitated any of these, Parsons surely hoped they would follow. He specifically names Christianity—all of Christianity—as the enemy of mankind.) The pilgrimage itself is not mentioned again in his surviving writings.

In *Ghosts & Scholars* issue 26, Jamesian scholars Rosemary Pardoe and Jane Nicholls discuss the possible literary and historical sources for James' Black Pilgrimage. They document James' knowledge of the apocryphal *Revelation of the Pseudo-Methodius* (fourth century) in which Chorazin is first mentioned as the birthplace of the Antichrist, as well as his familiarity with W. Bousset's *Der Antichrist*, published in 1895, which also documents the legend. James' favorite story by the early Irish horror writer Sheridan Le Fanu was "The Familiar," in which the phrase "the prince of the powers of the air" occurs. The phrase originates with St. Paul, who refers to Satan in this manner in Ephesians 2:2, and James would have known about its Biblical origin as well.

Pardoe and Nicholls also document James' familiarity with John Dee. James edited a list of Dee's manuscripts in 1921, compiling his list from several others and from original sources. One of the titles on Elias Ashmole's list was *Liber Peregrinationis Primae* (*The Book of the First Pilgrimage*). The authors speculate that this title influenced James' *Liber nigrae peregrinationis* (*The Book of the Black Pilgrimage*). This may be, but it only takes a basic knowledge of Latin to translate such a title. (Dee's book describes magical conversations recorded during a trip to Krakow in 1583.)

Pardoe and Nicholls excel when they show just how Parsons could've encountered James' story—and it occurred only months before he received his instruction to go on the Black Pilgrimage from Babalon. Samuel D. Russell wrote an essay on James which appeared in the Fall 1945 issue of *The Acolyte* (a fanzine). Russell and Parsons both frequented the Los Angeles Science Fantasy Society (LASFS), so it's fairly certain that James was discussed there. Parsons received his instructions on February 28, 1946, which seems to imply he had been reading James recently.

Unless further evidence appears, it appears that M.R. James invented the Black Pilgrimage as a literary device based on legends of Chorazin, rather than its being a genuine magical tradition. Parsons took inspiration for a magical working based on this concept, just as he had taken inspiration from other fantasy works (for instance, his favorite novel was Jack Williamson's supernatural thriller *Darker Than You Think*, discussed in chapter 4.) Recall Crowley's letter criticizing Parsons for taking such a low form of literature so seriously. Despite the criticism, Parsons continued to take his inspiration wherever he would find it.

James doesn't tell us how Count Magnus died; his death is a mystery, as is Parsons'. In contrast, however, Magnus had something that Parsons didn't. He had his "faithful messenger," the thing that he brought back from his Black Pilgrimage, the thing that protected his estate even after his death. Parsons doesn't seem to have brought anything back from his pilgrimage to protect him, and his messengers were few. The foremost of these were Cameron and Karl Germer, who preserved his writings and his message for future generations. They are gone now, and with the passing of Helen the story has come to a close.

Ruins of Chorazin

The starred crater, at 37° N latitude, 171° W longitude was named "Parsons Crater" in 1972 by the International Astronomical Union. Parsons Crater is on the dark side of the moon.

Parsons at the Parsonage.

John Parsons seen in the 1933 graduation photo from University School, top row, fourth from right.

Pasadena's private University School.

Photos courtesy of Pasadena Historical Museum

John Parsons stands above JATO at Arroyo Seco, June 4, 1943.

Arroyo Seco test site, 1936.

Photos courtesy of JPL Archive

In the Arroyo Seco Test Site, John Parsons, left, and Ed Forman, right, show greater caution than usual by wearing pith helmets.

Arroyo Seco Test Site in late 1936. John Parsons in dark vest, Ed Forman bending over in white shirt; Frank Malina is probably the individual bending over in a light-colored vest.

Photos courtesy of JPL Archive

Rudolph Schott, Amo Smith, Frank Malina, Ed Forman and John Parsons relax on Halloween, 1936.

Mannequins of the scene above used for the JPL Open House "Nativity Scene."

Photos courtesy of JPL Archive

Posed photo in August 1941 of Theodore von Kármán (in black), surrounded by Clark Millikan, Martin Summerfield, Frank Malina and
Captain Homer Boushey.

Photo courtesy of Aerojet

Parsons, second from left, Forman, third from left, Malina, center and
cohorts in an Ercoupe test.

Photo courtesy of JPL Archive

Very first Ercoupe flight in August 1941. The figure at left is either Ed
Forman or John Parsons.

200-pound solid fuel JATO cannisters, the invention of John Parsons, as
produced for Allied use in World War II.

Photos courtesy of Aerojet

In this photo, taken the last day of the Ercoupe tests in August 1941, Helen Parsons is seen among friends and family, third from the left. Parsons and Forman are once again seen fourth and third from the left of the test plane.

Photo courtesy of JPL Archive

Founding members of the Aerojet Engineering Corporation at Wright Field. Photographed in front of the Havoc Bomber are: Theodore C. Coleman, *director of Aerojet*; Parsons, *vice-president*; Edward S. Forman, *vice-president production*; Andrew G. Haley, *president*; Theodore von Kármán, *founder and chairman of the board*; Frank J. Malina, *secretary-treasurer*; Martin Summerfield, *vice-president engineering*; and T. Edward Beehan, *general manager*.

Photo courtesy of Aerojet

Monument at Jet Propulsion Laboratory celebrates its birthday, first erected on Halloween, 1968.

Photo by Greg Bishop

John Parsons believed the 1940 story, *Darker Than You Think,* presaged the appearance of Babalon. This is the cover of the 1948 edition.

DELL BOOK **591**

Super Science and Fantastic Death launch

ROCKET to the MORGUE

COMPLETE AND UNABRIDGED

ANTHONY BOUCHER

Rocket to the Morgue, published by John Parsons' sci-fi soirée friend, A.H. White, under the pseudonyms Anthony Boucher and H.H. Holmes, includes a Parsons-like character named Hugo Chantrelle, a Caltech scientist obsessed by Fortean phenomena.

The Parsonage of 1003 S. Orange Grove in Pasadena. The house no longer stands.

Aleister Crowley, the man John Parsons called "Father," making the sign of Pan.

Cameron's painting of Jack Parsons, "Dark Angel."

Cameron, mid-1940s.

Parsons and Cameron on the town.

Renate Druks in Kenneth Anger's *Inauguration of the Pleasure Dome*, filmed in 1954.

Parsons sits candlelit in the probable presence of Cameron.

Parsons' magickal black box discovered after his explosive demise.

Pasadena police officer with luggage probably meant for Parsons' and Cameron's impending Mexico trip at the house where Ruth Parsons committed suicide.

Pasadena criminologist Don Hardly inspects chemicals stored near the fatal site.

Officer Ernie Hovard at the scene of the explosion.

Appendix A Primary Bibliography

Anonymous. "Birth of JATO" (photo caption) in *Popular Science*. New York: *Popular Science*, July 1946. Pg. 74.

Anonymous. "The Daniel Guggenheim Graduate School of Aeronautics of the California Institute of Technology—A History of the First Ten Years" in *Bulletin of the California Institute of Technology*, Vol. 49, No. 2. May 1940. Pg. 17–19, 30.

Anonymous. "L.A.'s Lust Cult" in *People Today*. August 13, 1952. Pg. 60–61.

Anonymous. "Seeking Power" in *Popular Mechanics*. *Popular Mechanics*, August 1940. Pg. 210–213, 118A–119A.

Boucher, Anthony (as H.H. Holmes). *Rocket to the Morgue*. New York: Duell, Sloan & Pierce, 1942.

Crowley, Aleister. *Moonchild*. York Beach: Samuel Weiser, 1970. (Orig. 1929.) p. 107–110.

— *Magick In Theory and Practice*. New York: Dover Publications, 1976 (Orig. 1929).

— *Magick: Book 4, Parts I & IV* (Mary Desti and Leila Waddell, co-authors; Hymenaeus Beta, ed.). York Beach: Samuel Weiser, 1998.

— *Magick Without Tears* (Israel Regardie, ed.). Las Vegas: Falcon Press, 1989.

— *The Law is for All* (Louis Willkinson & Hymenaeus Beta, ed.) Scottsdale: New Falcon, 1996.

— *Liber Al vel Legis: The Book of the Law*. York Beach: Samuel Weiser, 1976. (Orig. 1938.)

— *777 and Other Qabalistic Writings* (Israel Regardie, ed.). York Beach: Samuel Weiser, 1973.

— *The Book of Lies*. York Beach: Samuel Weiser, 1980. (Orig. 1913.)

— *Confessions: An Autohagiography* (John Symonds and Kenneth Grant, eds.). New York: Arkana, 1989. (Orig. 1969.)

— *The Magical Record of the Beast 666* (John Symonds and Kenneth Grant, eds.). London: Duckworth, 1972.

— "*The Vision and the Voice* with Commentary and Other Papers," in The Equinox vol. IV, number 2. York Beach: Samuel Weiser, 1998.

Haley, Andrew. *Rocketry and Space Exploration*. Princeton: Van Nostrand, 1958.

Malina, Frank J. "Memoir on the GALCIT Rocket Research Project, 1936–38." June 6, 1967.

— "The Rocket Pioneers: Memoirs of the Infant Days of Rocketry at Caltech" in *Engineering and Science* No. 31. February 1968.

— "Memoir: The U.S. Army Air Corps Jet Propulsion Research Project, Galcit Project No. 1, 1939–46." October 10, 1969.

— "America's First Long Range Missile and Space Exploration Program: The ORDCIT Project at the Jet Propulsion Laboratory, 1943–1946.": September 23, 1971.

Martin, Robert E. "New Experiments with Rockets" in *Popular Science*. New York: Popular Science, September 1940. Pg. 108–110.

Parsons, John. *Analysis by a Master of the Temple*. Undated reprint, publisher unknown.

— *The Book of AntiChrist*. Edmonton: Isis Research, 1980.

— *The Book of B.A.B.A.L.O.N.* (Soror Chandria, ed.). Berkeley: Ordo Templi Orientis, 1982. (Also in *Starfire #3*. London: Starfire, 1990.)

— *Freedom Is A Two-Edged Sword, and Other Essays* (Marjorie Cameron Parsons Kimmel & Hymenaeus Beta, eds.). New York: Ordo Templi Orientis, 1989.

— *Songs for the Witch Woman*. Edmonton: Sothis/ISIS Research, 1982.

Rogers, Alva. "Darkhouse" in *Lighthouse* No. 5. February 1962.

Rostoker, Adam. "Whence Came the Stranger" in *Rapid Eye #3*. London: Rapid Eye.

Various. *Sandborn's Fire Insurance Atlas* for the city of Pasadena, CA. Vol. 1, pg. 211. Published 1910.

Williamson, Jack. *Darker Than You Think*. New York: Berkeley Books, 1969. (Orig. 1940.)

— *Wonder's Child: My Life in Science Fiction*. New York: Bluejay Books, 1985. Pg. 127–128.

Appendix B Secondary Bibliography

Anonymous. *L. Ron Hubbard: A Profile*. Los Angeles: CSI, 1995. Pg. 102–108.

Anonymous. *Revelation: Its Grand Climax At Hand!* Brooklyn: Watchtower Bible and Tract Society, 1988. Pg. 105–107.

Colquhoun, Ithell. *Sword of Wisdom: MacGregor Mathers and the Golden Dawn*. London: Neville Spearman, 1975.

Daraul, Arkon. *Witches and Sorcerers*. New York: Citadel Press, 1962.

Dee, John. *The Private Diary of Dr. John Dee* (James Orchard Halliwell, ed.). New York: Johnson Reprint Company, 1968. (Orig. 1842.)

Dunne, J.W. *An Experiment with Time*. London: Faber and Faber Limited, 1927.

Frazer, Sir James George. *The Golden Bough* (Abridged Edition). New York: Macmillan Publishing Company, 1922. Pg. 156–158.

Freedland, Nat. *The Occult Explosion.* New York: Berkeley, 1972. Pg. 144–146.

Gorn, Michael H. *The Universal Man: Theodore von Kármán's Life in Aeronautics.* Washington: Smithsonian Institution Press, 1992. Pg. 73–92.

Greenfield, T. Allen. "The Rocket Scientist and the Guru: Stargate 1946." (Unpublished.)

— *The Story of the Hermetic Brotherhood of Light.* Stockholm: Looking Glass Press, 1997.

Hyatt, Christopher S. & DuQuette, Lon Milo. *Enochian Sex Magick: The Enochian World of Aleister Crowley.* Scottsdale: New Falcon, 1991.

Hymenaeus Beta, ed. *The Equinox,* vol. III, no. 10. York Beach: Samuel Weiser, 1990. (Orig. 1986.)

— "Cameron Dies" in *The Magical Link,* Spring-Summer 1995.

James, Geoffrey. *The Enochian Magick of Dr. John Dee.* St. Paul: Llewellyn Publications, 1994 (Orig. 1984). Pg. xiii–xxvii.

Koppes, Clayton R. *JPL and the American Space Program: A History of the Jet Propulsion Laboratory.* New Haven: Yale University Press, 1982. Pg. 3–17.

Laycock, Donald C. *The Complete Enochian Dictionary.* York Beach: Samuel Weiser, 1994 (Orig. 1978).

Long, Frank Belknap. *Howard Phillips Lovecraft: Dreamer on the Night-Side.* Sauk City, WI: Arkham House, 1975. Pg. 190–191.

Marshack, Alexander. *The World in Space.* New York: Thomas Nelson & Sons, 1958. Pg. 140–142.

Martello, Leo L. *Weird Ways of Witchcraft.* New York: HC Publishers, 1969. Pg. 169–173, 191–200.

Mathers, S.L. MacGregor, trans. *The Book of the Sacred Magic of Abramelin the Mage.* New York: Dover, 1975. (Orig. 1900.)

— *The Book of the Goetia, or The Lesser Key of Solomon the King.* Mokelumne Hill: Health Research, 1976. (Orig. 1903.)

Melton, J. Gordon. *The Encyclopedia of American Religions.* Wilmington: McGrath Publishing Co., 1978. Pg. 256–259.

— & Moore, Robert L. *The Cult Experience: Responding to the New Religious Pluralism.* New York: Pilgrim Press, 1982. Pg. 132.

Moore, Patrick. *The Guinness Book of Astronomy Facts & Feats.* Pg. 47.

Pike, Albert. *Morals and Dogma of the Ancient and Accepted Scottish Rite of Freemasonry.* Washington: The Supreme Council of the Thirty-Third Degree, 1960 (orig. 1871). Pg. 291.

Regardie, Israel. *What You Should Know About the Golden Dawn.* Phoenix: Falcon Press, 1983. (Orig. 1936.)

Robertson, Sandy. *The Aleister Crowley Scrapbook*. York Beach: Samuel Weiser, 1988. Pg. 113.

Scholem, Gershom. *The Messianic Idea in Judaism*. New York: Schocken Books, 1971. Pg. 335–336.

Schueler, Gerald J. *Enochian Magic: A Practical Manual*. St. Paul: Llewellyn Publications, 1986.

— & Schueler, Betty. *The Enochian Workbook*. St. Paul: Llewellyn, 1995.

Sears, William R. "Von Kármán: Fluid Dynamics and other things" in *Physics Today* vol. 30 no. 1. New York: *Physics Today*, January 1986. Pg. 34–39.

Short, Nicholas M. *Planetary Geology*. 1975.

Spangenburg, Ray & Moser, Diane. *Space Exploration: Space People A–Z*. Pg. 52.

Staley, Michael. "Sorcerer of Apocalypse: An Introduction to John Whiteside Parsons," in *Apocalypse Culture*, Expanded and Revised Edition (edited by Adam Parfrey). Los Angeles: Feral House, 1990. Pg. 172–189.

Symonds, John. *The Great Beast: The Life and Magick of Aleister Crowley*. Frogmore: Mayflower Books, 1978. (Orig. 1971.) Pg. 339–340, 445–449.

Thayer, Joseph Henry. *A Greek-English Lexicon of the New Testament*. Grand Rapids: Zondervan, undated. (Orig. 1885.) Pg. 92.

Vallee, Jacques. *Messengers of Deception: UFO Contacts and Cults*. New York: Bantam Books, 1980. (Orig. 1979.) Pg. 12, 204, 210.

— *Dimensions: A Casebook of Alien Contact*. New York: Ballantine Books, 1988. Pg. 225.

The Visual Encyclopedia of Science Fiction. Pg. 235.

Wilson, Robert Anton. *Cosmic Trigger: The Final Secret of the Illuminati*. New York: Pocket Books, 1978. (Orig. 1977.) Pg. 140–142, 172.

— "A Sword is Drawn," in *Magical Blend* #27 (Michael Peter Langevin & Jerry Snider, eds.). San Francisco: *Magical Blend*, 1990. Pg. 43–45.

Appendix C Additional References

1. JPL oral histories

Charles E. Bartley, 10/3/94

Dorothy Lewis, 6/15/72

Frank J. Malina, 10/29/68 and 6/8/73

William H. Pickering, 1972

Walter B. Powell, 5/3/74

Robert B. Rypinski, 2/11/69

Apollo M.O. Smith, 9/23/86

Homer Joe Stewart, 1972

Fritz Zwicky, 5/17/71 and 4/27/72

2. Items from the JPL history files

GALCIT Project No. 1 Organizational Chart, 7/1/41

GALCIT Project No. 1 Organizational Chart, 5/24/42

Handwritten letter from Parsons to Malina, 5/5/42 (2 pages)

Parsons' handwritten "Description of Tests," November 1936 and January 1937 (5 pages)

"Proposal for a Jet Propulsion Experimental Station at the Guggenheim Aeronautical Laboratory of the California Institute of Technology," 4/18/39 (probably Malina)

von Kármán & Malina, "Beginnings of Astronautics," 1960 (lecture notes, 12 pages)

Letter from von Kármán to Malina, 1/13/58 (1 page)

Interview transcript w/von Kármán, 1/13/58 (3 pages)

Letter from Malina to John Reese, 4/10/59 (4 pages)

B. Huber, "Guggenheim: Extent of Early Participation" (6 pages)

Malina, "Memoir on the GALCIT Rocket Research Project, 1936–38" (21 pages)

"Life at Aerojet-General University," Chandler C. Ross, 1993

Memo from Parsons to T.E. Beehan, 8/14/44 (2 pages, unsigned)

Ditto, 8/15/44 (3 pages, signed)

Ditto, 8/17/44 (2 pages, signed)

Arroyo Test Drawing, Malina & Parsons, 8/28/36

Parsons, "A Consideration of the Practicality of Various Substances as Fuels for Jet Propulsion," 6/10/37 (13 pages)

3. Newspaper and magazine articles

Associated Press transmission, April 1938

Pasadena [unknown] (morning edition of *Star-News*, w/photos), 7/15/38

Los Angeles Examiner, 7/15/38 (w/photo)

New York Times, 1/26/38

Houston Chronicle, 1/26/38

"Exploring Our Universe" column in unknown magazine, possibly *Astronautics* (undated, w/photo)

Los Angeles Evening Herald & News, 5/6/38, 5/10/38 (photo)

Pasadena Star-News, 6/18/52, 6/19/52, (w/obituary), 6/20/52 (mother's obituary), 6/21/52 (w/obituary)

Pasadena Independent, 6/18/52, 6/19/52, 6/20/52 (w/obituary), 6/22/52

Los Angeles Times, 6/17/52, 6/19/52, 6/21/52, 6/24/90

Saturday Evening Post, 3/15/45

Astronautics, 6-38 (cover only)

— "Experiments with Powder Motors for Rocket Propulsion by Successive Impulses" by Parsons and Forman, no date (8 pages)

Malina, "The Jet Propulsion Laboratory: Its Origins and First Decade of Work" in *Spaceflight* Volume VI, No. 5 & 6 (12 pages, photos)

London Sunday Times, 1969

4. Miscellaneous

John Bluth, "Notes on Jack Parsons," August 1997, 3 pages

Michael D. Schlei, "An Investigation into the Death of Jack Parsons," 4/27/95 (29 pages)

U.S. Patents No. 2,573,471; 2,693,077 (3 pages) & 2,774, 214 (3 pages)

Pages from Sandborn's Fire Insurance Atlas showing 1003–1071 S. Orange Grove

"Aerojet—50 Years of History" (from web page)

The Lockheed Star, 11/8/68 (3 pages by Forman)

Malina's "Excerpts from Letters Home"

City directories (Pasadena, Los Angeles, Boston—ca. 1900 to 1952)

"Shadow of the Wing" and untitled files associated with it

John Parsons' FBI file

Cameron interview

"Is Smith A God?" (excerpt)

5. Correspondence

Crowley to Parsons, 6/2/45, 3/27/46, 5/19/46

Parsons to Crowley, 1/21/46, 2/2/46, 2/22/46, 3/6/46, 7/5/46, undated (1947?)

Crowley to Germer, undated (1946?)

Parsons to Germer, 6/1/49, 6/11/49, 6/19/49, 9/5/49, 3/31 (1950?), 4/29/52 (sic), 10/3/52 (sic), 11/2/52 (sic)

Parsons to Cameron, 10/5/49, 1/15 to 16 (1950?), 1/25/50, 1/27 (1950?), 2/1/50, 2/6/50, 2/8/50, 2/9/50

Jane Wolfe, magical record, December 1940

Wolfe to Crowley, March 1942

Crowley to Max Schneider, July 1943

Crowley to Wolfe, December, 1943

Parsons to McMurtry, December 8, 1943

Parsons to McMurtry, undated (ca. 1944)

Crowley to the Burlingames, February 1944

Parsons to McMurtry, December 14, 1944

Parsons to McMurtry, March 11, 1945

Wolfe to Germer, late 1945

Parsons to Crowley, early 1946

Parsons to Crowley, March 6, 1946

Parsons to Crowley, March 15, 1946

Parsons to all Agape Lodge members, March 16, 1946

Culling to Germer, May 12, 1946

Crowley to Germer, May 22, 1946

Crowley to Germer, May 31, 1946

Parsons to Crowley, July 5, 1946

Smith to Crowley, mid 1946

Parsons to Crowley, August 20, 1946

Parsons to Germer, early 1952

Crowley to Culling, October 1946

Cameron to Wolfe, December 15, 1952

Cameron to Wolfe, January 22, 1953

Cameron to Wolfe, March 17, 1953

Index

chapter title

chapter title